Advance Praise for *Deadly Valentines*

"You might think you know everything there is to know about Chicago's wild Prohibition days, but Jeffrey Gusfield will prove otherwise. With *Deadly Valentines*, he vividly tells **the twisted yet somehow moving love story of an iconic American gangster and his sexy, nutty gun moll.** Told with a driving, you-are-there narrative, it's a rigorous, sometimes astonishing, and consistently entertaining performance."
> —Douglas Perry, author of *The Girls of Murder City: Fame, Lust, and the Beautiful Killers Who Inspired Chicago*

"Gusfield's book gives **a thoroughly researched and colorful account of a bullet-ridden Jazz Age Chicago.**"
> —*Publishers Weekly*

"**Authoritative, fast-moving, and affecting,** *Deadly Valentines* tells a compelling true-life gangland saga that is loaded with action and, not least, the ache of romance."
> —Howard Blum, author of *American Lightning: Terror, Mystery, the Birth of Hollywood, and the Crime of the Century*

"Jeffrey Gusfield's *Deadly Valentines* is **an encyclopedic love letter to the Roaring Twenties** as embodied in its title characters, Jack McGurn and Louise Rolfe, each of whom succumbed to the seductive flash and drunken abandon of each other and the dark side of the American Dream."
> —Paula Uruburu, author of *American Eve: Evelyn Nesbit, Stanford White, the Birth of the "It" Girl, and the Crime of the Century*

"Jeff Gusfield's *Deadly Valentines* is **a wonderful exploration of not only Jack McGurn's life and violent career but also of that of Louise Rolfe herself.** . . . Gusfield's work does a wonderful job of clearing up much of the myth and misinformation surrounding McGurn and Rolfe, including in-depth examinations of their upbringing and their torrid yet all-too-brief life together."
> —Dan Waugh, author of *Egan's Rats: The Untold Story of the Prohibition-Era Gang That Ruled St. Louis* and *Gangs of St. Louis: Men of Respect*

"Skilled researcher and empathetic writer Gusfield steers us into the private world of Al Capone and the pugilist-turned-killer Jack McGurn—their clannish roots and gangland alliances—and explores the Machiavellian power that Capone directs toward McGurn and his failed dream of ringside glory. **If the underworld ever produced an American tragedy, this is it.**"

—Ellen Poulsen, author of *Don't Call Us Molls:*
Women of the John Dillinger Gang

"Over the years—meaning beginning many years before I first met him—Jeff has been 'pursuing' the subject of Jack McGurn. . . . During that time he has unearthed important public records pertaining to McGurn's life and death . . . in a masterful attempt to find the facts about this man, his second wife and alibi Louise Rolfe, and the events related to them. **Jeff is also an engaging storyteller.**"

—John Binder, author of *The Chicago Outfit*

DEADLY
VALENTINES

DEADLY VALENTINES

The Story of Capone's Henchman
"Machine Gun" Jack McGurn and Louise Rolfe, His Blonde Alibi

JEFFREY GUSFIELD

CHICAGO
REVIEW
PRESS

Published by Chicago Review Press, Incorporated
814 North Franklin Street
Chicago, Illinois 60610
ISBN 978-1-61374-092-7

Interior design: Jonathan Hahn

Library of Congress Cataloging-in-Publication Data
Gusfield, Jeffrey.
  Deadly valentines : the story of Capone's henchman "Machine Gun" Jack
McGurn and Louise Rolfe, his blonde alibi / Jeffrey Gusfield. — 1st ed.
     p. cm.
  Includes bibliographical references and index.
  ISBN 978-1-61374-092-7 (hardback)
  1. McGurn, Jack, 1905-1936. 2. Rolfe, Louise. 3. Gangsters—Illinois—
Chicago—Biography. 4. Organized crime—Illinois—Chicago—History. I. Title.
  HV6248.M46543G87 2012
  364.1092'277311—dc23
                              2011043257

Printed in the United States of America
5 4 3 2 1

For Ann Chrispin Gusfield

Zoccu a fimmina avi, l'omu u disia.
What the woman has, the man wants.

Contents

Part II: *Scorpion*

Part III: *Massacre*

Preface

I was "introduced" to Jack McGurn in 1953 when I was five years old, a sheltered suburban kid, my brain full of animated Disney characters. My father worked in the advertising department of the Hearst paper, the *Chicago American*. One Saturday morning there was an emergency, and he had to rush downtown to avoid a costly mistake. To my delight, he took me with him. It was my first trip to the *American*; I was enthralled by the adult seriousness of the place as well as the smells, noises, and sounds of a big city newspaper. I was a country mouse in a cathedral.

My father put me in the temporary custody of the only person he could find, his friend and legendary photographer Anthony Berardi, who visually recorded the Capone era in poetic black-and-white.[1] He was a small man in his forties, with the tough demeanor of a seasoned public eye. Being himself a father of four, he agreed to take me in tow.

His first question to me was, "Do you like pictures?" He took me downstairs to the newspaper morgue where all the photographic files were kept in walls of gray drawers. He walked his fingers through a familiar metal cabinet and threw a glossy positive down in front of me.

"This was the Saint Valentine's Day Massacre in 1929," he said.

Pinocchio, Bambi, and Peter Pan fled my brain, replaced by the tableau of seven murdered men, their blood and brains spattered like grisly confetti. I'd never seen a dead body before, although in black and white the violence of that photo seemed more bloody red than any in color.

The St. Valentine's Day Massacre, February 14, 1929. COLLECTION OF JOHN BINDER

Powerful feelings invaded me for the first time as I experienced an utter fascination with the kind of reality nobody had dared to reveal to a child. Mr. Berardi produced another picture, this one of a baby-faced, well-dressed young man with soulful dark eyes, a slightly bulbous nose, and a sweet, cherubic smile.

"This is the guy who did it, as well as lots more," he added, addressing me as if I were an interested colleague. "They called him 'Machine Gun' Jack McGurn."

I still remember the shock and the irony that such an innocent-looking fellow could cause such mayhem and death.

I stared at one, then another, my child's mind roiling with delicious waves of fascination, bloodlust, and that inexplicable desire to be closer, to look deeper into the wounds, to contemplate the horrible but undeniably hypnotic proof of violence and death.

Jack McGurn, 1929. PHOTOGRAPH BY ANTHONY BERARDI, AUTHOR'S COLLECTION

Anthony Berardi taught me a lot that morning, not the least of which was that a face can lie. It was just one of the enigmas that surrounded Jack McGurn, or Vincent Gebardi, his real name. Mr. Berardi pointed to the picture of that impossibly sweet face, tapping the surface of the old glossy. The nail of his index finger was darkened from countless immersions in developer solutions. "He was the nicest guy you'd ever want to meet. You'd never guess what he did for a living."

That was fifty years ago. I've been chasing Jack McGurn for half a century; the truth about him needs to be told. Moreover, his Blonde Alibi and future wife, Louise Rolfe, turned out to be just as fascinating. As I peeled back the layers on McGurn, Louise naturally revealed herself, presenting another dimension that was no less interesting or outrageous. Their story is one of the richest chapters of the entire gangster era of the Roaring Twenties. They grabbed at life and at America's abundant material wealth that was so seductive and waiting to be taken. They represented rebellious freedom, a new kind of antiestablishment that helped to make the post-Victorian sensibilities that existed before World War I a distant memory. Very much like the youth culture of the 1960s, they lived in a dizzying world of inebriated near-anarchy, drawn to the new music that offered a frenetic pulse to their world, rejecting social constrictions and morality. Their lives, surrounded and syncopated by the pounding beats and hollering horns of jazz, stood out as definitive

Louise and Jack on their happiest day, 1931. PHOTOGRAPH BY ANTHONY BERARDI, AUTHOR'S COLLECTION

examples of the human extremes that surfaced during the amazing decade of the 1920s.

McGurn utilized his intelligence and talents for criminal gain, but he still stands out as an amazing example of human achievement. As unfortunate as his choices may have been, one cannot deny the tremendous and lasting impact that he made on law, politics, popular culture, and criminal endeavor.

Jack and Louise's story is far richer than the previous attempts to describe them or the stereotypes that have become their legacy. As is the case for superheroes who are impossibly larger than life, at some point the humanity of these antiheroes must be revealed. Otherwise we can never understand the person who lives under the costume, whether it is Superman's Clark Kent or an immaculately dressed killer called Jack McGurn and his wayward middle-class minx, Louise Rolfe.

Cu rispettu,
JEFFREY GUSFIELD

Author's Note

Although I have portrayed some "common sense" emotions on behalf of a few people, please note that this is a completely documented and researched work of nonfiction; most of those instances were also suggested by my two anonymous sources, both of whom were extremely close to the Gebardi-DeMory and Rolfe families.

Obviously we cannot know the innermost feelings of those involved, but after more than forty years of work uncovering the details from libraries, historical societies, newspaper morgues, law enforcement and judicial files, and personal interviews, I have allowed the 99.9 percent that is fact to support the 0.1 percent of human behavior that is anecdotal.

The Capone Outfit, 1928

Alphonse "Al Brown" Capone: The Big Fella, head of the Outfit

Frank "The Enforcer" Nitti: Chief operating officer and tactician

Jack Guzik: Chief financial officer and bagman for political fixes

"Machine Gun" Jack McGurn (Vincent Gebardi): Head gunner, tactician

Ralph "Bottles" Capone, Lawrence "Dago" Mangano, and Charlie Fischetti: Beer distributors

Joe Fusco: Hard-liquor distributor

Johnny Patton (mayor of Burnham): Beer distributor and specialist in political fixes

Frank Pope and Anthony "Mops" Volpe: Gambling and handbook managers

Peter P. Penovich Jr.: Manager of floating casinos

James V. Mondi: Overseer of Capone takes from independents

Hyman "Loud Mouth" Levin: Chief collector for Mondi

Dennis "Duke" Cooney: Capone whoremaster in charge of brothels

George "Red" Barker, William J. "Three-Finger Jack" White, and Murray L. "Curly" Humphreys: Labor-racketeering specialists

Frank "Frankie" Cline (Frank Rio): Main bodyguard

Louis "Little New York" Campagna, Frank Milano, Frank "Diamond" Maritote, and Phil D'Andrea: Bodyguards

James "King of the Bombers" Belcastro and Joseph Genaro: Explosives specialists

Sam "Golf Bag" Hunt, Tony "Joe Batters" Accardo, Joey O'Brien (Joseph Aiuppa), Paul "The Waiter" Ricca (Felice Delucia), Rocco DeGrazia, Louis "Little New York" Campagna, John Scalise, Albert Anselmi, Joe "Hop Toad" Guinta, Rocco Fischetti, Willie Heeney, and Gus Winkeler: Drivers and gunmen

DEADLY VALENTINES

Prologue

Call Everybody!

Valentine's Day, 1929

L ike most participants in the sideshow of the Ages, police sergeant Thomas J. Loftus, star number seventy, hasn't a clue that he is poised on the brink of history. In the morning, he pulls his Arctics on over his shoes and buttons his shin-length blue wool coat against the fourteen-degree Chicago air. This day will see no sun and will only get four degrees warmer. As he leaves his apartment at 2737 Carmen Avenue to work the day shift, he is concerned only with buying some Valentine's candy for his wife and daughter.[1]

Sergeant Loftus, born in Chicago, is a veteran cop at fifty-four, his ginger hair rapidly receding, making him thankful for his hat on such a morning. The city is misty, dotted with clouds of steam that come from the thousands of smokestacks, sidewalk vents, and manhole spouts. By the time he arrives at the Thirty-Sixth District station house at 1501 North Hudson Avenue, it is fifteen degrees, and the air is filled with a light and picturesque snow, a Valentine's gift from Lake Michigan.

So far, it is a quiet Thursday morning. Loftus begins jawing with a local neighborhood cop fan, an eighteen-year-old named Billy Rudd, who occasionally stops by for coffee. At 10:45, as he and Billy drink the strong station-house java and watch the street through frost-coated glass windows, Desk Sergeant Harrity answers a phone call from a nearly hysterical woman identifying herself as Mrs. Landesman. Loftus catches part of

Harrity's side of the conversation as the sergeant tries to calm the woman on the other end of the wire. Harrity finally hangs up and turns to Loftus, explaining that there's a screaming Mimi over on Clark Street who says there's lots of gunfire at 2122 North.

Loftus is the only cop in the station; everybody else is out on patrol. Both Model A squad flivvers are gone, and Billy Rudd doesn't drive. A telephone-company electrician is working on the alarm switch box near the front desk. Loftus buttonholes him and asks him for a ride. Wanting to get in on the excitement, the electrician succumbs to human nature and nods his head. He'll gladly drive Loftus wherever he wants to go. Billy Rudd asks to come along, and the three of them bundle up and hurry out the front.

At that moment, one of the squads pulls up. Loftus runs over, yanks open the passenger door, and sticks his head in, informing the two officers inside that they should follow him to Clark Street. As with every call, it could be something or it could be nothing. Loftus slams the door and jumps into the passenger seat of the telephone truck, with Billy Rudd climbing in behind him.

Thrilled to be doing anything other than his job, the electrician, whose name is Charlie Corrigan, throws the Ford into gear. He plays policeman all the way, speeding around streetcars on the icy pavement. When they pull up in front of the Clark Street address, Loftus jumps out and spots a frantic woman in the open window of the second-floor apartment, which is situated over a tailor's shop. She is yelling and pointing down at the painted window that says SMC CARTAGE.

A small crowd is beginning to gather as Loftus opens the door, which is swollen from the harsh winter and proves resistant. He unholsters his service revolver. The other two officers haven't shown up in their patrol car yet, so Loftus enters with Billy Rudd following behind. The first thing the policeman becomes aware of is the dog inside, howling as if being tortured. Something is very wrong, very bad in there. He enters the foyer of the building, an office cheaply partitioned off from the long expanse of garage that runs perpendicular to Clark Street.

Loftus hesitantly steps forward and announces loudly that he is a police officer. The door closes. The frigid air is immediately sucked out and replaced by an overwhelmingly different atmosphere. Over the smell of concrete and gasoline is the odor of wet cloth, the pungent scent of cordite from ignited gunpowder, and something else that raises his hackles. Loftus carefully follows the sights of his Colt revolver through a partitioned hallway and into the garage. He takes a left at the end and slowly moves down an aisle braced with seven trucks and three automobiles.[2]

Twenty feet inside, Loftus spots a man trying to crawl toward him, quickly recognizing him as gangster Frank Gusenberg, whose nickname is Hock. Gusenberg is dressed in a dark suit and overcoat and leaves a smeared, crimson trail in his wake.

Half blind and dying, Gusenberg recognizes the police officer and begs, "For heaven's sake, get me to a hospital!" The words and the broken voice that utter them send a solid chill up Loftus's neck and spine. He runs over to the pathetic form, almost slipping when his shoes pass through viscous, spattered blood and the hundred brass cartridges that are strewn everywhere.[3] He commands Billy Rudd to go back outside and guard the door, his voice cracking as he yells, "Call an ambulance! Call Deputy Commissioner Wolfe and the bureau of investigation! Call the switchboard! Call everybody!"

Loftus kneels down next to Gusenberg. There are ragged bullet holes in the back of his coat, each oozing red. Placing his revolver on the concrete floor, he turns the man over as gently as possible. It's like squeezing a leaking paper bag.

Loftus looks at the fellow's thick neck and the spattered gore on his broad face. Gusenberg has been a familiar participant in Chicago crime for years, acting as a robber, gunman, and newspaper-union muscleman. Gusenberg and his crazy-eyed older brother Pete, nicknamed Goose, worked for Dean O'Banion's gang and are now associated with O'Banion's inheritor, North Side bootlegger George Moran, who uses the garage as a delivery depot.

Gusenberg has been shot so many times that his clothing is shredded. Blood spills from his shirt cuffs. He's taken bullets in the groin area, and his pants are glistening red. The dog maintains its tormented barking, getting louder as Loftus stands up and approaches. It is a maddening sound. As the whole panorama of the garage comes into focus, punctuated by the monstrous, unceasing noise of the crazed animal, Loftus gasps. He's seen his share of dead bodies in his thirty years as a Chicago cop, including many gunshot victims and dozens of stabbings. He's seen bloated corpses pulled out of the Chicago River and Lake Michigan, but nothing he's ever imagined is as evil or grotesque as the sight before him.

To his right is a wall of bodies. Light wisps of steam or smoke—he can't tell which—rise from a half-dozen decimated human shells, all frozen in a tableau of sudden, violent death. They seem to float on rivulets of blood that run toward a central floor drain. Four of the dead lie together. Three of them are perpendicular to the brick wall on their backs, and one is on his stomach, jammed up against the wall at their feet. A fifth corpse lies at a forty-five-degree angle to their left, a light-colored fedora positioned strangely on his chest, as if someone gently placed it there. To his left a sixth lies near the corner of the room, slumped against a chair. Several of them have been shot in the head, and two lie in lumps of their own brains, their skulls burst open like gourds that have fallen from a height to reveal their pithy innards.

This isn't Custer's dead Seventh Cavalry or the Argonne of the Great War. This is a garage in the heart of Chicago, a great, modern city. Loftus feels his scalp burning as a numbing shock pushes his own blood down through his body, making him feel like he weighs a ton. Moreover, the shocks keep coming. Loftus leans down and hears Gusenberg moaning over the ceaseless railing of the dog, its echo pounding against the brick walls and concrete floor. It looks like some kind of shepherd; it is chained to the axle underneath a truck that is being repaired. The animal is running and lurching insanely into the air, then violently being pulled back when it reaches the end of the tether.

"Do you know me, Frank?" Loftus yells.

The man's eyes flutter open. Blood seeps from between his red, gritted teeth. Gusenberg's eyes attempt to focus on Loftus. He coughs, spattering Loftus's wool coat and chin with bright-red droplets.

"Yes, you are Tom Loftus," gargles Gusenberg.

"Frank! Who did this? What happened?"

It is a question that will be asked by millions of people for a very long time.

Gusenberg groans, which turns into a gargling sound in his throat. "Won' talk."

There are police gongs ringing nearby, outside on Clark Street. There are the faint sounds of more people out on the sidewalk. Gusenberg moans and coughs, his body shaking. Loftus sees life slipping away. How can a person this decimated still be alive? He grips the man's coat, feeling his hands fill with blood, which has already saturated the wool like a sponge.

"You're in bad shape."

Gusenberg groans and closes his eyes. "For God's sake, ge' me to hosh-pital!"

Loftus tries again. "Who did the shooting?"

"I refuse to talk," manages Gusenberg.

Loftus shakes his head. These tough guys are all the same, all hard cases with a stupid code of silence. The dog continues to howl. Its intensity is the same, but its bark grows raspy as it chokes itself again and again on the chain. Loftus must feel like everything is unreal, as if he is watching himself from above, holding the dying Gusenberg.

"The wagon is coming, Frank. Is your brother here, too?"

Gusenberg tries to focus on the policeman. His eyes are black, like a dead dog's. "Yes," he gulps. Frothy blood bubbles across his rapidly bluing lips.

"Were you all lined up against the wall?"

Gusenberg's eyes are rolling up into his head. "Won' talk," he repeats.

The two lagging officers, Tom Christy and George Love, arrive along with the ambulance driver and attendant. Loftus orders them to hurry Gusenberg over to Alexian Brothers Hospital, which is the closest. As they load Gusenberg onto a gurney, Loftus spots Gusenberg's brother Pete, who is slumped in the chair in the far corner. He walks over and sees that Pete is gone. Loftus doesn't recognize any of the other victims. It occurs to him that someone else might be alive, although he doubts it. He yells after the medics to get a doctor. A few minutes later, a neighborhood doctor who has been summoned from his nearby office on North Clark arrives and quickly examines the other men.[4] "Jesus," he whispers as he goes from one bloody body to another. They are all dead.

Soon, from behind Loftus, through the cheap foyer of the SMC Cartage Company, from the frozen streets, come those who will report this to the rest of the world. It is the most shocking abomination of a still-young twentieth century, a virtual criminal earthquake that will vibrate around the world and define Chicago in popular culture. They all ask the same question: Who did this?

PART I

Arrival

1

I Came to America to Give a Better Future to My Children

1906

Giuseppa Verderame Gibaldi has brought the children to the main deck for their arrival in America; they huddle at the port railing of the steamship *Gregory Morch*.[1] They are from warm Sicily and have never known such cold. Giuseppa has them wrapped in every piece of clothing they have, including blankets. They watch gulls and winter birds wheeling over the skies near the Sandy Hook lighthouse. Twenty minutes later, after passing through the narrows between Brooklyn and Staten Island, the Statue of Liberty appears, floating like the Madonna over the white-capped harbor.

Baby Salvatore is in Giuseppa's arms, and she is holding four-year-old Vincenzo's little hand in a tight grip; he is an incredibly active toddler.[2] Clinging to them is Giuseppa's eight-year-old brother, Francesco. They can hardly hear over the howling wind, the deep thrumming of the steam engines, and the echoes of the harbor horns. The chilling, salty wind whips through their ebony hair, which the Anglo ticket agents in Palermo describe as "maroon."[3] They stare in wonderment at the *signura virdi* with her torch. They left Palermo on Thursday, November 7. Today—the day of their arrival at the port of New York—is Saturday, November 24. The four of them spent their eighteen-day journey in second cabin, a single stateroom with washing facilities, which was provided by Tommaso's money from America. It is almost a luxury accommodation compared to the steerage level that most Italian immigrants endure. Giuseppa has been watchdog, nurse, and mother to three little boys in an impossibly tiny space for over two weeks. She is strong, but still, the daunting task has worn her out. At times, she has certainly wondered if this is all worth the effort. The thought of dry land must be intoxicating.

The steamship *Gregory Morch*, 1906. ELLIS ISLAND FOUNDATION

Giuseppa will soon Americanize her name to Josephine. She has recorded her age on the passenger manifest as twenty-four, but in reality she is only nineteen.[4] She claims to be older because she is towing three children alone. She has been warned that most Americans do not favor fifteen-year-olds having babies.

The father of her two boys, Tommaso Gibaldi, awaits the arrival of his family at 14 Union Street in Brooklyn, an apartment building that sits right on the apron of the docks. It is inhabited largely by immigrant men waiting for their families to arrive. Having preceded them to America, landing on April 19, 1903, Tommaso is now nineteen, born the same year as Giuseppa.[5] He has slaved for twenty-two cents an hour for two and a half years as a longshoreman so he can bring his family over to America. He and his young wife want to escape the poverty and hopelessness of Sicily, where aspirations seem to wither, where Old World ways, cultures of vengeance, and murder remain the norm. They want to prosper without paying feudal extortion to Mafia or Black Hand criminals, who watch for signs of success like the familiar tarantulas that hide in wait to prey on fat insects. The Gibaldis desire a small place in America, where their hard work will move them forward in life, where their children will have choices, rewards, and freedom from tyranny.

Giuseppa sees Governor's Island as it appears on the right; ahead is Ellis Island. As the ship steers to port and enters the harbor, she turns toward the stern and surveys in wonderment the broken New York skyline. Everywhere she looks, the panorama is overwhelming. Her emotions wander from joy to awe to fear. America is already beyond anything she has imagined. She hugs Salvatore to her breast and squeezes Vincenzo's hand. She must feel tiny and insignificant, surrounded by the vast mountain range of concrete, smokestacks, and steel, with the unknown territories ahead.

Marked by cacophony and long waiting lines, the degrading and dehumanizing process of the immigrant arrival at Ellis Island awaits them. They are all questioned, examined, poked, and prodded, while Giuseppa struggles with the children. Her English is minimal. She tries her best to communicate with the officious American agents, who seem to have limited sympathy for the multitudes. There are only a handful of translators for the hundreds of Italians and none for the Sicilians. She juggles Salvatore, restrains Vincenzo, and keeps an eye on Francesco while the uniformed immigration Anglos hammer away at her.

She must think that perhaps she is losing her mind, especially as she physically fights to contain Vincenzo, whose energies seem endless. She yearns for Tommaso to help her as she brushes the tears from her cheeks, but he is waiting outside Ellis Island, having traveled there from Brooklyn, taking his first day off in many weeks to meet his family. He is terrified that he will lose his job on the docks, for there are hundreds of other newcomers ready to step in to replace him.

Many hours later, after the surreal torment blessedly ends, Giuseppa and all three boys prove themselves healthy and are released into their new world. Many others who have traveled with them remain quarantined on the island. Immigration doctors worry constantly about influenza, tuberculosis, and other diseases transmitted onto the mainland. At the end of a long promenade, Giuseppa spots Tommaso, a small man who now appears to be broader in his upper body from the hard labor. Giuseppa points him out to Vincenzo, and he runs to his father. Baby Salvatore was born after his father left for America; it is the first time Tommaso sees him. Nearly swooning with relief, Giuseppa weeps uncontrollably as she finally embraces her husband, as they become a new American family.

Before little Vincenzo Gibaldi lands in New York, his *arma gemella*, his soul mate, Louise May Rolfe, is born in Indianapolis on the seventh of May.

Causing her eighteen-year-old mother, Mabel, to scream in agony, Louise is already making her pay. She is pink and bloody, with white hair and blue eyes that will remain blue. She is bathed and put into her mother's arms. Nobody could look at this beautiful baby and imagine how much trouble she will be, certainly not her momentarily happy parents.

Mabel Clark, a hopeful teenager whose mother was from Kansas and whose father was from Iowa, had married Bernard Frank Rolfe when she was sixteen. For the Clarks, an American version of the Victorian farm family, it was as if the sky had fallen and hell had erupted up through the corn, for Mabel married Bernard thinking she was pregnant. It turned out she was wrong: all those strange physical symptoms she was experiencing were from her first sexual encounter. The simple fear of her sins made her nearly hysterical. Her body reacted accordingly to the stress, fooling her, causing her to assume the worst.

Bernard Frank Rolfe, who was born in 1877 in Missouri, the Show Me state, asked pretty young Mabel to show him, and she did. He was handsome, and she was mesmerized. He was twenty-seven, and she, like many farm daughters, wanted desperately to get out of Iowa for a big city, full of life and culture. He had not yet learned that everybody is beautiful when they are young. They married under duress in a country church full of grim Midwestern faces.

Realizing full well that Mabel's people wanted to impale Bernard on a pitchfork, they ran from that stoic prairie wrath to Indianapolis, where Bernard had family. Bernard wanted to be in advertising; his vision of the new century was one of a retail and marketing heaven. He was a communicative talker and a first-rate salesman. Who else could get a sixteen-year-old farmer's daughter to give up her virginity in her own father's barn?

After nine months in Indiana, she gives birth to Louise and presents her with the middle name of May, after herself and the joyful month. In the interim, Mabel has learned that Indianapolis isn't that much different from Des Moines; it's just another medium-size, provincial Midwestern town. She has yet to discover a true big city.

Six years later, Bernard, hungry to be in the advertising business that he finds so alluring, takes his young wife and daughter to Chicago. He becomes completely immersed in the world of selling and advertising anything and everything to the vast sea of eager new consumers in America's second largest city. While pregnant, Mabel gained sixty pounds, at least forty of which will remain with her. By the time they are ensconced on the North Side of Chicago, any affection Mabel and Bernard have for each other is evaporating like the morning mist on the Chicago River.

2

Sicily in Brooklyn

1907

The Americanization of the Gibaldi family has begun. It is a difficult challenge for any greenhorn immigrant, although the very young seem to have an easier time of it. Vincenzo—which means the same thing as "James," more or less—refuses to be called anything other than Vincent. Salvatore becomes Sam, and Giuseppa is now Josephine.

Brooklyn days are far more challenging than she has ever anticipated. At night, however, cloistered in their tiny apartment at 9 Union Street, she tries to direct Vincent's dreams. Each evening she puts baby Sam to bed and then rocks Vincent to sleep in her arms, whispering of her Sicily.

Josephine has found the American immigrant experience daunting, even frightening at times. The culture shock is immense. She takes sweet comfort in verbally reconstructing Sicily for her children. She transfers to Vincent her world and her perceptions so that many of his first childhood memories are his mother's very best recollections. She wants him to remember the land of his birth, for she sees how America takes over the spirit. She senses that, with time, they will all completely forget their homeland.

Josephine and Tommaso had grown up in the little village of Licata, near Agrigento, the largest city on the southwestern coast of Sicily. Like most young people in their world, they had children at an age so tender that they hardly knew each other.

Tommaso Gibaldi came from a line of market haulers who brought fresh vegetables and fruits up and down the coast. Little Vincent has almost no memory of Licata, where their tiny house caught the fragrant sea breezes from the Mediterranean. They lived in one of the true garden spots of the earth, but their Eden was ruined by poverty and violent criminals. This is exactly why Tommaso chose to bring Josephine and the children to America, where the opportunity is endless, poverty can be reversed, and laws protect the citizens.

As it still is to most immigrants, America is an immense challenge to Josephine. At first, she probably wakes up in the morning and wonders why she has traded the poverty of Sicily for the poverty of America. She misses the Sicilian coast more than she can express. On many hot Brooklyn nights, longing for her home while Tommaso works a brutal late second shift on the docks as a loader, she must feel claustrophobic. At night in Licata, the ocean sends cool breezes into town; on those gentle winds are fragrant hints of African orange blossoms and Greek olive trees. Licata smells of wild orchids and other subtropical coastal blossoms, of *scupazzu*, the dwarf palms that grow everywhere, sweating in the hot sun. It is an identifiable combination carried subtly on the breezes of the Sicilian coast, that made Josephine feel heady as if from wine.

She whispers of these things to Vincent, high up on the asphalt roof above the streets of Brooklyn. She re-creates a romantic, perfect Sicily for him. She speaks to him in Sicilian, which contains threads of Arabic and Spanish, even though it sounds close to Italian, which is actually a dialect of Tuscan. Sicilian has no future tense and, like Sicily itself, no future for Josephine and her family. America is all about the future.

Yet Josephine relates to her son that the sands of the Sicilian coast are the richest witnesses in the world, having seen the arrival of the Greeks, Phoenicians, Romans, Vandals, Carthaginians, Saracens, Normans, Germans, and Spaniards. He is fascinated by the history of Sicily, by the thousands of years of cultural invasions, and thus the true complexity of being *Sicilianu*. Like all good mothers, each night Josephine must exhaust her already tired body and mind trying to get Vincent calmed down by telling him stories.

Josephine insists on calling Vincent "Jimmy" (in her strong accent it comes out "Jeemie"), for which he rebukes her. He is Vincent Gibaldi, and he doesn't like the name James. Even though it is a solid American name, he refuses to let anyone call him anything but Vincent. He makes fun of his mother's thick accent when she tries to say "Jimmy." She is the only person who will ever call him this.[1]

The children in the Brooklyn schools are unusually tough and often violent. They have inherited a legacy of brutal behavior from the unfortunate traditions of the Five Points area, mirroring the adults in their lives. Even in the youngest grades, the public schools are alarming examples of survival of the fittest. It becomes the sad duty of all immigrant parents to go about converting their sweet children into survivors.

Josephine tells Vincent old Sicilian stories about strong-willed youngsters who were forced into violent, adult actions in order to avenge the wrongs done to their loved ones. These are the Sicilian versions of Robin Hood and the romanticized American West, imbued with a liminal coming-of-age mystique. They will hopefully better prepare Vincent for the streets of Brooklyn.[2]

The folk tales are epic, about the outlaw heroes of Sicily, mythologies that have been expanded from generation to generation and grow with each telling. They recount adventures of violence, robbery, and revenge that have acquired a patina of Sicilian mores over many hundreds of years, imparting the wisdom of the peculiar codes of conduct, justice, and honor. For Josephine, they define much of what she's been taught about men, although she knows that her own husband toils more fearsomely in America than the protagonists of her stories. She wants to make sure, however, that Vincent understands the responsibilities of manhood from her Sicilian perspective. She relies on the entertainment value of her son's imagination.

Vincent loves every sport; he is always moving, always running. Getting him to sleep is still a never-ending struggle. He denies he is tired until he literally drops, which makes Josephine feel close to dropping as well. She combines her lessons of manliness with the only method she knows to get him to bed: he can be counted on to beg for a story. Josephine will always give in, because it is still their tradition and she feels relieved to have him remain still.

She recounts to Vincent tales of *vinnitta*. He will be restless with feelings of pride as he hears about resourceful Sicilians carrying out their revenge. Vincent must feel the hot rush of blood to his face, little needle pricks of emotion, spawned by the overwhelming, self-righteous sense of justice. These cathartic rhythms simmer inside him. He is already tightly in control of his emotions, having learned this from the rare hours spent with his father. Life is demanding, and men are serious. From these stories, Josephine is able to instruct him, hopefully giving him a better ability to see what is coming in the schoolyard and on the streets before he becomes a casualty.

She wants their share of the promises of America, but education for the poor comes with a high price. She expands her storytelling to include all of the cautions that reflect her gravest worries for her greenhorn children out on the mean streets. The immigrant experience, especially in New York, is initially a dialogue of survival.

Josephine doesn't need to worry. Her little Vincent is a splendid survivor. Taking his cues from the oral tradition of his Sicilian heroes, he is fearless. He is naturally prepared. Vincent will know to take the enemy by surprise, for only a stupid cow marches into battle; better to be a scorpion and wait for the adversary in his shoe. He will learn that victory always depends on great preparation, that the better the sketch, the better the finished painting. In a fight, he will learn always to aim for the head—a man with a bleeding, broken nose will almost always cease his attack.

He will be cautioned never to fight angry, which will make him lose his senses. He should always retreat and return another day with a plan. He is admonished to always walk away from trouble smiling, because to avoid blame, one must seem innocent. He is cautioned to remain a good man, *un omu di rispettu*, and harm nobody who is innocent. This way the people will stay behind him and remain his friends.

He is also warned never to boast, to talk of nothing concerning his affairs to others, not even to his friends. In addition, Josephine's Sicilian tales certainly teach him the virtue of *silenziu*, always to keep his mouth shut and his eyes open.

From what the future will prove, Josephine also insists that her children always be polite and display good manners. In their home there is great respect for elders, the ever-present reminders from their Roman Catholic traditions. However, Vincent certainly learns early that family life and street life demand different rules. As in the home of his future boss, Alphonse Capone, who also lives nearby in Brooklyn, his mother's table is a sacred place, the most important sanctuary. Good sons speak differently at home in front of their parents than they do outside, where dog eats dog. It is a masculine code to conduct personal business away from one's family. This duplicity seems to be an unwritten law in immigrant homes, like wiping one's feet before entering. Life is hard in America, too. A man doesn't complain.

One of the guiding concepts in most Sicilian families is honor. Shame and disgrace result from dishonor, which seems to be worse than death itself. Moreover, they subscribe to an old-world version of honor; to Sicilians, it is the total definition of any human being, the cornerstone of Sicilian culture, even in Brooklyn. A person is either honorable or not. Surrounding Vincent is a world of men who bend the laws to get by in America. Nevertheless, each one is judged in his own community by his sense of honor. As in other cultures, this might be considered hypocrisy, but it is the basis of life in Sicily, where a righteous man can be a killer and still remain honorable, perhaps even well liked.

To his dismay, Tommaso Gibaldi finds that the Black Hand gangsters have become just as entrenched in America. The extortionists and murderers who prey on the vulnerable in Sicily have moved their operations to Brooklyn, where they urbanize their modus operandi. Their activities have become so widespread and notorious that the state's attorney in Kings County recognizes their milieu and gathers his troops to combat this Sicilian menace. A headline in the *Brooklyn Eagle* claims THE FIGHT AGAINST THE BLACK HAND IN THE CITY WILL NOW BE UNDERTAKEN IN EARNEST.[3]

In another world, the Rolfes live in a three-bedroom apartment at 632 West Addison Street, a few blocks from Lake Michigan on Chicago's growing North Side.[4] Both parents adore Louise while suffering a growing estrangement from each other. Bernard is rarely home, his ambition taking him downtown to the Loop as well as to other cities in the Midwest. Consequently, Mabel spends all her time with Louise. When Bernard comes home on his increasingly infrequent visits, he spoils his daughter, trying to make up for his growing absence.

Mabel feels more and more like a prisoner in their apartment. To assuage her growing claustrophobia and loneliness, she eats rich foods and reads movie magazines. Her body has transformed into a matronly heft, with thick ankles and a sagging bosom. She tries to hide it all under tent-like flowered dresses. Bernard, whom she and everyone else call Frank, will look at anyone else but his wife.

Louise is bright and hears everything. Like most children, she understands the nuances of adult emotions, something that her parents probably sense but deny. The growing distance, resentment, and bitterness in their home hang like heavy curtains. Little Louise knows from the time she is two that her parents don't like each other, but she also knows they put whatever love they do have in her direction. She quickly learns to accept it, use it, and abuse it. As a toddler she becomes a grand manipulator, sensing opportunity and weakness in her parents and utilizing it whenever she can. She is completely adorable, and they must find it hard to say no to her. They are miserable in their tenuous union, but as long as Louise appears happy, they continue with their domestic charade, which will not last long.

3

He's Capable of Learning Many Things

1911–1917

On Union Street, the Gibaldi family grows larger when a third son, Frank, arrives on January 15, 1910.[1] Daughter Angela, called Angelina, is born nine months later. Vincent at nine is completely athletic, constantly finding new outlets for his formidable energy. He attends the nearest public school, most likely the original incarnation of P.S. 29 at 425 Henry Street, which is about half a mile away, the closest to his home. He excels in almost every sport, having a natural ability at anything physical. He has also learned English; his accent is rapidly fading into typical Brooklynese, though his father remains mostly unable to read or speak the language of his new country. This is mainly the reason why Josephine chooses to speak mostly Sicilian at home, laboring to learn only the most essential English.

There is the expected stress in the Gibaldi home, with Tommaso almost never there except to eat and sleep. If he and Josephine hardly knew each other before they were married in Sicily, they spend even less time together now. Like most immigrant fathers, Tommaso often works more than one strenuous shift, a physically exhausting life that takes its toll on the little man. In the early winter of 1911, he contracts a strong, invasive virus and dies in bed before the New Year. There is no record of his interment in any of the Brooklyn cemeteries; it is likely that his body is cremated. This is a core, tragic loss for his children. For Josephine, it is devastating. She is now alone with four children and no financial support.

By the spring of 1912, Josephine is a single, overwhelmed mother. She is attractive and still young; thankfully, her Brooklyn parish doesn't let her suffer for long. The women of her neighborhood take care of their own, making sure that she is introduced to grocer Angelo DeMory, who is modestly prosperous and open to inheriting the full load of Josephine's children.

They have a swift, polite courtship. Mercifully, Josephine is not bound by the societal restrictions of Sicily that dictate a prolonged period of mourning—America offers the alternative of expedience. By early autumn, Angelo DeMory has become the man of the house, assuming the financial burden, apparently without a qualm.

On April 15, 1913, Josephine gives birth to Anthony, the first DeMory son. He is a magnificent child, with brown eyes, black hair, and perfect features.[2] His eleven-year-old stepbrother Vincent adores him, eventually becoming almost like a surrogate father to the baby, forming a special bond that will last their entire lives.

Meanwhile, Vincent has met the tough streets of Brooklyn as well as the youthful violence of the schoolyard. Street gangs are everywhere, still carrying on the nineteenth-century traditions of the infamous Dead Rabbits and their Five Points pals. One of the fiercest gangs is the Five Points Juniors, comprised of eager adolescents copying their ruthless fathers and brothers. Because of this, Angelo DeMory has encouraged Vincent to learn to box, for he is small for his age, a natural target for bullies.

Vincent immediately falls in love with pugilism. He learns boxing's twelve Queensberry rules, but in order to protect his precious five cents of lunch money and to fend off the meaner, truly aggressive children, he develops quickly into a fist fighter. He is oddly fearless and as fast as he is small. His resolve and intensity at any sport, especially this one, is impressive.

Vincent is unusually tough for someone so young. He has already learned that thievery and extortion are part of everyday grammar-school life. The strong always prey on the weaker. As he experiences more of the realities of schoolyard mayhem, he practices his boxing with greater intensity. He quickly learns that his immigrant status and especially his Sicilian ancestry make him a potential victim of the gangs. He knows that sooner or later he will face them. No doubt he's had a few small skirmishes in his years at P.S. 29 that are more like rehearsals and child's play than real violence. By the time he is in sixth grade, pushing has evolved to fist-fighting, as the height and weight of the children have increased. At eleven, Vincent is still smaller but noticeably tougher than most of them.

Josephine hates the violence but is even more afraid of the larger children hurting Vincent (she continues to call him Jimmy, to his chagrin). As he passes through elementary and middle school, he begins to box in gymnasiums and YMCA rings. By the time he is in high school, he is serious about fighting as a welterweight anywhere he can. He is known in the neighborhood as a fierce competitor with the gloves on; bare-fisted, he is merciless. Josephine seems to ignore her son's growing reputation of preferring to beat on others rather than be beaten. Stepfather Angelo is proud that his boy, who is small of stature, is respected for his physical fierceness. They encourage Vincent, each in their own way.

In 1917, as America enters World War I, Vincent, fifteen, is attending his sophomore year in high school, his last year of formal education.[3] Two monumental awakenings have directed him toward his own path in life. Relatively intelligent and a dreamer, he realizes that working twelve hours a day as a manual laborer like his birth father is not for him.[4] In addition, he has also seen how many of his peers prefer an easier road, taking advantage of the rich pickings of America in less than legitimate enterprises. Also living out their youth in Brooklyn are the future spine of Chicago crime: Alphonse Capone, though a few years older than Vincent, often hangs out at a club on Carroll Street with an assortment of Italian and Irish thugs. Frank Nitti and Louis Campagna (who will be nicknamed "Little New York" when he comes to Chicago) are also growing up in those streets.

There are no known police records attesting that Vincent Gibaldi is anything but a dedicated young athlete who wants to box in the professional ring, where the prestige and riches are almost unimaginable. It is the dream of many tough young men who would love to climb out of their poverty and into the spotlight of the fight world. Well-known boxers walk the streets of Brooklyn with impunity, worshipped by everyone. They are the star athletes of their day, practiced and tough, making more money as they progress in the game. This is how Vincent must see himself. He wants to be tough with style, like the heroes in the dime novels and crime magazines sold in Brooklyn, such as Bat Masterson and Doc Holliday.

Vincent's other awakening is spurred by the game of golf. He is introduced to the links and works as a caddie at one of the few country clubs in or near Brooklyn. The Dyker Beach Golf Course, built in 1896, is only six miles from Carroll Street, and it's accessible by streetcar. It is a lovely course, near the Narrows, directly across from Staten Island. Though caddying begins as a way for Vincent to hustle a quarter, it instills in him a love for golf, which will eventually bring him to a professional venue and a moment that will define his life. Once Vincent swings a club, he discovers he has an astonishing gift, a natural kinship with a very difficult sport.

Vincent has always been an athletic mimic, able to play any sport with considerable success. Besides boxing, golf becomes his passion. There are a few Catholic clubs and youth organizations that make the learning of the game available to youngsters who might not otherwise have the opportunity. It is predominantly a rich person's pursuit, but its popularity will continue to grow, welcoming a larger spectrum of players. Vincent develops a good swing almost immediately, although he cannot afford to truly play the game, certainly another reason to achieve financial success as soon as possible.

Vincent learns quite a lot about the wealthy country-club golfers, the people he will regard as "swells" in the 1920s, who will eventually help to make him comfortable with them on any golf course. With his baby face and polite comportment, he must be popular as a caddie. At the end of the season, the best caddies sometimes get tossed a "rock"—a coveted, magnificently heavy silver dollar.

Vincent must certainly take notice when Bobby Jones wins the 1917 Southern Amateur Championship. He and Jones are the same age. Perhaps this serves as an inspiration, furthering Vincent's resolve to excel at his own chosen sport of boxing. At the very least, young stars like Jones must serve as icons to Vincent, giving him further impetus to play golf, which comes so easily to him. Between both boxing and golf, Vincent is finally able to effectively channel his powerful resources of teenage energy.

Louise Rolfe's mother, Mabel, is isolated, unhappy, and middle-aged long before her youth is over. She has hosts of fears and worries, many of which she projects on Louise. The guilt of her polluted virtue and her transformation from dutiful Iowa daughter to corpulent, unhappy hausfrau have her convinced that her eleven-year-old daughter must be warned away from that terrible reality. Even though she has ample money from Frank, she is miserable. She preaches to Louise about every possible pitfall, advice that will have exactly the opposite influence, nourishing the seeds of rebellion.

Mabel is concerned with the typical moral imperatives of her post–Victorian era sensibilites. She will warn Louise to always keep her wits about her, that alcohol is the devil's tool, and that no real lady ever goes out alone at night, a habit left to streetwalkers. With the new fashions exploding into the stores and modesty being whittled away daily, she will no doubt warn Louise that a lady always covers up her body. She will reason that men only want one thing and that there's no need to encourage them to take what is not theirs. She will warn her daughter that men are like wild animals—they have no control.

Louise knows better. She is a child of earthy instincts. Whenever her mother says that men are this or men are that, she is really referring to one man. Mabel will quote the commandments of her lost youth: A man needs to respect a woman. A woman must never give herself to just any man. A man should be home with his family. A man has different interests and needs than a woman has. Louise understands perfectly that when her mother speaks of men, she is speaking of all the things that she does not get from her man. And when her mother speaks of women, it is a litany of regrets, things that she has failed in doing herself.

At eleven, Louise has learned that, rather than adopt her mother's myriad worries, she should choose to ignore and even embrace them. She must begin to see her mother as a spoiled, plaintive, and pathetic victim.

Like eroding sand in an hourglass, she begins to lose respect for her. To Mabel's utter dismay, Louise is completely gregarious as well as increasingly rebellious, already rejecting even the slightest constructive suggestions out of hand.

To make up for his expanding absence, Frank Rolfe gives his daughter anything she might desire out of guilt. She forms a habit that will come to define her as a woman. She becomes spoiled by the primary man in her life at a very early age.

4

She Who Is Born Beautiful
Is Born Married

1918

Vincent Gibaldi's sixteenth year brings a tidal wave of tremendous changes. America becomes embroiled in a world war. Stepfather Angelo is slightly too old to be drafted, and Vincent is not old enough. Moreover, with the war making the grocery services busier than ever, Angelo DeMory doesn't lack for gainful employment. In addition to attending high school, Vincent trains several mornings a week at a gym or the YMCA. He has a lot of confidence, loves music, is always lively, dances well, and has become popular with young women. Life seems full and promising; he is carefree, acting on his dreams as well as his responsibilities.

For some reason, perhaps to honor a wish of his father's, Vincent alters his name from Gibaldi to Gebardi.[1] Depending upon the situation, he will even claim his stepfather's name, DeMory, sometimes spelling it Demore. But he will mostly prefer to be known as Vincent Gebardi. He is already confusing the issue of his true identity, a habit that he will maintain for the rest of his life.

In October 1918, with the Spanish influenza outbreak exploding all over the country, and particularly in New York, life seems to take on a pervasive hardship that alters everyone's existence. Six hundred to eight hundred people expire each day; the month of October will be the deadliest in the nation's history as one hundred ninety-five thousand Americans fall to the pandemic, an enormous toll.

The fear reaches every corner of New York, with influenza precautions listed on posters and flyers and in the newspapers. People live with their mouths covered, wiping surfaces with bleach and boiling anything and everything, all the while grieving. The influenza pays no heed to the importance or economic status of its victims. Rich and poor alike suffer, adding to the near hysteria in New York and everywhere else. Though Franklin D. Roosevelt, Woodrow Wilson, and America's darling, Mary Pickford, all survive the disease, several of Vincent's acquaintances will succumb to it.

With the growth of the Gebardi-DeMory clan, Vincent wants to contribute in order to ease the family's increased financial burden. As he is a dutiful son and loving brother, he leaves high school for a job on the docks, where the workers labor with masks over their mouths and noses until spring. He doesn't train at any of the gyms; everybody is too terrified of the flu, avoiding close human contact. However, the constant lifting nature of his work keeps him extremely fit, giving him a more muscular upper body, even though he is still small for his age.

Vincent keeps himself emotionally buttoned up as if he is one of the men of the house, even though he knows that he is still closer to being a child. Although he is intelligent and did well as a student, he didn't mind leaving school. Most immigrant children of his generation will achieve only an eighth-grade education or, at best, two years of high school. Moreover, it is an honor to work for his family. He has his entire life to learn what he needs to know. Certainly he doesn't expect to spend that life breaking his back like his father. He believes he is worth more, that his own world will hold better things. This is the message he has learned in Brooklyn, that there are opportunities that didn't exist in Sicily. After all, isn't that why they came to America?

In the aftermath of the influenza, there are severe economic problems in New York. Angelo DeMory believes that the grocery business is far less competitive in Chicago, where some of his friends have prospered. Angelo is tough in business and gentle with his family. He has ideas on how to make an even better living to support his formidable brood. Josephine agrees that they should go to Chicago, to the Sicilian enclave of Little Italy on the West Side, known by Chicagoans as "The Patch." There, the Sicilians are extremely ethnocentric, even refusing to be regarded as Italian. Angelo has business connections in that neighborhood. His feeling, like that of many immigrants who experience life in New York, is that it certainly might be easier to make a good living in the slower-paced, more provincial Midwest.

This news isn't so good for Vincent's dreams. As well as being torn loose from everything in the world that he knows, he won't even be able to box in Chicago. Since 1900 and the fight called the Big Fix, when Joe Gans fought "Terrible Terry" McGovern at Chicago's Tattersall's Arena, boxing has been illegal in the city.[2] Seventeen thousand fans watched McGovern knock out the African American Gans in the second round. The fans went berserk and broke up everything they could find on their way home.[3] The blame was cast on the sport of boxing rather than on the idiotic, drunken mob. Consequently, a few days later, the mayor and the city council voted to ban professional boxing in Chicago.

With this turn of events, the great fighters are forced to go elsewhere, including Europe, for their important bouts. If a fighter wants a legitimate match, he has to go outside the city limits. Yet "benefit" matches are allowed, and of course the large subculture of fight fans and gamblers still show up to conduct their wagering on the side.

Nevertheless, Vincent decides his family is more important than his career. His mother and his siblings have cast their lot with Angelo DeMory. Instead of suffering in poverty in the tenements of Brooklyn, they will be a large, happy family in a city that is smaller and perhaps more likely to afford them prosperity.

By the time 1919 comes to an end, 571 Sangamon Street has become the Chicago home of the Gebardi-DeMory clan. On January 1, 1920, the census shows the large, combined household of nine individuals,[4] all named "Demore," which the census official spells incorrectly. Angelo is listed as the father, Josephine is the wife, and the children are listed by age in descending order as James (Vincent), Sam (Salvatore), Frank, Angeline, Antonio (Anthony), Charles, and sixteen-month-old Joseph. Charles and Joseph both arrived while the family still lived in Brooklyn.

Also making his appearance in Chicago at nearly the same time as the Gebardi-DeMorys, young New Yorker Alphonse Capone comes to work as a bodyguard for Johnny Torrio, a relatively mild-mannered criminal who is a cousin to Chicago's colorful crime boss "Big Jim" Colosimo. Colosimo owns brothels with his wife, Victoria Moresco, as well as the hugely popular restaurant and cabaret Colosimo's, his pride and namesake.

Colosimo either knows or is connected to almost everybody in the city, the most successful survivor of the old underworld of the Levee district. He has welcomed cousin Johnny Torrio from Brooklyn because there's plenty for everybody in Chicago. Young Al Capone's first job for Johnny Torrio is to be a bouncer and a "capper" at the Four Deuces, Torrio's brothel-club at 2222 South Wabash Avenue. A capper stands outside and tries to lure men in, saying things like "We got a lot of nice girls in here." It's a job that requires the brazen spirit of an undeniable tough who can withstand verbal or even physical rebukes. Capone has already lived a life of criminal violence in Brooklyn, and he can be so menacing that few people challenge him.

As the Gebardi-DeMorys spend their first Christmas in Chicago, a monumental happening occurs right after the New Year that will guide the destiny of Vincent Gebardi. At the stroke of midnight on January 17, 1920, which ironically is also capper Alphonse Capone's twenty-first birthday, the "noble experiment" begins: the Volstead Act, which makes it illegal to drink alcohol, becomes the law of the land.

The government, in a great, self-righteous attempt to legislate morality, opens the door to almost thirteen years of Prohibition, thus giving birth to the grand era of the bootlegger. The smugglers, home distillers, and especially the gangsters will construct an empire that will provide libations to the thirsty masses. Many historians will claim that the dry laws will further promote the grand party of the Roaring Twenties. The legislation, draconian and puritanical, will prove to be one of America's most unfortunate mistakes, giving birth to a sense of rebellion as well as a generation of criminals who will help pave the pathway to the Depression with a trail of booze and blood.

Edward Behr best explains the people and bent ideology behind the Volstead Act in the introduction to his excellent book *Prohibition: Thirteen Years That Changed America*. He regards the "noble experiment" as "the rearguard action of a still dominant, overwhelmingly rural, white Anglo-Saxon Protestant establishment, aware that its privileges and natural right to rule were being increasingly threatened by the massive arrival of largely despised (and feared) beer-swilling, wine-drinking new American immigrants."[5]

In the cities of America, the only people who are eager to clean, repair, or do the hard work of construction are beer-swilling, wine-drinking immigrants, who work harder and longer than anybody else. They have naturally become the backbone of the urban workforce. Noted sociologist Joseph Gusfield (cousin to the author) expresses the multifarious forces that conspire to enact the Eighteenth Amendment in his book *Symbolic Crusade*, published in 1963: "Coercive reform became the dominating theme of Temperance. It culminated in the drive for national Prohibition. The Eighteenth Amendment was the high point of the struggle to assert the public dominance of old middle-class values. It established the victory of Protestant over Catholic, rural over urban, tradition over modernity, the middle class over both the lower and upper strata."[6]

In many ways, the Volstead Act represents the deepest prejudices in 1920s America. Moreover, it is just as conflicting a time for the average native-born American. As the true modernization of the United States picks up momentum in the 1920s and stress increasingly becomes an integral part of daily life, the traditional western form of relaxation becomes illegal.

Out of this enormous change will appear the bootlegger and a new generation of gangster; their time is now. They are a warrior class, archetypes of that breed of rebels who give the people back what their government has taken away, including booze, gambling, and prostitution. They will kill each other for a cut of the new rich pie, emerging from various ethnically defined neighborhoods. They will follow the middle-class model of Sinclair Lewis's George Babbitt, dressed for success like bankers, mirroring the big business barons like Rockefeller and Carnegie. Most are charitable to the people around them, although they are not exactly Robin Hoods. They do represent the needs and desires of the working-class American, especially when it comes to the imbibing of alcohol. They stand to make cascading waterfalls of money. If necessity is indeed the mother of invention, Prohibition is the father of the bootlegger.

The gangster bootleggers will actually provide a quality control that will save many lives in the coming decade. With alcohol illegal and professionally made commercial products unavailable, the country is soon flooded with substitutes that are hazardous to human health. Dangerous amateurs make libations like "Jamaican Ginger," a mixture that contains enough wood alcohol to harm the nervous system and cause blindness. Others will brew up "Yack Yack Bourbon," a moonshine flavored with iodine and burnt brown sugar. Out of thousands of private stills will come "bathtub gin," which is ethanol mixed with oil of juniper. In contrast, the gangster bootleggers will for the most part provide a non-life-threatening quality of illegal alcohol products, but they will never hesitate to threaten the life of anybody who opposes them.

The very balance of Eurocentric culture, going back to the explorers and their ships, is threatened by the Volstead legislation. People know that even the lowest-ranking seaman on the most decrepit sailing ship got his rum ration. This intrusive attempt to legislate morals is an insult to most law-abiding Americans. Never in history will such imposed "moral" behavior create such immorality.

That initial bleak winter, as the country deals with its rude new reality, Vincent Gebardi learns about Chicago. He finds the closest gymnasiums where he can train. He learns that the Maxwell Street police station at Maxwell and Morgan Streets has an upstairs gym where the neighborhood kids are welcome to work out. There are jump ropes, punching bags, and barbells. A few months before he becomes a professional fighter, he accepts the generosity of the Sixteenth District cops and trains for free.[7]

There is a traditional belief among researchers of the Capone era that Vincent becomes associated with the 42 Gang not long after he arrives in Chicago. Soon he will expand his circle to the Circus Gang on North Avenue, but this is relatively far from his home. His connection with the 42s of Little Italy makes more sense, since any young tough will be introduced to the people of his neighborhood sooner than later. Vincent is a fast-talking wise guy from the streets of Brooklyn, speaking the jargon of the day. His persona, similar to so many in his milieu, will be the model for the James Cagney and Edward G. Robinson films of the 1930s. With sound in cinema will come gangster-speak and colorful colloquialisms that will define the decades of the 1920s and form the foundation of the 1930s.

Vincent communicates this way with his new friends—1920s hip, with seasonings of attitude that emanate from each individual's emotions or lack thereof. The retorts are quick, low, and often humorous. The wild boys no doubt have great affection for their new pal Vincent Gebardi.[8]

Louise Rolfe's life with both parents together becomes altogether distasteful. Her father and mother close in on a permanent separation, which will provide relief from some of their agony. Any anger or scarring that Louise has incurred is already beginning to show. She is demanding and contradictory, and she loves to shock. She is a real version of F. Scott Fitzgerald's Ardita, the spoiled, angry flapper-philosopher[9] who invents what will become the American teenager's psychological anthem: No child ever has a bad disposition unless it's her family's fault! Whatever I am, you did it.

Like most good Lutheran mothers from Iowa, Mabel Rolfe is greatly concerned for her blossoming, rebellious daughter, who is like no one she has ever seen. To her, a good reputation is essential to living in a civi-

Teenage model Louise May Rolfe, 1920.
CHICAGO TRIBUNE ARCHIVES

lized world. She is still constantly reminding Louise of "proper behavior," warning her of the dire punishment polite society levels on people who ignore those lessons. Her fears fall on deaf ears, as Louise and many others of her generation will amply prove in short order.

A proper young lady doesn't flirt. A proper young lady doesn't laugh with her mouth open or out loud at the dining table. It is not proper to slouch or climb trees or play with boys. Proper people never spend time on street corners or in parks. A proper young lady never loiters. A proper young lady never straddles a chair; she keeps her knees tightly together. And a proper young lady would never drink alcohol, especially as it is now illegal. Ultimately these become Louise Rolfe's to-do list, which galvanizes her contrarian nature as gasoline nourishes a fire.

Louise is essentially a nice young girl, with a charming demeanor and angelic looks that compel people to like her. She is an early teenage victim in the unfortunate tug-of-war between her estranged parents. She suffers from the familiar confusion of trying to assuage the ongoing battle in her home life. She is determined not to become like her mother, whose obvious unhappiness is intertwined with her fears and regrets. The crucible of the Rolfe home has produced a different kind of young woman.[10] Whatever kinds of abuse and conflict help to form Louise, she will have a startlingly large sisterhood out in the world. Unlike her mother, she will rarely be alone. Louise craves attention, smitten by the seductiveness of fame. From his connections in advertising, Frank Rolfe gets his daughter into a corset ad, which runs in the Chicago papers. Her debut is humble, but it feeds her teenage dream. She falls in love with her own image, although it is a face shot, defined by a simple, screened newspaper engraving. With this, she truly believes she is on her way to stardom.

5

Boxing

1921

Vincent Gebardi has come to a crossroads. At twenty, he is about to realize his goal of fighting in a professional venue. His childhood dreams of success in the boxing ring actually seem to be within his grasp. He is scheduled to fight on the card on the USS *Commodore*, a Naval Reserve training ship that is essentially a huge wooden warehouse-size building, built on a barge that is docked at Lake Street and the Chicago River. The *Commodore* has been moored around town since before World War I. When it was lashed to the State Street Bridge in 1917, it was the headquarters of the Naval Militia.[1]

The Navy Post of the American Legion holds bimonthly fights onboard, with part of the gate being contributed to various veterans' groups. Charity events and benefits are the only way legally to have a boxing match in Chicago; the military, however, gets double dispensation because the ship is technically not part of Cook County. Just like the riverboat gambling that will appear in the United States in the 1990s, the *Commodore* is a floating exemption from the law.

This is an enormous opportunity for Vincent, who is new to the city and already has a sweetie—a quiet, dark-haired Sicilian girl named Helen Cannazzaro. Their young love affair extends to Vincent's family, who adore Helen. Luck seems to be on Vincent's side, for he is also in the right place at the right time: he is noticed by fight promoter and matchmaker

The *Commodore*, Chicago's floating boxing arena, 1921. *CHICAGO DAILY NEWS* ARCHIVES

Jim Mullen, who has been putting together fight cards since 1920.[2] Mullen and many others keep a close tab on the various gyms and training clubs, and they discover Vincent at Silvio Ferretti's. He has probably worked some kind of legitimate job for at least a few months, because the fees and costs to train are not something he can ignore.

Jim Mullen notices Vincent's talent and sparring record, appreciating the delicious irony of his incredible baby face. Vincent is a charming, genuine kid to anybody who doesn't threaten him. Only serious adversaries ever see his street side, which is more ruthless than ever and always at hand. Mullen magnanimously offers him his first big break and arranges for him to debut in the floating ring of the *Commodore*. Vincent Gebardi must think he's in heaven and that every one of his most fervent prayers has been answered. On October 1, he will be facing another welterweight named Jimmy Ford in a professional six-round match.[3]

Because he's known the grueling drudgery of the docks, Vincent has avoided becoming a workaday stiff, another invisible member of the American labor force, dying young and poor. Because he has talent and can employ discipline, he has achieved a rare chance at one of those American dreams that are supposed to be so plentiful but are really quite elusive. One may have ability, but luck is the true deciding factor. It is probably

McGurn's first professional opponent, Jimmy Ford, 1921. *CHICAGO DAILY NEWS* NEGATIVE COLLECTION, SDN-062451

what will make him a dedicated gambler all of his life. This stroke of precipitous luck will boost him directly into the grand arena, a gladiator with an early chance at the gold American ring. For Vincent, it is a stunning breakthrough.

The tough kid from Brooklyn is now a dedicated boxer in Chicago. He's learned some hard lessons already about his new city, but one thing does not change: Italians are held in disregard and suffer from widespread prejudice. Just as in New York, Irish and Jewish fighters dominate the game in Chicago. There are Italian battlers, but they don't fare so well, so many of them change their names to sound Irish. Vincent Gebardi decides to make his professional name Jack McGurn.

This choice of a moniker very possibly begins as a joke, "kidding on the square." Vincent invents the Irish name, choosing Jack, which is somewhat similar to his "real" name of James, and McGurn because it is the toughest-sounding Irish moniker, having a "grrr" of intimidation in it. Also at this time, McGurn's Handball Court, a revered boxing and sporting academy, is extremely well-known in the city. It was founded by the great Chicago boxer Happy Gilmore in 1887.[4] It is a swanky, forty-year-old club where Italians are not welcome; perhaps that irony tickles Vincent. The name Jack McGurn is an almost comical parody of a tough, black Irish stereotype. If he fails in the ring, Jack McGurn will bleed on the canvas for Vincent Gebardi.

After a few months, since he is new to Chicago, everyone outside of the neighborhood except his family knows him as Jack McGurn.[5]

This taking up of a nom de guerre becomes something much deeper than simply adopting a different name. Vincent Gebardi begins to disappear in many ways, creating a tough persona to accompany his new identity. From now on, he will become Jack McGurn, a variation of his former self, a more violent and ultimately dangerous young man who begins to lead a life of extreme action, both in the ring and on the street. Somehow this molting occurs rather quickly, almost as if Vincent is ready to step into a new skin. He is immediately comfortable being Jack McGurn, not only in his professional life but in his inner being.

McGurn continues to train at Ferretti's on Lake Street, just west of the Loop. This is where the toughest Italians in the city watch young fighters work out and spar. Gamblers and gangsters frequent the gym, all looking for some betting action. Most are South Siders, but even some of the North Side toughs visit Ferretti's.

In this world full of scarred mugs, McGurn looks as if he's somebody's young, visiting son. He is classed as a welterweight, weighing 140 pounds. With his clothing on, he could pass as a late adolescent. With his shirt off, his physique is mature and hard, as he has been pummeling bags and other boys for eleven years. With the gloves off, McGurn is still essentially a nice guy until someone threatens him. Then he takes the slightest physical provocation to a medieval conclusion, always to his advantage. When he leaves the gym and the rules of the sport are no longer binding, he is capable of the hardest mentality. His boot camp was Brooklyn, and although the males of his generation are no less tough in Chicago, there seems to be another level of street hardness in New York, simply because of its size and history. To the young gangsters in Chicago, Jack McGurn is already like a noncommissioned officer, which is why he will be an immediate candidate for promotion.

Being absorbed in the pugilistic culture of Ferretti's, McGurn begins to learn more about Chicago boxing history. He knows that some Chicago fighters have enjoyed great success in New York, such as Packey McFarland, who'd been born in Chicago's stockyards neighborhood and had fought Mike Gibbons, the "Saint Paul Phantom," in 1915 at Brooklyn's Brighton Beach arena. It was a huge draw, ending in a dead-even contest, but the classiness of both fighters is memorable. This is the style of boxer

McGurn dreams of becoming. His first opportunity is a battle that is waiting for him, floating over the Chicago River.

The *Commodore* is overly packed with people on October 1. The military and veterans get so many seats that the tickets are always at a premium. Police are supposed to watch the numbers of the crowd closely so that the barge doesn't turn over or sink, but the capacity is always overflowing. Gamblers and underworld figures all adore the fights and the fighters, and since most of them smoke, there is always the concern of fire in any wooden corner of Chicago, the city that returned from the flames.

Bootlegger Johnny Torrio is no doubt attending with his young lieutenant, Alphonse Capone. Many of those gathered are wondering who shot independent mobster "Big Jim" Colosimo four months ago, with the lion's share of surmise drifting in the direction of Torrio and his imported New York help. Colosimo, who had recently married a beautiful young singer named Dale Winter, was ignoring the inevitable; he was a holdout to bootlegging. His energies were directed elsewhere as he enjoyed his extended honeymoon. To his associate Johnny Torrio, this was like rejecting gold that is falling from the sky. Torrio, with a brilliant mind for business, knows they are poised to make money hand over fist. Consequently, Brooklyn gangster Frankie Yale, who was Al Capone's first mentor, visited Chicago and allegedly gunned down Colosimo. Writers such as John Kobler have always felt that Capone planned the setup and perhaps even drove for Yale.

There is an enormous shift in the underworld as Johnny Torrio takes over the fallen Colosimo's vice concerns with the savvy of a Fortune 500 mogul. He is gifted in all the right areas, even though his business is unfortunately illegal. He is a civilized gentleman who believes in communication rather than violence, a negotiator among men dealing in absolutes. Al Capone prospers in many more ways being mentored by Torrio, but the bottom line will always seem to revert to New Yorker Frankie Yale's method, which is murder.

The mild-mannered Torrio is well-known in the sporting milieu and is a devoted member of the boxing culture. He was a fight promoter in his early years in Chicago, managing Kid Murphy, who eventually became a world champion. The fight cards on the *Commodore* are wildly popular, considering how rare boxing matches are in Chicago, and Torrio and Capone often attend. They are both notoriously active gamblers.

Capone, like his boss, has his eye out for young fighters to manage. He is crazy about pugilism, a brutal fist fighter himself in his relatively recent youth and in his capacity as a capper. He is also in need of muscle for their organization, which is expanding daily now that Colosimo is no longer an obstacle. The gymnasiums and fight clubs are full of young toughs who need to make a living; Capone is constantly scouting those prospects. One of the fighters he will eventually manage is Paul Dazzo, who will become the Illinois amateur bantamweight champion (although Dazzo will move on to other management).

In the first bout on the *Commodore* card is Mike Dundee, the son of a fruit grocer in Rock Island, Illinois, whom Capone will also end up managing. Dundee's real name is Michael Posateri, another example of Anglo camouflage. The featherweight Dundee steals the evening at the onset by knocking out his opponent, Frankie Tucker, in the middle of the first round. It is an almost comic couple of minutes as Tucker comes out at the bell, dancing energetically around Dundee. No more than a minute later, Dundee moves in and gives Tucker a fierce, double tap to the head, sending him to the canvas.

The crowd is a Chicago mixture of veterans, navy, the fashionable rich, gangsters, politicians, and bankers; they all go wild. It is likely that this is where Al Capone makes the mental note that Mike Dundee is his kind of fighter and decides to pursue him.[6] If Capone stays for two more fights, he will see an equally impressive young Jack McGurn, who will nearly repeat the first round knockout on his own opponent, Jimmy Ford, putting him down for a full seven count. Ford is able to get to his feet and to his corner, where his people frantically try to patch him up. Miraculously, he returns to spar with McGurn for another four rounds. McGurn comes back hard in the sixth, however, and wins the decision.

This is a wonderful moment for Jack McGurn, who must be gleefully certain that his future in the ring will be bright. He is applauded by everybody and congratulated with countless slaps on the back as well as a bit of prize money. His dreams are becoming fulfilled, and his sense of destiny must be weighty. Perhaps Johnny Torrio and Al Capone introduce themselves. If it isn't this night, it will be soon.

The rewards of victory begin paying off as the promoters immediately book McGurn again for the November 4 card on the *Commodore*. He will fight "Battling" Williams in another six-round bout. Their match is the semi-windup fight, taking place before the headliner, in which bantamweight Pal Moore decidedly beats Earl Puryear.

As his fight begins, McGurn comes out swinging like a dynamo, knocking Williams down four times in the first four rounds. Frank Smith of the *Chicago Tribune* notes that Williams stays down for several counts as "McGurn's left hook landed on the button."[7] In the fourth round, Williams revives and "knocks McGurn all over the ring."

The fifth round is an even match, although the sixth round almost proves deadly for McGurn, who is floored, hitting the canvas after Williams lands a right cross. He bounces back up in time to defend himself at the end of the round. The decision, "the shade," goes to McGurn because of his excellent pummeling of the first three and a half rounds. Jack McGurn, with the impossible baby face, has won again.

McGurn is getting noticed now, as he has won two fights. The word is out: the kid with the angelic features knows how to hit but apparently has difficulty sustaining the battle for six whole rounds. The true challenge of the sport is that with every fight, the opponent becomes harder to beat. The onus is on McGurn now, with expectations growing. He hears the term "promising welterweight" thrown in his direction, but he also knows he has weaknesses to overcome. But for now he is undefeated, with stars in his eyes.

Everything in his life has changed. He tastes a small bit of fame and glory with his first victories. Heady with triumph and the indomitable confidence of youth, he is so sure of his future that he impetuously marries his girlfriend, Helen Cannazzaro, on November 24, 1921. They are married as Mr. and Mrs. Vincent Gebardi, and she is welcomed into the family; sometimes she will also use their DeMory name.[8] Because he comes from a close family, even as extended as it became, Vincent also becomes a family man. The grand festival of the remainder of the decade, with its excesses and outrageous machinations, is on the near horizon. But for the moment, he follows the traditional model of his parents. Twenty-year-old Vincent Gebardi is now the husband and prizefighter Jack McGurn, battling his way up.

Louise Rolfe, fifteen and basking in the small glory of having had her picture in an advertisement, yearns for more. She constantly begs her father to get her into more print ads, but the agencies suggest to Frank that she prepare by attending a modeling school. Mabel wants her to continue at Senn High School for a proper education. She is too young to spend her days down in Chicago's Loop, where the streets are teeming with danger for comely teenagers. In the recent past, hundreds of young lasses have been grabbed and brought into the Levee district's many bordellos, their lives enslaved by prostitution and drugs, Mabel Rolfe's worst fear. But her daughter has a stubborn streak and an iron will. Every day seems to be twenty-four hours closer to an inevitable reckoning for the lovely Louise, whose aspirations are nothing like her mother's.

6

If You Don't Do What I Want, I Won't Be Happy

1921

In Chicago, Louise Rolfe's father prospers when advertising becomes increasingly more important in the early 1920s. It is a gigantic new industry as millions of washing machines, vacuum cleaners, radios, automobiles, and movie tickets are sold throughout the decade. Postwar manufacturing and retail are giddy. If there is ever a time to celebrate with alcohol, it is now, which is exactly why most people will continue to do everything they can to break the dry laws.

Louise is only fifteen, but her body is more mature. She is beautiful, constantly noticed by men, and straining at the leash that is rapidly slipping out of her mother's hands. She loves to be the center of attention, anywhere, any time. She and her best friend Jenetthlyn "Jennett" Fredericks enter Senn High School together, where they immediately became hypersocial, toying with boys and drinking anything they can find that won't explode. A popular gateway concoction is "syllabub," a mixture of port wine, milk, and sugar. Louise probably learns quickly to do without the milk and sugar.

Like most other well-to-do girls, they will wind up the Victrola and put on 78 rpm records of the new jazz played by the African American musicians like Joe "King" Oliver, whose exotic Creole Jazz Band plays at the Lincoln Gardens Café on East 31st Street and Cottage Grove Avenue. Louise, Jennett, and many of their more precocious friends are no doubt eager to go there. They deem themselves ready to enjoy the world of the seductive, adult music. They've been told about the chicken-wire ceiling festooned with maple leaves and the licorice gin at two dollars a Prohibition pint. But of course, they are too young to get in the door.

Instead, they find their way to the Friar's Inn at 343 South Wabash Avenue, on the Near North Side. It's a rundown, sinister-looking dive where the bands play the "slow drag" and the "two-four one-step." Those who are underage are still banned, but they are allowed to stand outside near the doorway and listen to the wonderful music. They pass slim silver hip flasks among themselves and get "spiflicated" out there on the sidewalk. The visionary young foundlings of the jazz generation congregate here on weekend nights, as if apprenticing themselves to the music. This is as close as they can get for the moment.

The New Orleans Rhythm Kings start playing the Friar's in December. They are eight white boys who play black jazz, emulating King Oliver. Louise and the other teenagers who love the new music loiter in the Chicago cold until the Friar's Inn is forced to close their front door to keep the heat inside.

Louise and her friends realize that they can read the African American paper, the *Chicago Defender*, to find out where the bands are playing. Louise's main dream is to find older boys who are of age to take her to any of the hot joints. Because she possesses a mature look and attitude, she is frequently able to achieve this. In the winter of 1921, the big news is at the College Inn, where Chicagoans are flocking to hear the Isham Jones Orchestra, with Frank "Tram" Trambauer on the saxophone. Their signature number, "I Wish I Could Shimmy Like My Sister Kate," is an instant anthem for Louise's generation, who buy records with African American labels like Okeh, Paramount, Vocation, Black Swan, and Brunswick.

"Race music" is the rage, the cat's pajamas, especially in Chicago, with its wonderful infusion of transplanted New Orleans musicians who have been slowly migrating to the city by the lake. The older generation doesn't approve of the kids dancing to such suggestive music. Conservative and fundamental groups all over America are horrified, a reaction that is, of course, the finest kind of publicity. This turns out to be the second time white youngsters will rebel and trump their parents' racism, a happy tradition that began with the white acceptance of ragtime after the turn of the century.

The old fogies bitterly complain about how harmful the new jazz is to their children, while at the same time they reluctantly foot the bill for the purchase of the records. Since Frank Rolfe has decided to move out of the apartment and divorce Mabel, he certainly makes sure that his daughter has money for the current hits such as the Dixieland Jazz Band's "Livery Stable Blues" and the Fletcher Henderson Orchestra's "Shanghai Shuffle." When he finds the ever-shrinking time, he dotes on Louise, inviting her to his country club where she learns to play golf and sneak drinks of Prohibition booze, rubbing shoulders with her eager, blossoming generation of rich kids. Frank must think everything she does is cute.

The truth is that at fifteen, Louise is almost as wild as any adult. She already has a plan to be the center of attention in larger arenas, perhaps the theater and silent movies. She has the same "look" as film stars Carol Dempster and Lillian Gish, which further convinces her that she can be an actress or a model. She is dangerously spoiled by her guilty father, quickly becoming a dedicated pleasure seeker and hedonist with appetites beyond her years. But she is special. Not only does she drink any alcohol she can find and experiment with every kind of sex, but a month before her sixteenth birthday, Senn High School student Louise Rolfe kills her first man.

Frank Rolfe has left Mabel and now has an apartment at 5925 Magnolia Avenue, where Louise visits him as often as possible. On March 27, 1921, she steals her father's Cadillac limousine, after which she and Jennett Fredericks pick up two boys, Edward Madigan and Frank Mawicka, who provide a couple of flasks of booze.[1] They go joyriding, and on Winthrop Avenue, where Louise removes her eyes from the road to take a swig, she crashes into an automobile driven by a man named Charles Ulberg.

Ulberg's front-seat passenger is an attorney from north suburban Evanston named Frank A. Lasley; in the backseat is the automobile's owner, Philo L. Crawford. Louise's huge limo spins Crawford's car into the oncoming limousine of Illinois attorney general Edward Brundage, who is traveling south on Winthrop, with his sister and his two children.

Brundage's chauffeur, Harry Moore, and the children are uninjured, but the attorney general and his sister, Margaret Friesinger, are taken unconscious to Chicago Union Hospital, where they both will recover.

Louise and the other three people with her are shaken but able to walk away without medical attention. Ulberg is thrown out of the car, yet he is miraculously unharmed. Crawford and Lasley are pinned in the twisted metal of their Ford, sandwiched between two grand limousines that are at least twice as heavy. Crawford survives, but his unlucky passenger Lasley dies in Lake View Hospital the next day.[2]

Frank Rolfe puts up the sizable legal fees to get his daughter dismissed from the charge of vehicular manslaughter. It is expensive to get Louise off the hook, for she is obviously guilty. However, because she is underage, mercy is directed her way. Some of this may be due to her performance in court, for she seems to have cunning guile and at least enough theatrical ability to appear appropriately contrite. Her youth tends to be on her side, and no doubt she affects as innocent a physical appearance as she possibly can, including tears at the propitious moments. She already has a natural instinct to attempt to manipulate a courtroom.

For whatever reason, the judges who hear her case apparently feel that it would not serve justice to ruin this teenager's life as well, hence Louise escapes the nightmare without due punishment. It has to cost Frank Rolfe a small fortune, but it is nothing compared to the cost to Frank A. Lasley, who was never aware of the dangers of being on the road with Louise May Rolfe.

But nobody left alive escapes the wrath of Attorney General Brundage. The rotund, dynamic lawyer and politician is enraged; he and his sister file a civil suit in circuit court on July 14 against Frank and Louise Rolfe as well as the unfortunate Philo Crawford, the owner of the car Louise hit. They ask for fifteen thousand dollars in damages for their injuries.[3]

Louise sees that her immediate troubles are far from over, yet shockingly the opportunity for some publicity does not escape her. She displays an astonishing narcissism and self-awareness that will continue to define her. She makes certain that a *Chicago Tribune* reporter is given one of her professionally photographed portraits, which the paper compliantly reproduces for the article announcing Brundage's lawsuit. In the tiny picture in the paper, another line engraving taken from her corset ad photograph, she is young and fresh, with huge eyes and plaited blonde hair. Her practiced glance is casual, somewhat inviting, and slightly bemused. She seems naked below her neck, the cropped head shot taken from her first advertisement. Her wake of death and destruction notwithstanding, Louise is totally thrilled when the glamour shot ends up on the front page.

In court, justice is served, but it is not perfectly directed. Philo Crawford is judged not liable because his automobile was first hit by Louise. Frank Rolfe, ever his daughter's pigeon, ends up writing a check for fifteen thousand dollars to the attorney general of Illinois and his sister, a formidable settlement in 1921.

The budding performer Louise skips away. The future moll has one notch on her driver's license. For most young women, this terrible episode would be life changing, a shocking, wisdom-earning, soul-searching catharsis. It would turn most people around in a hurry.

Louise Rolfe is just getting started.

Vincent and Helen begin their married life in the DeMory home. Helen learns Josephine DeMory's finest Sicilian cooking tricks, including a gravy-thick sauce that will survive in the family to the present day. With Vincent (his family does not call him Jack) absent many hours at a time as he trains for his next fight, Helen becomes like a DeMory daughter, cooking, helping her mother-in-law, and patiently waiting for her young man to come home each night. She is dutiful, in love, and happy with her new extended family.

7

Everyone Wants to Earn More Money

1922

The newlywed Jack McGurn is now training for his third fight, which is scheduled to take place in Kenosha, Wisconsin, on February 3, 1922.[1] It is first announced that he'll be fighting Al Hennessey, who soon gets dropped and replaced by Eddie Mahoney.[2] Then the entire match gets postponed, with the card being juggled around again. McGurn's third opponent ends up being a tough Jewish welterweight named Vic Hirsch. This time it's an eight-round bout, which is the next step up in the professional ring.

Vic Hirsch proves to be a formidable fighter, but McGurn puts up a good fight himself. Both boxers sustain some bruises as they last all eight rounds. The fight is a draw. Even though Jack McGurn is not the winner, he is still undefeated. Half of the purse is better than nothing; his grand dream is still intact. No doubt he is happy when he returns from Wisconsin to heal up and train for another fight as soon as possible.

The desire for boxing matches is as innate in Chicago as it is in New York. Large sporting events are the most exciting things in the world to Americans. The USS *Commodore* is fine for holding the thinly masked charity benefits, but prizefighting is meant to be enjoyed by large crowds. The prohibition of pugilism in wooly, brawling Chicago makes any decent-sized town outside of Cook County a likely venue for a larger event.

This is exactly why entrepreneur and fight promoter Jack Sager decides to accommodate the popularity of the sport of kings by building an open-air arena in nearby Aurora. It is a quaint Illinois town some sixty miles west of Chicago in the Fox River Valley. Sager is partnered with matchmaker Jim Mullen, who will create the fight cards. He purchases a natural pine bowl in the countryside known as "Noble's twenty-seven acres," where he puts his five-thousand-seat arena, planning the opening event for May 29.[3]

Jim Mullen wants Jack McGurn to fight in the grand opening, and he signs him to take on Eddie Mahoney, a popular Irish welterweight, in one of the eight-round preliminary bouts. The main event is a ten-rounder between Joe Burman and Sammy Mandell. The newspapers report that tickets will go on sale at three locations around the city—on Dearborn, Clark, and Thirty-Ninth Streets. The incredible deluge that follows surprises even Jack Sager, who is forced to add on another thousand seats, which are also sold out in a couple of days. Not only will Jack McGurn fight his fourth match in front of six thousand people, he will help make boxing history as one of Sager's openers.

McGurn and Mahoney turn out to be evenly matched. They have similar fighting styles and weigh nearly the same. They trade off body blows for eight rounds, and then the referee raises both their hands for a draw. McGurn must feel both relieved and disappointed, having put up a decent fight against an opponent who is slightly higher ranked. He is still undefeated, but he is a fierce competitor with a strong desire to win. He is being bet on by more and more gamblers, and he knows he can prosper only with victories, not draws. After four fights, he is one of the most watched welterweights, so Mullen has hopes for him, putting him on the card again at Sager's on June 24.

McGurn is relentless and completely confident that he'll fare better this time. He knows what he's capable of doing to another man outside on the street; he is certain he can accomplish the same thing with the gloves on. There will be lots of money hanging around the ring for a big fight card like this one. The gamblers and fight buffs are always eager to find somebody to back with their dough. If he does well in Aurora, perhaps one of them will pick him up.

On June 24, the gate takes in an impressive fourteen thousand dollars, but the private betting surrounding the matches makes that amount look puny. Fight fans have come from all over the Midwest to see the headliner bantamweight Pal Moore, the "Memphis Flash," confront Bud Taylor from Terre Haute, Indiana. The fight goes ten full rounds and ends in a draw. The semi-windup before that main bout is between "Battling" Jack McGurn and Bud Christiano. Apparently McGurn liked the moniker of his prior opponent, "Battling" Williams, adopting it for himself. According to Sam Hall, who covers the fight for the Associated Press, "Christiano had a good shade" by the end of the eighth and final round.[4] To his profound dismay, Jack McGurn suffers his first loss.

McGurn has been fighting professional welterweights who are legitimate contenders. Several of them will fight their way to a modicum of fame. At this point, he has achieved a level of professionalism that gets him noticed by Al Capone, who is constantly around, gambling and managing fighters. It is during this period that Capone and McGurn form a friendship. Apparently from the very beginning, they enjoy great chemistry.

It becomes fairly clear that as McGurn fails to prosper in the fight realm, he needs to seek other sources of income. He remembers the cost and brutality of gainful employment to his birth father, as well as his own labor on the Brooklyn docks. He wants more. He wants to play golf. He wants a good life. More important, his young wife, Helen, becomes pregnant.

As Capone continues hiring the toughest guys as muscle for Torrio's operations, two of his richest fields of recruitment are the gangs and the fight gyms. This includes young Jack McGurn, who already is as hard as they come. Without the restraining gloves on his hands, McGurn is deadly with his fists. He is aided by his natural camouflage—his disarming, sweet, innocent face.

While the other tough guys practice looking threatening, McGurn harbors the ultimate surprise, the cupid who is capable of unimaginable violence, although what naturally emanates from McGurn's business side may be the hardest "look" of all. This rarer face of McGurn's is the one nobody wants to see. His features become hard, his eyes flinty like those of a western gunfighter. What is there instead is the sallow face of a dangerous man who broadcasts the inevitability that he will go all the way.

Following his fight with Christiano in June, McGurn does not get another scheduled bout until the following May 1923. The logical conclusion is that he already supplements his unsteady ring income by at least part-time work for Capone. Growing up on the hard streets of Brooklyn and in the world of prizefighting has made him an extremely marketable muscle, for which Torrio and Capone are willing to pay. The fact that he is also quite intelligent makes him even more appealing.

Many of the young men conscripted into the Outfit from the street gangs like the 42s and the Circus Café on North Avenue will be used as muscle for newspaper and labor disputes. Vitally important for anyone bootlegging in Chicago is the strong-arming of voters on election days. It is essential to have the right politicians on the hook. However, the muscle will mostly guard shipments of illegal alcohol. As their competitors begin to prosper, Torrio and especially Capone know that having the more ruthless army will be not just beneficial but necessary.

Their associates are also ruthless people: the Genna brothers run the West Side in Little Italy, while Dean O'Banion and his gang occupy much of the North Side. There are two O'Donnell gangs—oddly unrelated—and an assortment of smaller groups and independent operators who are all smuggling or making as much illegal alcohol as they can. Needless to say, the demand has constantly grown while the supply has vanished. Only the gangsters can provide what people want and what will not kill them after they drink it.

McGurn's fierce courage and his clever mind will elevate him quickly in the Torrio organization, but he does not stop his training; he is still determined to gain glory as a welterweight. He straddles both careers for the last six months of 1922, with one foot in the gym and the other planted in the rapidly growing Outfit.

Louise, now sixteen, acts like she's twenty. After her deadly accident when her daddy saves her from whatever fate the courts had in store, she drops out of Senn High School. This is not even slightly directed by remorse or humiliation for having killed a man, but because she sees her classmates as children and beneath her. As a student, she lacks discipline, the ability to focus, and even the slightest aspiration when it comes to her education. She is now completely determined to be an actress, or at the very least a model. She is way beyond most of the teenagers her own age, so she still seeks out older people, a spoiled world of wannabe flappers and collegiates who steal their rich fathers' illegal alcohol, drive their rich fathers' cars, and have furtive, cramped sex with each other in the backseats. They are all transfixed by the music, each with a growing collection of jazz records.

Louise leads a wild existence, drinking and dancing. She hooks older boys into taking her to the summer fraternity parties at the swank Chez Paris on the North Side, where King Oliver and his band are playing. If she's lucky, she ends up hearing King Oliver and Louis Armstrong play dueling coronets at the Friar's Inn. Young, acne-plagued, and already married Alphonse Capone also frequents the Friar's. It is a true hot spot.

On one of her wild nights, Louise catches the attention of a good-looking, somewhat shy young man, who politely introduces himself as Harold Boex. She thinks he's cute; they dance and she flirts. At sixteen, Louise has powerful charms. She drinks from a garter hip flask. He has a few drinks himself. They have an enchanted evening, and he gets her address.

When Boex shows up for a date a few nights later, he charms Mabel Rolfe, not an easy maneuver. He is twenty-three, originally from Fond Du Lac, Wisconsin. His father, Anthony Boex, who arrived in the United States in 1876, and his mother, Nana, are Dutch immigrants.[5]

Boex is just the kind of fellow Mabel understands, having been raised in a small, rural town in the Midwest by strict, decent parents. He is nothing like the boys in the fast group whom Louise has been seeing or who inhabit Frank Rolfe's country club. His manners are impeccable, and he has a job. Uncharacteristically libated, he watches Louise dance the Black Bottom, which is her forte. It is a joyful but aesthetically challenging dance with a lot of foot stomping, somewhat akin to clogging. It works magic on Dutch lad Harold Boex, who is quickly falling in love. To him, she is a golden angel. She has dyed her dishwater hair blonde, and her spit curls and waves are a gleaming corn yellow. Apparently Louise, smitten as well, stays on her best, slightly reserved behavior.

Mabel, praying that her daughter's wild cycle is near an end, envisions married life and perhaps grandchildren in the near future. After all, she herself was married at sixteen, which, although ruinous for her, might be just the thing to straighten out her wayward teenage daughter. The near future turns out to be nearer than she ever expects.

Louise envisions Boex, who is twenty-three, taking her to all the black-and-tan cafés on the South Side, where the best musicians are consistently making history. This is a dream come true for her, the perfect way to ensure she'll get all the nightlife she needs, partnered with a man who is already old enough to vote.

Impetuous and always full of surprises, Louise elopes with the naive, hypnotized Harold on September 23. They drive up Sheridan Road about forty miles into neighboring Lake County, where they are married by justice of the peace Julius V. Bork in Waukegan, Illinois. Louise presents a fake Illinois automobile operator's license, claiming she is nineteen.[6]

Louise still harbors the growing desire to be a performer; she will tell friends much later in her life that Harold shared this same desire—although from all accounts, he is gainfully employed despite any interest in the theater. They start out hopeful, but Louise is too self-involved to cater to anybody for very long. Their fledgling marriage is a time bomb; Harold has little insight into the wild creature he has so spontaneously wed.

PART II

Scorpion

8

Terrible Misfortune

1923

At the age of twenty, Jack McGurn, the fresh Torrio-Capone muscle, has begun to make a good income; he even purchases an automobile. Although he still claims to be a boxer, his neighbors near the DeMorys' apartment on South Sangamon Street notice that he is never without money, whether he fights or not.

McGurn begins emulating his new mentor, Al Capone, buying flashy suits and shoes, looking "snorky," the slang for "elegant" in 1920s haberdashery. It is also Capone's private nickname inside his intimate circle. Capone believes in dressing for success, like all the corporate magnates. But, unlike Rockefeller and Ford, he also believes in luminous and even bilious colors. His custom-tailored, handmade suits can be bright purple or sea green, an ostentatious affectation that ends up giving "snorky" an entirely new connotation. The beautifully dressed McGurn is more conservative, preferring brown and light blue or gray suits, sometimes three-piece, and usually with his own small flamboyance, a garishly flowered necktie.

Along with his regular training at Feretti's, McGurn reports to the Outfit's headquarters in Cicero. His stepfather, Angelo DeMory, is also prospering. He has opened a small grocery business at 700 East Vernon Park Place, within walking distance of his home. Angelo labors in the center of a modern fiefdom, that of the "Terrible Genna Brothers," consisting of "Bloody" Angelo, cultured Anthony ("Tony the Gent"), and Mike "Il Diavulu" (The Devil). There are also Jim, Pete, and Sam, who play their own roles in the family business. These six Sicilian brothers rule their West Side neighborhood of Little Italy like feudal lords. Instead of exacting taxes from their poor immigrant peasants, the Gennas pay them to make illegal alcoholic products in their tiny apartments. They dole out five-gallon stills to hundreds of immigrant families, paying them fifteen dollars a week to monitor the fire and whatever is brewing. Most families can produce up to thirty-five gallons a week with one still, usually tended by the women of the household. On any temperate Chicago day, one can amble down Taylor Street and smell the wafting odors of fermentation exuding from the hundreds of individual apartment distilleries.

The Gennas seem to have the complete cooperation of the police. Their factory and warehouse, licensed to make industrial alcohol, are within four blocks of the Maxwell Street police station, where McGurn worked out during his first year in the city. The thousands of gallons of raw alcohol distilled by the individual home brewers also end up in the factory, where the additional noxious ingredients of creosote, iodine, burnt sugar, fusel oil, cane sugar, and oil of juniper create an incredibly strong odor. The Maxwell Street policemen, most of whom are on the Genna payroll, ignore everything that is going on around their station house.[1]

McGurn's stepfather, Angelo DeMory, has gravitated to the bulk distribution end of the bootleg business. He delivers out of his "grocery" for Joseph Montana, an "importer" who has his own store at South Morgan Street and Blue Island Avenue.[2] That Montana is allied with the Gennas means that Angelo delivers bulk goods for the Gennas as well. But the business of bootlegging is so lucrative and promising that Angelo decides to branch out and take on other customers. He purchases a flatbed truck. After all, isn't initiative why he came to America, where ambition and opportunity are abundant?

Thirty years later, municipal court judge John H. Lyle, famous for his unabashed positions against the Chicago gangs, will recall that Angelo DeMory was the Gennas' chief alky cooker, but this seems to be a tremendous exaggeration.[3] Angelo merely procured bulk goods and delivered for the Genna organization, distributing the dry good ingredients for the stills.[4]

In the intimate web of the neighborhoods, the word of Angelo De-Mory's "extended success" leaks out to the overfed, brutal Gennas. The brothers have the proprietary philosophy that the people of Little Italy can only serve one master: them. They farm out the problem of DeMory to their intimate group of killers, led by Orazio "The Scourge" Tropea and his crew consisting of Vito Bascone, Ecola "The Eagle" Baldelli, and Tony Finalli. These dangerous men often supplement their incomes by extorting the residents of Little Italy in the manner of the Sicilian Black Hand terrorists. Consequently, Tropea and his boys offer Angelo DeMory one chance, sending him a Black Hand–style letter with a grave warning to get out of town or die.[5]

In the neighborhoods, Tropea is a very tough gunner, who superstitious Sicilians claim has the "evil eye." He and the others are the Gennas' first line of offense, instilling fear as if the West Side were a Sicilian village. For whatever reason, Angelo DeMory sees fit to disregard their letter, perhaps not aware that it comes obliquely through the Gennas. On the other hand, maybe he knows full well and initiates an appeal to the Gennas through his associate Joseph Montana. Regardless, Angelo is not that easy to intimidate; he has many mouths to feed, and besides, isn't that another reason they came to America, to escape the fear of the Black Handers and the extortion of the Mafia? It is Angelo's fatal error.

Early on the morning of January 8, 1923, Angelo DeMory is shot to death on his way to work when two men from the Tropea crew jump out of an automobile in front of 936 Vernon Park Place. The gunmen run through an alley beside the building and drop their two .32-caliber revolvers, gangland-style. The automobile with the other two men comes around the block, picks up the killers as they emerge from the alley, and speeds away. A neighbor, Vito Spinelli, and his son William, who live on the first floor of the apartment building where Angelo is murdered, hear the two men come through the alley. They tell the police that they heard seven shots. Angelo DeMory absorbed five of them.

A bakery truck driver sees the killers emerge from the alley and reports this to lieutenant David Fitzgerald of the Maxwell Street police station. The driver is the sole witness who can identify the shooters, but he will never dare to testify against them.

The grief and devastating sorrow that erupts within the Gebardi-DeMory family is overwhelming. Neither Josephine nor any of the six children would ever have expected their new dreams and good life to vanish in an instant. As Angelo's blood fuses with the icy street of Little Italy, Josephine's tragedy of dire loss seems to be the second act of her pathetic opera. To make matters much worse, she has discovered that she is pregnant.

Four police sergeants from the Sixteenth District station arrive on the scene to find a dozen people surrounding the quickly chilling corpse of Angelo DeMory. Sergeants Sugg, Landa, Ahern, and O'Malley answer the call and find weeping and wailing Sicilians, including a baby-faced young man holding his grief-stricken mother as she kneels on the frozen sidewalk, cradling her dead husband's decimated head.[6]

The reportage in the *Tribune* the next day describes Angelo DeMory as an "olive oil and macaroni salesman."[7] He is considered "a victim of the political feud in the old [Ninth] Ward," and the small story is illustrated with the icon of an automatic pistol, a familiar *Tribune* affectation during the early 1920s to indicate news with a criminal or bootlegging connection. It is a little editorial reminder of the vice that has arisen, now associated with the dry laws. No death notice for Papa Angelo appears on the obituary page.

McGurn loved his stepfather, considering Angelo DeMory the grandfather of his unborn daughter. Angelo saved the Gebardi family from their destitute paralysis after Tommaso's death, giving Josephine and her children an immediate second chance at a decent family life. The cops who see McGurn's innocent face on the street that morning have no idea that he is a muscle for the Torrio Outfit, although they know he is a boxer from the fight results in the papers. Many of them still remember him from when he worked out in the gym above their police station.

The *Daily News* reports that DeMory's "twenty-four-year-old stepson Jimmy" (McGurn will actually be twenty-one in July) told them his stepfather had received a Black Hand–style death threat three weeks previously. But McGurn knows very well the order of things in Little Italy. Extremely few, if any, people are murdered in the Genna gang's territory by someone other than the Gennas.[8]

It is at this point in the story of Jack McGurn that myths are born. Some suggest that the murder of Angelo DeMory is the catalyst that eventually brings the grief-stricken stepson into his life of crime, which is absolutely untrue. Another often repeated myth is that McGurn buys a BB gun and learns to shoot a firearm by popping at birds on telephone wires. In actuality, by this time McGurn carries a .32-caliber revolver and is already beginning to live the gangster life, surrounded by the denizens of the fight game and the burgeoning Torrio-Capone mob. Decades later, in his memoirs, Judge Lyle will confirm this, quoting John Stege, Chicago chief of detectives, who is informed that McGurn has become a muscle while still prizefighting. He is already on the Torrio payroll when his thirty-seven-year-old stepfather is gunned down.

Sadly, the tragedy of Angelo DeMory is compounded as Josephine, her body racked with the physical shock of sorrow, miscarries. Heartbroken, she names the child Thomas, perhaps after McGurn's birth father, Tommaso. In the second week of January, Angelo DeMory and the tiny remains of his son are lowered into the frozen ground at Mount Carmel Catholic Cemetery. His headstone, with a popular pictorial engraving of Jesus pointing to his merciful heart, will reflect the dual mortality: DEMORY—GRANDPA, 1885–1923. SON THOMAS, AT REST 1923.[9] Unfortunately, now the family must face the excruciating process of the legal system and its casual disdain toward immigrants and especially Sicilians. If anything, the demeaning experience will help make Jack McGurn into a sardonic adversary of law enforcement.

9

We Remain Tormented in This Land

1923

No arrests of Angelo's killers are made in the following weeks, leading to a coroner's inquest on February 1, 1923, the proceedings of which are recorded word-for-word by a stenographer. Since there are no key witnesses who are willing to come forward, there will be no trial. The coroner's inquest is all that exists, besides the police reports of the murder of Angelo DeMory.

A tremendous amount of insight into Jack McGurn at the age of twenty can be gained from this transcript. McGurn tells the court that his name is James DeMora, not DeMory.[1] The inquest is presided over by deputy coroner S. L. Davis. McGurn, his mother, and his brothers attend.[2] McGurn already has things to hide, not the least of which are his employment in the Torrio Outfit and his stepfather's role as a bootleg grocer. He has subtle theatrical talent and plays up his act as the forlorn, lost little boy, oddly mixed with a quiet machismo. His accent and abuse of English become expanded and intensified. His demeanor is almost a Sicilian immigrant version of the shuck-and-jive act that African Americans in the South will sometimes put on during this period for whites with authority:

Deputy Coroner Davis: And are these people all witnesses?

McGurn: No, that is the wife and the sons and I am a son, too.

Davis: You are a son too?

McGurn: Yes.

From the tone of the transcript, Davis seems glib and condescending. There are many instances when McGurn cannot be heard clearly, and Davis has him repeat what he has said. McGurn has a soft voice, which in confluence with his accent and his purposeful act makes him difficult to understand. As the inquest proceeds, evidence is furnished that Angelo DeMory had received the threatening letter, telling him he had fifteen days to get out of Chicago. McGurn admits to Davis that he too had received the same kind of letter. Davis has learned from all the Maxwell Street cops that McGurn—or James DeMora, as he is calling himself—is a pugilist:

Davis: Where are your headquarters?

McGurn: Silvio Ferretti's gymnasium.

Davis: Are you a teacher of boxing?

McGurn: No, sir, I box myself.

Davis: And haven't you any suspicion who this is sending this [threatening letter] to you?

McGurn: No.

Davis: Have you got any [suspects]?

McGurn: It might be the same fellows, I don't know.

Davis: When was the last engagement that you had?

McGurn: You mean, what I have had?

Davis: Boxing engagement?

McGurn: Oh, that was three months ago.

Davis: Three months ago?

McGurn: Yes, sir.

Davis: Did you knock him out?

McGurn: No, sir.

Davis: What was it, just a sparring exhibition?

McGurn: A fight.

Davis: Here in Chicago?

McGurn: Aurora.

Davis: Where?

McGurn: Aurora.

Davis: Aurora, Illinois, oh, yes. What do you fight as?

McGurn: Welterweight.

Davis: Who did you fight with last?

McGurn: Mahoney, Eddie Mahoney.

Davis: You know him pretty well, do you?

McGurn: Yes, sir.

Davis: He would not be likely to send you any letters?

McGurn: No. God, no; if it was the rest of the boys, I would have a million letters, if that was the case.

Davis asks him what he is doing to protect himself.

McGurn: I tried to get some help from the police by trying to get a permit [for a gun]. So I know it is no use. So what am I going to do? Sometime when I am out alone, am afraid to take a chance. I am scared that somebody might come and I would lose gun and everything.

Davis: And what does your mother think about it?

McGurn: Well, she won't even make me—if I have to go out, she wants to go out with me because I am the only one in the family to take care of the family. We ain't got no relatives at all. I tried to get help from the police; that is all.

Davis points at Frank Gebardi and asks how old "the next one" is. McGurn says he's twelve years old and that he'll be thirteen in two months. Davis asks him his own age, and McGurn tells him the truth, that he'll be twenty-one in July. Davis snidely makes a remark about his brother being seven years younger, to which McGurn answers, "Yes, sir; well, I had another brother and sister, but they died." Apparently he's referring to a little daughter, who, according to New York gangster expert William Balsamo, fell to her death from a Brooklyn fire escape as a toddler.[3] He is also referring to the baby his mother has just miscarried. At any rate, McGurn seems to be going for additional sympathy for his mother here, not content in the least with Davis's condescending, interrogative attitude, but he hides his feelings well.

Davis is ready to throw in the towel, seeing that there are no witnesses who have come forward to help and that McGurn knows nothing. Davis can't seem to determine any motive for killing Angelo DeMory other than what the *Tribune* has already reported: it's a part of old Ninth Ward "feuding." Davis and everyone else obviously knows it's related to bootlegging, especially since Angelo is not robbed after he's shot; he still has four rings, a watch, a ten-dollar gold piece, and sixty-eight dollars in his pocket.

Davis: Well, I don't see how we can do anything.

McGurn: No, if the chief of police can't do anything, I don't see how you can. I got to take it as it comes; that is all.

Davis: What?

Again he doesn't understand McGurn's put-on accent.

McGurn: I say, we got to take it as it comes.

Davis is genuinely surprised by this remark. It strikes him that this young fellow with the innocent face doesn't seem to be very fearful. It doesn't seem quite right.

Davis: Well, you certainly take it very complacently, I must say. I would hate to have something over my head and going around town and expecting a short gun shot.

McGurn feels himself being cornered, so he tries to snow the coroner.

McGurn: You would have to run away.

Davis: What?

McGurn: You would have to run away.

Davis: That is what I'm going to do; I think I would live over at the Maxwell Street [police] station.

McGurn: That wouldn't do you no good. They would get you, if you live in the President's building.

That's an interesting and fairly prophetic statement, especially coming from someone who is becoming a killer. It's the yet-to-be-heard voice of a first-class urban assassin. It's also a good show, and it works. Neither the police nor Deputy Coroner Davis would consider that this young man who claims to be "James DeMora" is capable of killing those who murdered his stepfather. Even though Davis suspects a bootlegging motive to this murder, he has seen dozens of cases like this, and since he's not a street detective, his job is finished.

This semi-ignorant immigrant act is pro forma for McGurn whenever confronted by authority in the earliest days of his career. He is able to put it on like theatrical makeup. The inquest provides a wonderful picture of that rather pathetic persona—in reality, McGurn is only two years away from becoming Al Capone's main killer.[4] The transcript also indicates what happened to the only known witness to Angelo DeMory's shooting. When Sergeant O'Malley is called, Davis asks him, "Now, Mr. O'Malley, have you done anything with reference to these men, the perpetrators of this deed?"

Sergeant O'Malley: No, nothing has been accomplished. The only further information I have to tell you is that the man who called the police is a grocer [the bakery truck driver] in the neighborhood and he was notified to be here.

Davis: Is that grocer here? I thought he would be here. [*To the bailiff, who shakes his head*] No?

O'Malley: He was notified to be here.

With the system's failure to find any suspects or witnesses who aren't in mortal terror of the Genna brothers, Davis rules murder by persons unknown.

McGurn, who is hardly surprised, takes a blood oath for *vinnitta*, as any dutiful Sicilian son would be expected to do. Sadly, he is continuing the very same vendetta tradition that his parents sought to escape by coming to America. He's a lot more knowledgeable about the status quo on the West Side streets than anyone would ever suspect. The Gennas own the Sixteenth District police, so McGurn no doubt expects very little in the way of justice, but it will simply be a matter of time. He is well aware of who his enemies are.

10

I've Been Living in This City for Three Years

1923

The powerful Genna brothers are lucky. For the moment, Jack McGurn is preoccupied with training through his grief; he has a fight on May 21 against Iowan Glenn Mulligan. Angelo DeMory's death notwithstanding, it is a tremendous opportunity to get back into the ring. It is even being held in Chicago at the Ashland Boulevard Auditorium because it's a charity benefit for Saint Malachy's alumni association. Jim Mullen is once again the matchmaker. He still believes McGurn can put up a good battle, so he invites him onto the card.[1]

The main event features the extremely popular Jewish fighter Sammy Mandell from Rockford, Illinois, against Chicagoan Eddie Walsh. McGurn and Mulligan will fight the second preliminary match of the evening. Walter Eckersall of the *Chicago Tribune* gets McGurn's name wrong, instead writing "Jack McCarthy of the West Side."[2] Regardless, McGurn triumphs again. The two 138-pound welterweights begin in what Eckersall describes as a "whirlwind fashion," as they fight themselves out in the opening round, which is scored as even. In the next seven rounds, McGurn proves more aggressive, landing cleaner punches. He is the clear winner.

The promoters can also see that McGurn has displayed a pattern of ferocity out of the gate, then a loss of power because he hasn't paced himself. He puts out so much in the beginning of the fight that he prematurely tires himself out. His exhaustion in the late rounds leads some of those who are watching to surmise that he hasn't got the "true fighting heart," which will be proved ridiculous, but not in the boxing ring.

McGurn is scheduled to fight once more before 1923 ends, but it doesn't happen. He is put on the card at George Oswego's East Chicago Arena for December 3. East Chicago is actually in Indiana and therefore allows pugilism. The main event is once again Sammy Mandell versus Eddie Brady from Brooklyn. McGurn will be matched with Frankie Harvey in an eight-round bout. Something changes this; either McGurn backs out, which is most unlikely, or the promoters at Oswego's prefer another fighter. Welterweight Andrew Williams is substituted for McGurn.

McGurn will never fight in the ring again. Apparently his entry into the Torrio Outfit has usurped his boxing dream. In addition, he has realized his own limits and has decided he is better off earning a "steadier" living, following the diamond-studded carrot that has been dangled before his eyes. He is a dutiful son, and with Angelo DeMory gone, he intends to support his family.

Whatever else that will be said about Jack McGurn, his brief boxing career is modestly commendable, contrary to the claims of many writers. He wins three fights, draws two, and only loses once. He works his way up to eight-round welterweight matches during the worst possible time for the sport in Chicago, since it was still outlawed. The future will attest to the fact that he doesn't lack for a fighting heart and certainly not killer instinct. With the protective coloration of his young, angelic face, he is still the most unsuspected of dangerous men, so tough that he is already creating fear.

There will be two joyful events for McGurn before the year ends. At least a small part of the void left by Angelo DeMory and his unborn son is filled. Late in the year, McGurn becomes the father of a baby girl, whom he names Josephine after his mother. Helen and her infant daughter still see him as Vincent Gebardi at home, although much less frequently. He has begun to work long and late hours.

Helen is willing to accommodate her husband on every level and has the patience of the Madonna. She grows even closer to her mother-in-law and Vincent's siblings, tethered quietly to the bosom of the DeMory family.

Jack and Louise, the future star-crossed lovers, neither of whom should ever be a parent, both experience the same dubious joy in 1923. Louise Rolfe Boex becomes pregnant almost as soon as she and Harold are married. She turns seventeen in May and becomes a mother when her daughter, Bonita, named after Harold's sister,[3] is born on July 6.[4]

Perhaps, for the moment, Louise has convinced herself that having a family is her destiny. In a whirlwind, she has traveled from obstreperous teenage flapper to wife and mother. She has not a clue how to be either, nor, as it turns out, the inclination. She has instantly become everything that she does not want to be, playing house with an infant and a young man who still has no idea whom he has married.

Louise is the vanguard of a new, growing American phenomenon. Like many children of unhappy upper-middle-class marriages, she is angry, rebellious, pampered, and cynical, with a worldview that is relatively narrow, despite the exponentially changing music and technology. Her early life experiences give her a completely different perspective from most young women her age.

For the first time in American popular culture, youth are becoming quite influential, especially in the marketplace. There's no end to the demand for anything that is "all the rage." The fad itself becomes a fad, from goldfish swallowing to waist-length beads to cloche hats to any number of dances, all advertised in waves of newspapers as well as on the exciting, burgeoning radio. All of this stimulates Louise, sounding harmonic chords in her. With a new infant, she worries that she will miss out on the fun. After recovering from the birth of her daughter, she is once again ready to rejoin the ongoing bacchanal. A friend who is extremely close to the Rolfe family believes, in retrospect, that Louise appears to suffer from severe postpartum depression but "rallies" as soon as she is able to go out for the evening.

Harold Boex, as it turns out, is a boy scout or, in the language of the time, a real stiff. To her dismay, Louise discovers that he isn't totally out of line with temperance and the dry laws. Now that he has a family, he puts his nose to the grindstone, which he learned from his decent, conservative Dutch parents. Mabel Rolfe is crazy for her little granddaughter, Bonita, and will take care of her any time she is asked. She sees a chance to enjoy innocence and perfect love for a child once again, hopefully to succeed where she has already failed with her own daughter. As a grandmother, she becomes more of a mother.

Mabel hires Frances Connors as a housekeeper and maid. Frances will often care for Bonita and will be an intimate witness to Louise's hedonistic obsessions.

With her mother looking after the baby, Louise expects her husband to take her to clubs for drinking and dancing. If he refuses, she simply goes on her own, escaping what she perceives to be asphyxiation in their apartment, which always smells like a baby, a constant reminder of her burdensome duties. She will run to a hot spot, perhaps to hear Jelly Roll Morton, who is a sensation at the Lincoln Gardens, where she'll drink, dance, and draw attention to herself.

At least by being married she has eluded becoming a statistic in the damning "report" of the Illinois Vigilance Association, a church-oriented, draconian group that claims that the downfall of more than a thousand girls can be traced to the influence of jazz music. They begin building the myth that the wild, outrageous generation of young people is being perverted by the music to which they snap their fingers. This will become a tradition of prejudice and fear that ensuing generations of Americans will also find familiar, particularly in the 1950s in Michigan, where a partially racist state house will attempt to ban early rock 'n' roll because it is performed by people of color.

In the 1920s, the mostly African American art form is called "race music" by worried whites. The same critics seem to vilify the Jewish composers also coming into prominence. Their contention is that "music from Negro brothels of the south" and "Semitic purveyors of Broadway melodies" are directly to blame for their wild, wayward young people.[5]

To her credit, Louise Rolfe Boex, teenage hausfrau and errant mama, nurtures the seeds of rebellion against that status quo. Relatively uneducated and decidedly wild, she will maintain her loyalties to the burgeoning 1920s party culture and the African American musicians. Despite her brand-new family, she still has a lot of living it up to do.

11

This Man Knows Precisely What He Wants to Do

1924

By the winter and spring of 1924, McGurn has become close to Al Capone and his brothers. More important, they completely trust him. He has already proved to be fearless, loyal, and extremely likable. Despite his contradictory looks, he proves he is a very tough guy on the street. With his athletic antics, he also is capable of making them laugh.

Alphonse buys a plain two-story red-brick fortress, built in 1914, at 7244 South Prairie Avenue. He adds steel lattice covers to the windows that will keep out bombs and grenades. Capone lives in the seven rooms with his mother, Teresa; his sister, Mafalda (who is enrolled nearby in the private Richards School for Girls); his wife, Mae; and his son, Albert Francis, known as Sonny. Al's brothers Matt and John (who is called Mimi) live in back bedrooms. Frank Capone, the second eldest of the brothers, lives nearby. Al's older brother, Ralph "Bottles" Capone, occupies the second story with his wife, Velma, and his son, Ralph Junior.

McGurn is one of the few Capone lieutenants who is invited to eat dinner with the family on Prairie Avenue. His mother, Josephine, forms a friendship with Teresa Capone. Mafalda has an adolescent crush on the good-looking, athletic McGurn.[1] He is accepted like another little brother, being a few years younger than Al. He will never, however, be mistaken for a Capone. In his book *Capone*, biographer John Kobler gives a wonderful description of the Capone brothers, who shared a strong family resemblance, with "thick, heavy bodies and blunt features, and when assembled in family council, they suggested a small herd of ruminating bison."[2]

The spring of 1924 is primary season; Joseph Klenha, the front man and mayor of Cicero for three terms, is up for re-election. Johnny Torrio knows for a certainty that he must make sure Klenha wins so that his Outfit will receive immunity from the law in any enterprise they undertake. Beer running, booze making, prostitution, gambling, and racketeering are all approved on the agenda. Torrio and his political cronies cannot afford to see the hated reformer, Mayor William Dever of Chicago, get a foothold in Cicero. Al and Frank Capone receive the charge from Torrio to prevent this from happening.

Al utilizes McGurn and every other man he has, including paid mercenaries from allied gangs, to invade the primary. Capone leads the troops like a crusader knight, getting his hands dirty, for the young underboss is still essentially a brawler. Two hundred thugs hit the streets to do a little "hard campaigning." In the polling places, voters are shown whom to vote for by the hoods; they're slugged or beaten if they're the least bit defiant. It is a day that belongs to the lead-weighted leather sack known as the blackjack. In several instances, poll watchers and election officials are dragged off as captives. Wherever they're held, they're given a drink and a wink and then released when the polls close.

It is also April Fool's Day, but nothing that happens in Cicero is a joke. People are shot, stabbed, and thrown out of windows. A policeman is blackjacked into unconsciousness, causing a group of terrified people to seek aid from Cook County judge Edward K. Jarecki, who promptly deputizes seventy police officers. He sends fourteen cars full of heavily armed detectives and uniformed men into Cicero. Gangsters and cops sporadically engage in gunfights and brawls all afternoon.

Toward dusk, a flivver with five cops pulls up to the corner of Twenty-Second Street and Cicero Avenue just in time to spot Al and Frank Capone with their cousin, the brutish Charlie Fischetti. The three of them have

automatic pistols and are intimidating voters near the enormous Western Electric plant that comprises much of the industrial base of Cicero,
employing several thousand workers and thus voters.

The cops explode out of the unmarked black limousine with shotguns and rifles. Detective sergeant William Cusick, as well as the rest of
the men with him, are wearing plainclothes, having been deputized off
their shifts in the election emergency. To Capone and his boys, they could
just as well be rival gangsters. As they move quickly toward the Capones,
Frank seems to panic and points his automatic at patrolmen Phillip J.
McGlynn and Lyle Grogan, but when he pulls the trigger, it is on an empty
chamber. As if the punch line to an April Fool's joke, the two officers
shoot Frank Capone down with their shotguns. Al is already half a block
away, running down Cicero Avenue. He is able to escape after holding
another squad of cops at bay with his revolver. (Al is never arrested for
this.) Charlie Fischetti is picked up and released.

The Torrio-Capone Outfit is devastated. Frank's death is a heavy price
to pay to keep Mayor Dever's reformers out of Cicero. The funeral is
huge, attended by all the unshaven, sullen Capone brothers. The obsequies are festooned with elaborate gangster chic, including huge flower
arrangements from North Side gang chieftain Dean O'Banion's flower
shop, Schofield's, on State Street.

Al Capone is inconsolable and begins drinking heavily. He is haunted
with the thought that he ran away while his older brother was gunned
down. His bender lasts for several weeks as he maintains a constant,
drunken state. It is during this period after Frank's death that Jack McGurn
becomes more like an adopted Capone brother.

Al remains in deep grief. He is constantly angry, tormented, and as ill
humored and volatile as he can be. On May 8 he nearly blows everything
when he erupts in defense of his obese Jewish money man, Jack Guzik.
A mean, drunken hard case named Joe Howard slaps Guzik around in
Henry Jacob's bar on Wabash Avenue. Al, unreasonably infuriated, goes
down to the saloon and empties a revolver into Howard's head. It isn't
known whether McGurn is present, but whichever Capone men accompany the enraged Alphonse quickly drag their berserk boss away and into
hiding.

Al is eventually able to weasel his way out of the Howard mess, just as the jolly North Side florist Dean O'Banion almost brings Johnny Torrio to his doom. Short, stocky, and somewhat sadistic, O'Banion shares gambling and bootlegging interests with Torrio, but their relationship is rocky. Torrio, quiet and reserved, must suffer the highly animated O'Banion and his Irish "hail fellow well met" bluster.

O'Banion—onetime singing waiter, jack roller (mugger), and robber—has been one of the princes of the North Side underworld since 1920.[3] Underneath, he is a genuinely tough little Napoleon—he is always well armed with at least two guns and has a penchant for acting out. Often quite likable, he has a duplicitous, aggressive personality. Like Johnny Torrio, O'Banion is a dedicated husband, but away from home, he seems to yearn for confrontation. He is described in Rose Keefe's biography, *Guns and Roses*, as "shrewd and streetwise but totally bereft of caution."

The wacky O'Banion hatches a devilish little plan to remove Torrio's Outfit from competition in the Chicago beer trade: he offers to sell Torrio his interest in the Sieben Brewery, at 1470 North Larrabee Street, where they are partners. The price to Torrio is an extremely fair five hundred thousand dollars, but what he doesn't suspect is that O'Banion knows from an informant that Chicago police chief Morgan Collins has already scheduled a raid on the brewery for May 19. Like selling a mansion that is slated for demolition, O'Banion beautifully sets up Torrio, who is on the premises when the police arrive. He is arrested for his second Prohibition violation, which carries with it a mandatory prison sentence. He even suffers the indignity of not being able to bond out, because Collins hands him over to federal agents, so his lawyers cannot get him released. O'Banion revels in his prank.

Al Capone is enraged. He is extremely loyal to Johnny Torrio, but he is nowhere near as phlegmatic. O'Banion's death sentence is sealed, but Capone first consults with the president of the Chicago chapter of the Unione Siciliana, the beloved, philosophically nonviolent, and democratic Mike Merlo.

Merlo is more in tandem with Johnny Torrio in his inclination to negotiate everything like a gentleman, wisely aware of the recriminations of violence. Merlo has lost weight in recent weeks; unbeknownst to everyone outside his immediate family, he is stricken with a late stage of neck cancer. He is extremely ill and particularly empathetic to both sides, and he requests that Capone not kill Dean O'Banion.

Capone completely respects the obviously emaciated leader, and out of deference to this great man, Capone honors his charge. For the moment, the North Side prankster O'Banion lives by the good graces of Mike Merlo, but this uneasy stalemate lasts only as long as the doomed Unione president.

12

Dean Is More Clever than Intelligent

1924

Although Jack McGurn takes no part in the most famous killing of 1924, it will define future courses for him and everybody in his milieu. The killing of Dean O'Banion in his flower shop by a mixture of Genna and Torrio-Capone gunners will initiate the gang revenge wars. It is the genesis of a violent conflict that will continue for five years, culminating in an act that will shock the entire world. The murder of O'Banion will set things in motion that will eventually make McGurn into Al Capone's commanding general.

Before they can get around to killing him, O'Banion also creates political havoc for the Torrio Outfit by swearing to carry his North Side wards for Republican Robert Crowe for Cook County state's attorney in the upcoming November election. Torrio's political interests are diametrically opposed because he needs Democrat Michael Igoe in the state's attorney's position, a crucial requirement for his Outfit's business. The future of any of the gangs hinges on those relationships between politicians, including mayors, state's attorneys, judges, and as many cops and detectives as money can buy. McGurn and every other muscle are fully mobilized on November 4 to slug, kidnap, or even shoot voters and election officials in order to get the required political outcome.

Once again, Election Day turns into a roving battle—rival gangsters shoot at each other, attack polling stations, and constantly try to evade Chicago Police Chief Collins's detectives, who are also heavily armed and driving around in thirty-six squad cars. The explosive wards by the Chicago River and in pockets all over the West and South Sides are literal battlegrounds. Only twenty-eight thousand Chicagoans cast votes, braving the insanity and violence in the streets. As history tends to note, the dead are well represented in the ballot boxes, a Chicago tradition.

To Capone's anger, O'Banion and his North Siders rule the day, ultimately getting the Republicans their victories. O'Banion's charge by the seated Republican Party members inspires him to motivate all of the North Side wards in a desirable response. Even the heavy-handed, all-out efforts of the Capone minions to win for Michael Igoe fail in comparison. McGurn evades arrest or worse, but dozens of boys from every gang keep the defense lawyers in Cook County busy and well fed for many months to follow.

O'Banion has truly underestimated the enmity of Alphonse Capone. The nutty little Irishman's influence and huge effort to sway the election are the final straw. Capone, like the good lieutenant that he is, has taken over most of Johnny Torrio's work since O'Banion's crafty Sieben Brewery setup, a debt that certainly must be paid one way or another. It is maddening to Capone that O'Banion is dancing triumphantly around in the ring as if he's a contender, challenging the efficacy of the Torrio organization.

Capone decides he needs help and elicits the conspiratorial aid of his allies the Genna brothers, who are O'Banion's worst enemies. Even though Capone is trying to keep the Gennas out of the leadership of the Unione Siciliana—which they also desperately desire—he makes a deadly pact with the brothers. The enemy of his enemy has become his friend.

The Gennas offer the services of their thoroughbred killers, imported Sicilians John Scalise and Albert Anselmi. Mike Genna, who hates O'Banion even more than Capone does, volunteers to be the driver. Capone suggests providing another man to gain an introduction to O'Banion's flower shop, somebody with whom he is already acquainted. He knows that O'Banion will no doubt have his customary two guns, which he is apt to use with minimal provocation. The assassination, still on hold, starts to gel.

Everything begins happening at once on Saturday, November 8, when Mike Merlo succumbs to his cancer, dying a natural death, the last president of the Unione Siciliana to do so for a very long time. His passing is monumental, providing Capone an opportunity to seize the Unione. With Merlo gone, Capone and the Genna brothers decide to kill Dean O'Banion immediately.

The Murder Twins, Anselmi and Scalise, 1927. PHOTOGRAPH BY ANTHONY BERARDI

The circumstances of Merlo's death also establish a third man to help kill O'Banion. Frankie Yale, Capone's first mentor, will be coming to Chicago from Brooklyn for Merlo's funeral. Chicago police have always suspected New Yorker Yale in the murder of Big Jim Colosimo back in 1920, the event that bought Johnny Torrio his lion's share of the Chicago underworld. Capone and Yale correspond, and the execution of O'Banion is set.

On November 10, O'Banion is as busy as a bee, producing magnificent and expensive floral arrangements for Mike Merlo's huge funeral. The wreaths and displays can cost up to ten thousand dollars apiece. Mike Genna borrows a dark blue Jewett sedan from his associate, West Side thief and bootlegger Jules Portugese (whom McGurn will end up killing). Genna picks up Scalise, Anselmi, and Frankie Yale, and, while he keeps the Jewett running, Yale and the Murder Twins walk into Schofield's Flower Shop on State Street. Yale is immediately recognized by O'Banion, who greets all three men and chats with them for a few minutes. Then O'Banion offers his hand, and in what has traditionally become known as the Chicago handshake, Yale immobilizes the florist's right hand, his gun hand. Scalise and Anselmi step forward and shoot him in the face, then four more times in the neck and chest.

The dangerous little O'Banion is dead, but rather than rebalancing the powers of gangland, his death opens a vast abyss of perennial violence and revenge.

O'Banion's North Side boys are stricken. The fallen leader's protégé, Hymie Weiss, whose real name is Earl Wojciechowski, has always been psychopathic and prone to migraine headaches. He is nearly immobilized with grief and rage. Weiss, George Moran, Vincent "Schemer" Drucci, and Louie "Two Gun" Alterie inherit O'Banion's Outfit, intending to run it as a council, although Weiss's twitchy, alpha-dog personality propels him into the leadership. Naturally, their first order of business is to seek retribution from Torrio and the Gennas. The newspapers have made it clear whom the police suspect in O'Banion's murder, as well as whom they've questioned. Weiss, who adored and idolized O'Banion, is motivated less by business than by personal revenge.

To Al Capone's profound surprise and anger, as soon as Mike Merlo is buried at Mount Carmel Cemetery in a massive funeral that sets the all-time standard for obsequies in Chicago, Angelo Genna elbows his way into the presidency of the Unione Siciliana. Capone is obsessed with the Unione and the power base the organization holds, not the least of which are all the thousands of home distilleries in the Sicilian neighborhoods. Because Capone prefers to remain the power in the background, he continues to provide puppet candidates for its presidency, the best way he can dominate the Unione. His vision of an expanding empire for his Outfit, especially in terms of racketeering, includes a dependable and controllable Unione chief, someone who will do his bidding in Chicago.

Frankie Yale, who is extremely brutal but also very smart, has always preached to Capone that there is enormous wealth to be taken from the American labor unions; Johnny Torrio and Big Jim Colosimo were also tied into various union interests. In addition, Capone constantly seeks a façade of legitimacy, which is exactly what the Unione would be for his enterprises. The Unione is also a direct, neural pathway to the thousands of Sicilians and Italians in the neighborhoods, as well as to their businesses.

When the Gennas immediately grab control of the Unione, they blindly initiate what will eventually be known as the War of the Sicilian Succession, creating yet another front in addition to bootlegging for Torrio and Capone to do battle. This will necessitate excellent leadership of the troops, and Capone will discover that he already possesses this asset in Jack McGurn.

Louise Rolfe Boex is completely out of place in the world she has made for herself. She realizes almost immediately that she is not designed to be a mother. Life is a grand party, and she is married to a young man who is increasingly disgusted by her rather close relationship with alcohol and her constant pursuit of Chicago's nightlife. Everything Harold Boex knows about family life is the complete opposite of Louise's own experiences. Actually, he is much closer in life philosophy to Mabel Rolfe. He is certainly shocked and disappointed that the golden-haired goddess he went so crazy for is a wild, lewd, narcissistic partygoer.

Louise, the married mother, is still a teenager in an era that is rife with liberated, rule-breaking, mold-shattering, independent girls. A growing portion of the women she knew in her two-year dalliance at Senn High School will go on to universities.[1] But Louise is the prototypical anti-intellectual, interested only in the pursuit of pleasure. The silent flicks that inspire her are "flaming youth" stories with actresses such as Clara Bow, whom Louise emulates and reveres.

To Louise, Harold Boex is a huge mistake. She must wonder what she had been thinking. Had the pressures to be who her mother wanted her to be simply gnawed away at her, until she impulsively exploded into doing what she did?

Harold and Louise spend a few months trying to reform each other while grandmother Mabel cares lovingly for little Bonita, who rarely sees her own mother. Louise goes out most nights and sleeps late into the afternoons. Perhaps she spends a little time with her daughter when she finally manages to wake up, before the evening festivities are resumed. She attempts to completely circumvent her husband, already bored with their thinly veiled charade.

Louise has a lot of temptations, for 1924 is a marvelous year for music and pleasure in Chicago. The jazz, the bootleg gin, and the needled beer fuel the scene. The "live for today" attitude and carefree philosophy is like an aphrodisiac to the young, whose childhoods were interrupted and scarred by World War I. For Louise's generation in particular, Prohibition only makes the continuous sense of festivity more appealing. It almost seems that by living faster, they will never become as old as their parents seem to be.

And how can Louise ignore the opportunity to hear Paul Whiteman, the "King of Jazz," and his huge orchestra of twenty-three musicians? Whiteman is playing at the Edgewater Beach Hotel, which is within walking distance of Mabel's apartment. The current Whiteman hits are the demure "A Pretty Girl Is Like a Melody," the brassy "To a Wild Rose," and the quintessential classic "Song of the Volga Boatman." The orchestra will also play the George Gershwin megahit, the symphonic "Rhapsody in Blue."

And how can a girl who is as alive as Louise babysit an infant and a clueless husband when the great Louis Armstrong and his singer Ollie Powers are playing the Dreamland Café on South State Street? Couldn't she use Harold's help in getting her into that opulently mirrored black-and-tan café? Isn't that why she married him? The guy is a flat tire, and here she is, brimming with magnetism. No matter, for she'll go anyway, either by hooking onto some other sucker or simply using her spurious ID.

Halfway through the year, Louise packs up Bonita, leaves Harold in their little apartment, and moves back in with her mother, who will end up raising the baby, of course, with the help of housemaid Frances Connors.

Louise still fancies herself a model from the job her father got her when she was fifteen. She wants to pose for more underwear ads, and she still entertains the fantasy of becoming an actress. She worships the ones who play flappers, adopting all their subtitled slang and sounding like an early Hollywood writer when she talks. Like the characters the women play, she enjoys smoking in public, drinking, and dancing the nights away. She spends her father's money on the zingiest fashions and shops at the best women's boutiques. She's in top form in her French heels, a real doll who turns heads wherever she goes. In terms of fashion, Louise is actually an antiflapper, preferring haute couture ensembles rather than the boyish A-line look of the early flappers, who bind their breasts and wear strangely masculine work shoes with the laces left untied. She plucks her eyebrows into needle-thin lines. In her mind, she is already in show business, living out her ambitions.

13

You Don't Have to Say Anything

1925

North Side gangsters Hymie Weiss and George Moran decide to shift the balance of power and get revenge for their fallen mentor O'Banion. They are not exactly visionary strategists, and they make a fatal error by trying to assassinate the moderate Johnny Torrio, who is once again out of jail on bond. This deed would give twenty-six-year-old Alphonse Capone the top spot in the Outfit. Weiss, Moran, and Vincent "Schemer" Drucci underachieve this by failing in an attempt to kill Torrio on January 24, 1925. It will prove to be the most influential botched murder in the legendary history of Chicago crime.

In an act that is more reminiscent of a dark silent comedy, the three North Siders shoot Torrio in front of his home while he is unloading packages from his car, in front of his wife. He suffers wounds in the chest, stomach, arm, and throat. Moran walks over to put a .45 automatic pistol to Torrio's head for the coup de grace. But he has lost count of his shots, and his gun miraculously doesn't fire. An automobile approaches, and the three stooges are forced to flee, leaving Torrio terribly wounded but alive. He will recover and retire after he serves nine months for Prohibition violations from the Sieben Brewery setup.

Torrio is always promoting peaceful negotiations between the gangs. To honor this, while Torrio is hospitalized and being guarded by Chicago police, his young protégé Capone refrains from going after crazy

Johnny Torrio recovering from his botched assassination, 1925. PHOTOGRAPH BY ANTHONY BERARDI, AUTHOR'S COLLECTION

Hymie Weiss and "Bugs" Moran, his Sancho Panza. However, Capone is absolutely seething, counting the minutes until he will retaliate. Whatever kind of adversary the North Siders thought they had in Johnny Torrio, all bets are off when they inherit Al Capone and, consequently, Jack McGurn.

At this point, the other players, the West Side Genna brothers, are also essentially at war with the North Siders, having yet to answer to Hymie Weiss for helping to kill Dean O'Banion. In addition, the Gennas are also now targeted by Capone, who will stop at nothing to regain control of the Unione Siciliana. This presents a propitious confluence of revenge and business for Capone and McGurn. It will never be clear who actually kills Angelo and Tony Genna, whether it's solely the North Siders to revenge O'Banion or perhaps even a joint effort with Capone, whose intention is to seize the Unione. Of course, McGurn is more than eager to kill the Gennas and their henchmen to thoroughly avenge his fallen stepfather, Angelo DeMory. Since 1923 he has been patiently waiting for the opportunity, and now, with Capone behind it, McGurn is in line to pull the trigger as soon as he can.

Fortuitously for Capone, the North Siders do his bidding and begin their assault against the Gennas on May 25, 1925. Angelo Genna is ambushed on Ogden Avenue, when a closed sedan containing four men tries to outrun his roadster and the men begin firing at him. He jerks one of his two guns out of its holster and begins firing back as he accelerates.

The two cars race down the street with the occupants exchanging shots. As the sedan catches up to him, Genna loses control trying to turn onto Hudson Avenue, crashing into a lamppost. Before he can get out from behind the steering wheel, the sedan pulls up and several shots are fired at him, including a shotgun blast that shatters his spine.

The shooters in the sedan speed away. Bystanders in front of Schmidt's Meat Market on Ogden Avenue witness the murder. When they reach Angelo Genna, he is only barely conscious and still clawing at his other gun in its shoulder holster.[1] He dies in the hospital before saying who shot him.

Even though eradicating the Gennas and their power in the Unione Siciliana will greatly benefit Al Capone, the police identify the men in the sedan who shoot Angelo Genna as North Side killers. The police records suspect Schemer Drucci, and there are three others with him.[2] Since they work together often, George Moran, Frank Gusenberg, and perhaps even Hymie Weiss have always been logical candidates. Though they are successful in running down and shooting Angelo Genna, their signature style—impetuous, harrowing, and haphazard—is evident. As marksmen, the North Siders will prove time and again in the future that they are mediocre at best. This time, they get lucky.

In an ironic surprise, it is the Chicago police who eliminate Mike "Il Diavulu" Genna in a shootout on June 13 after he is involved in the slaying of two police detectives, thus cheating Moran and Drucci of further revenge. Notably the most vicious of the brothers, Mike is cornered and gunned down. His femoral artery is hit. When an ambulance attendant leans down and tries to help him, he tries to kick the man in the face, groaning, "Take that, you son of a bitch," before he expires, leaving a legacy worthy of his reputation. With him are Salvatore "Samoots" Amatuna, the Gennas' payoff man, and the Gennas' imported Sicilian assassins, Albert Anselmi and John Scalise—the Murder Twins. (The "twins" are only identical in their professional attributes; Anselmi is short and thickly built, and Scalise is tall and thin.)

The twins also kill two police officers, patrolmen Harold Olsen and Charles Walsh, and seriously wound sergeant Michael Conway. Amatuna runs away, but the police catch Anselmi and Scalise. When they are arrested for murder, they are immediately represented by Al Capone's lawyer, Pat

O'Donnell, an associate at Nash and Ahern. On Capone's behalf, it is a clever, duplicitous act because it makes the Torrio Outfit appear to still be supporting the Gennas in their time of need.

Samoots Amatuna immediately forms a legal-defense fund for Anselmi and Scalise, strong-arming every citizen of Little Italy who has two nickels to rub together. After two years of legal battles that grab headlines, Anselmi and Scalise will be acquitted of shooting the police officers on the grounds of self-defense. Capone's attorneys will convince several juries that Anselmi and Scalise were only protecting their lives from the police, a justification that of course shocks the public. Even more outrageous, at the culmination of their final trial their attorney brings out a booklet found on Mike Genna's body that lists the payoffs for four hundred Chicago policemen who are on the Gennas' payroll.[3] Out on bond, during that period of 1925 to 1927, Anselmi and Scalise eventually go to work for Capone as subordinates to Jack McGurn.

On July 8, the gentrified and community-conscious Anthony "Tony the Gent" Genna is lured out of his penthouse by someone he knows. He's shot five times in the back by two gunmen, whom witnesses describe as "one short and one tall."[4] Weiss probably offers Joseph Nerone up for the task of luring Genna out of his apartment. Nerone, at one time a Genna associate, was shafted by the brothers and has gravitated to Chicago Heights, the south suburb that is Torrio-Capone territory. Nerone gives Tony the Chicago handshake, and Drucci comes up from behind, emptying a .38 revolver into Genna's back.[5] Tony's dying words in the hospital are interpreted as sounding like "Cavello." However, he is apparently trying to say "Il Cavaliere," Nerone's nickname because he has an aristocratic persona.

It has taken forty-two days for the North Siders to kill all three Gennas, unknowingly fighting Capone's war for the Unione. Nothing is certain in the circles of gangsters, for many of them are real characters. One of the most colorful, Samoots Amatuna, apparently sees his moment. Besides his defense fund for Scalise and Anselmi, Amatuna does something else that will seal his doom. He foolishly decides to grab the presidency of the Unione Siciliana. He rounds up tough barkeep Eddie Zion and bootlegger Abe "Bummy" Goldstein, both veteran Genna gunmen; they are his "campaign managers." The three of them invade the Unione

Siciliana headquarters and pronounce Amatuna the new president. No doubt Capone puts his fist through a few walls after hearing that news, a harbinger for the rash Amatuna.

In September, with the Genna family all but eliminated, Capone moves his Outfit headquarters from Cicero to the seven-story Hotel Metropole, at 2300 South Michigan Avenue. Capone takes the fourth-floor corner suite of eight rooms for himself and six rooms on the sixth and seventeenth floors for the boys in his inner circle. Two of those rooms are set up as a gymnasium, where Al makes sure his troops regularly work out. He brings in punching bags, weight sets, rowing machines, and, for the more athletic boys like McGurn, a trapeze and horizontal bars. According to Capone biographer John Kobler, McGurn likes to skip rope to stay fit, his favorite training exercise.

On October 30, the evening before Halloween known as Beggars' Night, Jack McGurn makes his debut in the criminal courts. Al Capone has made an effort to provide his soldiers with legitimate business covers. This entails paying off various factories and warehouses to keep time cards for his muscle, a plan no doubt provided by Murray L. "Curly" Humphreys, who is the young racketeering genius in the Outfit. All the boys have to do is check in and punch the time clock, and when their ghost shifts are up, someone will punch them out. This gives Outfit men ready-made alibis for their whereabouts, plus a source of supposedly legitimate income, although the money these jobs pay would hardly cover their Sistine satin neckties.

On this night—when trick-or-treating officially takes place—Chicago cops are especially vigilant, looking for any prankster activity. When officer Joseph Benson of the Maxwell Street station spots McGurn walking in front of 812 West Harrison Street, his instinct urges him to roust the lone young man with the baby face and fashionable suit, who seems out of place and is definitely not in a Halloween costume. McGurn tries to use his charm and perhaps even his stuttering immigrant act to divert the policeman's suspicions. He tells Benson that he is an employee at the Sawyer Biscuit Company, a couple of blocks away at 1049 West Harrison Street.

Benson isn't buying it; he certainly recognizes McGurn from the neighborhood. The policeman frisks him, finding a .32-caliber revolver inside his jacket. McGurn claims he is a night watchman at Sawyer and that he simply came outside for a stroll and a cigarette. Benson arrests him for carrying a concealed weapon off the premises of his job site, introducing him to his first pair of Chicago police handcuffs.

After being booked at the Maxwell Street station, McGurn is given his phone call. He contacts Capone's lawyers and is then driven downtown to the Criminal Courts Building. First he sits in a holding room with an assortment of drunks, bums, and other miscreants waiting to be arraigned. When they finally call his name, he is led into a courtroom, and his manacles are removed. Two bailiffs escort him in front of the bench. A brass nameplate reads JUDGE WILLIAM R. FETZER. McGurn will become one of Judge Fetzer's hobbies.

The bailiff begins reading the charge, and the court stenographer begins typing, her mouth silently moving as if she is repeating every word. The prosecuting attorney announces to Judge Fetzer that the defendant is Mr. Jack McGurn, who was arrested in front of 812 West Harrison Street under violation of Section 4 of Senate bill 348, carrying a concealed .32-caliber revolver on his person.[6]

Benjamin Feldman appears at McGurn's side. Judge Fetzer is familiar with young counselor Feldman as well as the gangsters he usually represents. Feldman will make a wonderful living from Jack McGurn. The judge asks how the defendant pleads this charge.

Feldman robustly announces, "Not guilty." It's simple, really—his client was at work guarding his place of employment and went outside for a cigarette, forgetting he was armed, "which is a dutiful part of his profession." This must be humorous to McGurn, for nothing could be truer.

The judge queries if the defendant has ever been arrested before. McGurn shakes his head. With that prompt, Feldman tells the judge that his client is a law-abiding citizen and has no criminal record. Fetzer asks the attorney why his client was three blocks away from his place of employment. Feldman explains that Mr. McGurn likes to walk when he smokes; certainly that isn't a crime. The judge agrees but states that carrying an unlicensed concealed weapon is.

Since this is a first offense, Fetzer finds McGurn guilty and sentences him to one year's probation. After the judge slaps his gavel down, Feldman and McGurn are led to a processing room, where they are handed a paper with the name and telephone number of probation officer John Devine, who will supposedly be overseeing McGurn.

On November 10, Hymie Weiss's lieutenant, Vincent "Schemer" Drucci, once again liberates the Unione Siciliana when he's suspected of gunning down Samoots Amatuna in Isidore Paul's barbershop on Roosevelt Road.[7] Three days later, as he is returning from Amatuna's funeral, Samoot's "campaign manager," Eddie Zion, is also gunned down. Three days after that, his partner Bummy Goldstein is shotgunned to death. The Unione is once more up for grabs as the body count rises.

Capone seizes this opportunity to help install his man Tony Lombardo as president. Putting up an intense furor, the North Siders support Lombardo's friend Joey Aiello, who is more sympathetic to their needs. To placate them, Capone allows Aiello to become copresident, but in name only, which enrages the Aiello family. The Aiellos had originally sponsored Tony Lombardo's immigration to America. This prompts them to join the North Side constituency, a move that will cause more bloodshed and eventual doom for the Aiellos.

As November progresses, Officer Devine does not hear from his probationer Jack McGurn in a timely fashion. Therefore, on November 25 he pays his first visit to the apartment that is listed on McGurn's sheet. McGurn will prove to be characteristically elusive. Attached to his probation report are only five interview attempts by Devine:

11/25/25 | Called at 1230 Oregon St. and inquired on 2 floors where I was informed that he did not live in that building. There was nobody at home in the 3rd floor – the people I saw were all Italians – Devine.

12/21/25 | Called again at 1230 Oregon St. 3rd. Floor; said works for Sawyer Biscuit Co. $28.00 week – Devine.

1/23/26 | Called 1230 Oregon St. 3rd floor, nobody at home – left my card with notation for him to report every month without fail – Devine.

2/9/26 | After a lot of enquiring by calls and notices to come in and report he finally appeared and said he was working for the Sawyer Biscuit Co. at $28.00 week – Devine.

3/24/26 | Called and found nobody at home – he reports irregularly and when he comes in said he works – Devine.

After that March notation, Officer Devine gives up. With his list of probationers constantly growing, Devine turns his attentions elsewhere, and Jack McGurn slips through his first official crack in the system.[8]

Louise Rolfe Boex enrolls in one of the downtown modeling schools. Many of these are fly-by-night affairs that last just long enough to con a large number of young women out of their money, although there are always a few who do train models to be professionals for print advertising. Even though the fashion industry is centered in Manhattan and Paris, there are fashion photos needed for newspapers, advertisement flyers, and consumer catalogs in Chicago.

Louise is in heaven with the nightlife and especially the music in 1926. It is another important year for the evolution of jazz and big bands. She spends her days sleeping late, attending her modeling classes, and then hitting the hottest spot for the evening's wild entertainment. She ignores her ex-husband and lets Mabel and her maid care for little Bonita.

During that summer, Louise probably spends a few adventurous nights lining up with mostly working-class white people to get into the Midway Dancing Gardens at 60th Street and Cottage Grove Avenue. It is one of the rage spots in Chicago where the young folks pay only a dollar to dance to an eleven-piece band that plays all fast music. Sixteen-year-old Chicagoan Benny Goodman, who will soon be the anointed king of the clarinet and the jazz orchestra, plays the licorice stick in the house band.

The Midway was originally designed by Frank Lloyd Wright to be the home of a symphony orchestra, but the quickly changing times and revenues demanded that it be converted to a splendorous cabaret and dance land. The house band is the Frank "Tram" Trumbauer Orchestra; it numbers ten men, including the fast-emerging, revolutionary coronet player Bix Beiderbecke on horn.

Some of the greatest music ever heard wafts on the warm Chicago breezes, often smelling of the Union Stock Yards. Louise sips from the ever-present hip flask that is fastened to her leg with an elastic garter. There is a signature movement that women make on the dance floor, where they bend to their side, slip a hand under their skirt, and deftly remove the flask for a swig.

The pounding beats and heady aromas of Chicago jazz fill up Louise's life. She frequents the clubs where Al Capone and his friends are also attending more often to hear the music. She and Jack McGurn are in the same places on some of the same nights, but it is not yet their time together. Still, they share parallel lifestyles.

The winter of 1926 arrives. Louise knows where the hot kids are and very likely hears Satchmo Armstrong play at the Dreamland in November, where his wife, Lil Hardin, leads her own band. In December, the place to be is the Vendome Theater on South State Street, which is only three blocks from the Dreamland in the heart of the music universe. The Vendome is all elegance, requiring its patrons to wear tuxedoes. Satchmo introduces the world to "Poor Little Rich Girl" at the Vendome near Christmastime. It will become a huge hit for him, and it echoes the familiar angst of the Louise Rolfes everywhere, whose fathers' money still can't assuage their tremendous inner pain.

According to Mabel Rolfe's maid, Frances Connors, Louise takes off for California to perform in a dance chorus that excels in the Black Bottom, Louise's specialty. She will only stay a few months before returning to the Midwest, but the journey will allow her to discover Sonoma, which will one day become her home. When her limited tour experience in California ends, she is forced to return to Chicago.

14

I'd Like to Buy a Hat

1926

L ike the year that has preceded it, 1926 will be another period of
extreme gang violence, which for McGurn becomes much more personal. With the vengeful North Siders decidedly ridding the world of the
Genna brothers, Capone gladly accommodates McGurn by ordering the
executions of the Gennas' most effective killing crew. Bossed by Orazio
"The Scourge" Tropea are Vito Bascone, Ecola "The Eagle" Baldelli, and
Phillip Gnolfo, four of the names that had also been mentioned in the
murder of Angelo DeMory.[1] Tropea, Bascone, and Baldelli have been long
suspected of sending Black Hand letters to people in the Sicilian neighborhoods in their brutal extortion business.

McGurn is no doubt thrilled on getting word from Al Capone that the
very men he wants to kill the most are sanctioned for death. It is a bus-
man's holiday to be paid to do what he will relish, although to avenge his
stepfather he would probably work pro bono. There is no known record
of how much McGurn makes, but the assumption is that he is paid a
high salary and frequently an additional bonus, all in cash. He is already
Capone's favorite boy, treated preferentially by the Big Fella.

For these murders, McGurn partners up with movie-star-handsome
Johnny Armando, one of the gunners who is associated with the Jewish gangsters and politicos around Maxwell Street. Armando is the size
of a horse jockey, a bantamweight at five-four and 120 pounds, but he is

Jack McGurn, 1926. PHOTOGRAPH BY ANTHONY BERARDI

as lethal as he is diminutive. He is normally employed in the fiefdom of
Twentieth Ward boss Morris Eller, whose son Emanuel is a circuit-court
judge. They are a politically powerful family with strong ties to Johnny
Torrio and now Al Capone. Eller, with interests in bootlegging, also supports the extinction of the Genna organization. Armando is likely Morris

Eller's contribution to the workforce that is finishing off any Genna men who might try to seize power.

The boyish murder team of Jack and Johnny take out the serpent's head first when they shoot down Orazio "The Scourge" Tropea on February 15.[2] Tropea is the most dangerous Genna killer, believed to have the *malu occhiu*, the evil eye, by the more superstitious residents of Little Italy. The Scourge owns a café where his old-world-style Black Hand extortion plots are hatched, including the one that took Angelo DeMory's life in 1923. He walks with impunity, with the cloak of fear, the kind of pride that comes before a fall. He is almost completely unaware when Armando and McGurn drive their automobile slowly by him. A twelve-gauge shotgun opens up from the passenger seat, blowing away Tropea and both his evil eyes.

The press calls Tropea's murder part of an "alcohol gang vendetta," connecting it to the murder a month earlier of gangster Henry Spingola. Words such as "vendetta" and "Mafia" are used because these murders are occurring in the neighborhoods of the Gennas, which the papers have long associated with old-country Sicilian criminals. Spingola, who was shot sixteen times outside Amato's Restaurant, a favorite haunt for Italian opera singers, was a brother-in-law of the Gennas.[3] That Tropea, who is suspected in the Spingola shooting, is murdered himself leads the police to suspect that Little Italy is blowing up with internal, unfinished Genna business. McGurn utilizes this natural distraction and subterfuge to do his business, which the law will only realize in retrospect.

Next on McGurn's death list is Vito Bascone, another of Angelo DeMory's suspected slayers. Bascone, a wine dealer and amateur opera singer, also frequents Amato's. He is friendly with visiting opera stars as well as members of the Chicago Civic Opera Company, such as tenor Tito Schipa. He is often seen with Desire Beirere, the baritone stage manager of the Civic, and Giacomo Spadoni, the assistant conductor. However, underneath this cultural cladding, he is a killer and a thug or, as the police put it, "he conferred in the councils of the Mafia, where the deaths of enemies were plotted."[4]

McGurn and Armando know just where to find singing Vito; they pick him up off a street corner and take him for what will become known as the one-way ride. His body, with several bullets in his head, is found out on the suburban prairie, west of the city, on Sunday morning, February 21. Two revolvers are dropped near the body.[5]

Bascone is widely known to be a close friend and business associate of Tropea. The police are puzzled. This was supposed to be one thing, but it smells like another. These colorful Mafia characters (Bascone has a second, previously unknown wife who appears at his funeral) with Italian and Sicilian names seem to be lining up in the Cook County morgue. Somebody is killing them in obvious competition for booze, but the growing constant and methodical nature of the shootings is unsettling.

The citizens of Little Italy now avoid spending time on the streets for fear of getting caught in a gang shooting. The automobiles of the day tend to backfire, emitting blackish smoke with what sounds like a gun report. People visibly react whenever this happens—the common event is usually followed with a nervous laugh.

McGurn waits only forty-eight hours to kill Ecola "The Eagle" Baldelli, who is found on an ash heap in an alley with many bullets in his body. The Eagle was Tropea's driver; he probably drove the automobile on the day Angelo DeMory was killed. Along with the combination of .32 revolver and .38 automatic bullets in his body, Baldelli has been given "the buckwheats," 1920s gangster jargon for a hideous thrashing. His body is bruised and beaten. McGurn gets some personal revenge for his stepfather with a serious pummeling before he and Armando empty their guns into the Eagle.[6]

In Baldelli's pocket, the police find a return application card for the Chicago police department, which had been filled in. They theorize that the Eagle was killed by his fellow gangsters because he was going to join the police force. Apparently, with everybody dying around him, Baldelli was thinking of seeking refuge in the safest place he could imagine. This really confuses the detectives. A huge dragnet is launched; police begin raiding every blind pig, speakeasy, fruit stand, grocery, and storefront on the West Side. Consequently, a hundred men are picked up for questioning. The public is demanding protection, and the quickest way to make it look like something is being done is to simply roust anybody who "looks suspicious"—an action that turns into a mass law-enforcement profiling in which dozens of Italian and Sicilian immigrants are summarily carted to the lockup.[7]

The remnants and supporters of the Genna Outfit, as well as the North Siders led by Hymie Weiss, are now all aware of the dangerous role that Jack McGurn plays in the Capone organization. On March 2, somebody sends four men to kill McGurn. Cruising the West Side in their large touring sedan, they spot McGurn in the alley behind his mother's apartment at 622 South Morgan Street. Three of them emerge from the car and pull revolvers, but McGurn is too fast and too lucky for them, ducking as they blow his hat off his head. These were either Genna loyalists or North Side gunmen, possibly the Gusenberg brothers, Frank and Pete. If it was the Gusenbergs, they will find it hard to believe the future consequences of their ill-aimed shots. They are the opening salvo in an escalating private war with the baby-faced Jack McGurn, whom they have tremendously underestimated.[8]

McGurn escapes the failed attempt and is eventually found by the police several hours later. After being questioned, he is unable to offer any reason for the attack. This time he reports his name as James Gebhardt, his address as 1230 Oregon Avenue. He claims he was walking in the alley behind the apartment of his "mother-in-law, Mrs. Josephine Memony [sic], at 630 South Morgan Street." None of this is remotely accurate, but by this time the innocent immigrant act is probably gone. McGurn has Al Capone and his crack lawyers behind him now. He no longer finds it necessary to give lip service to anyone, especially to Chicago policemen, many of whom are on Capone's payroll anyway.

This assassination attempt results in McGurn's first mention in a newspaper in his role as gangster. It will become customary for the press to pick up the lies and misinformation that McGurn feeds to the police. On this particular day, he doesn't fool the *Tribune* reporters in the least; they identify him as "formerly a pugilist known as Jack McGurn."

With the war heating up between the South Side and North Side gangs, McGurn is already targeted by Capone's enemies. His reputation begins to spread throughout the underworld of Chicago. With each successive killing he gains new adversaries, including the possibility of vengeful relatives. He is quickly becoming an integral part of the familiar gangland death cycle. There are already a score of candidates who would prefer to see him dead.

The very next day, March 6, McGurn is suspected of killing Joe Cale-breise, aided by John Scalise and Hop Toad Guinta.[9] The Chicago police also suspect him of killing Joseph Staglia and Jeffrey Marks on March 17, aided by Myles O'Donnell.[10] Each one of the targets is associated with North Side beer sellers. There are no witnesses, at least none who will admit to it after finding out who the person is in the police mug shots they are shown. Fear overwhelms the moral imperative in every case. The killings are all committed with revolvers, which are dropped at the scene. The guns are picked up for evidence and will eventually undergo new forensics testing, but this does not occur until 1929.

On March 18, Murder Twins John Scalise and Albert Anselmi receive the most outrageous acquittal in Chicago judicial history. In their first trial they were found guilty of shotgunning police officer Charles Walsh during the shootout that killed Mike Genna. They were sentenced to fourteen years. In their second trial, for the murder of officer Harold Olsen, Capone lawyers pull off a dark miracle. Defense attorneys Thomas Nash, Michael Ahern, and Pat O'Donnell are able to convince the jury that Anselmi and Scalise were within their rights to self-defense when they killed the policemen.

When the judge, William Brothers, reads the verdict, Anselmi performs a strange gesture: he half rises from his chair and bows to what the press will call "the cop-hating jury." Both killers then shake hands with the jurors, who all smile warmly. It is the worst insult to policemen anyone can imagine; even the bent cops on the gangster payrolls are angry. This is the beginning of the idea that nothing and nobody is sacred in Chicago.

A *Tribune* photographer snaps a picture of the Murder Twins personally thanking the members of the jury, setting off a flashbulb. Since photographs have been prohibited by Judge Brothers, the only person going to jail will be the photographer, whom Brothers sentences to ten days for contempt of court.[11] This shocking verdict will aid Capone attorneys in winning a reversal of the first conviction; killers Scalise and Anselmi are free to go back to work for Capone and McGurn.

In April, the beer wars escalate. The Sheldon gang is shooting at the O'Donnell gang, with Capone's people adding their own contributions to the mayhem. This all leads up to the April 13 primary, in which the slate of candidates aligned with state's attorney Robert Crowe are all supported by the Outfit gangs, who honor a truce for the duration of the voting. Capone has already learned to live with Crowe out of necessity.

Crowe's assistant, young William McSwiggin, is a dynamic attorney who grew up with several of the gangsters on the North Side. He loves publicity and has been part of many of gangland's most famous cases. He eventually was the one who interviewed Capone about the murder of Joe Howard in 1925. He got himself appointed to the investigation of the O'Banion murder and suspiciously helped in the weak prosecution of Anselmi and Scalise in their second trial for the shootings of the two police officers. Along with his triumphs, there are rather interesting failures, such as when he unsuccessfully prosecuted Myles O'Donnell and Jim Doherty for the murder of gangster Eddie Tancl. McSwiggin is the gangster Doherty's boyhood chum. It is clear that McSwiggin, though Robert Crowe's right hand, smoothly plays both sides. He appears to be Chicago's best and brightest assistant state's attorney, but his duplicitous loyalties put him directly in harm's way.

This culminates when, on April 27, McGurn helps Al Capone and Louis "Little New York" Campagna make a significant error in judgment: they kill the wrong man. It will exhibit to the world that nobody is immune to gang retribution. Capone's gunman Willie Heeney spots rival bootleggers Jim Doherty, Thomas "Red" Duffy, and archenemy Myles O'Donnell in a green Lincoln sedan; Myles O'Donnell is on Capone's short list. Willie calls Capone, who has allegedly been drinking. The boss rushes the boys out in several cars to intercept Heeney, who is trailing O'Donnell's automobile. Tommy Ross, a relatively new Capone driver, grabs the wheel, with McGurn, Campagna, and Capone seated in the Cadillac with a Thompson and a fifty-round drum.[12]

They spot Heeney, who is following the Lincoln, near Madigan's Pony Inn at 5615 Roosevelt Road. Doherty and Duffy, a Crowe precinct captain in the Thirtieth Ward, step out of the car, along with their surprise guest, assistant state's attorney William McSwiggin, who isn't recognized by Capone and his boys. McSwiggin is out for the evening with his chums, never suspecting that he has picked the absolutely worst night to be in their company.

It is either McGurn or Capone himself who mows down Doherty and the two others. Only one Thompson is used, the barrel sticking out the window of the Cadillac, which Mrs. Bach, who lives above the Pony Inn, describes as something that "looked like a telephone receiver spitting fire."[13] Duffy is seriously wounded, but he is able to crawl behind a tree in an empty lot. Doherty dies instantly, cut nearly in half by sixteen of the bullets, while young Bill McSwiggin absorbs his share and crumples to the ground, also dead.

The Capone cars speed off as Ed Hanley, the driver of the green Lincoln, and Myles O'Donnell raise themselves from the floorboards, emerge, and haul the riddled corpses of Doherty and McSwiggin into the backseat. They dump the bodies in suburban Berwyn and the blood-spattered Lincoln in Oak Park.

When Capone finds out it is McSwiggin whom he killed, it is too late for damage control. The papers are screaming the question "Who Killed McSwiggin and Why?" This particular murder is unnerving because the young fireball was a respected and honored state's attorney. The ensuing investigation by Robert Crowe will last for many months as McSwiggin's entire life is examined with the scrutiny of a microscope. Eventually, Capone will tire of the huge public debate over McSwiggin's duplicitous activities. In 1928 he will tell the reporters, "I paid McSwiggin. I paid him a lot and I got what I was paying for."[14]

William McSwiggin dead, 1926.
COLLECTION OF JOHN BINDER

15

The More One Works, the More One Earns

1926

O n July 14, McGurn is suspected of killing twenty-one-year-old Jules Portugese, ex–Genna gunner and hijacker. Portugese is a dark, good-looking, smaller version of the Genna brothers who has always been suspected of complicity in the murder of Dean O'Banion. His automobile, a maroon Lincoln, is identified circling the block at the time of the shooting. Some accounts have Portugese lending his automobile to the Gennas for the occasion; others have him acting as a possible lookout to block the cars that might give chase to the killers. He is considered a rising young star in the bootlegging game, and his multifarious alliances have him marked for extinction by Capone.

Portugese is lured out to Cicero in his automobile to discuss phony plans for a payroll robbery. Out in the country, his passenger, believed by the police to be McGurn, shoots him in the head at point-blank range, then empties the gun into his torso.[1] His body is quickly pushed out at the junction of Milwaukee Avenue and Glenview Road in the north suburb of Glenview. He is found crumpled and tossed away like refuse, another definitive example of a marked man being taken for a ride.[2]

Police believe that South Side gangster Joe Saltis (formally known as an ally of Jack Zuta) accompanied McGurn, but the motive for killing

Portugese has never been completely understood. Most theories suggest that Portugese had grown ties with Louis "Big" Smith, who is a thorn in everybody's side. Imported from New York to be a bodyguard, presumably for one of the North Side bootleg chiefs, Smith forms his own gang, which gathers at a gambling house on West Roosevelt Avenue. They hijack anybody and everybody's alcohol shipments. Smith is psychopathically brutal; he kills almost indiscriminately and is so outrageous "even the outlaws have outlawed him."[3]

The papers point out how universally disliked Smith is, bringing up the fact that many of the gang leaders have popularity in their neighborhoods because they are often charitable but that "Big" Smith has "no Robin Hood in him." Apparently Smith has made the fatal error of crossing the Outfit; Capone puts him on McGurn's short list. But before Smith can be dealt with, there is political business that must be addressed.

Capone utilizes McGurn and most of his gunners and muscle to "canvas" the voters, since it is once again election time. Capone has expanded upon the lessons he has from his mentors that the key to his business is a gangster-populist treatment of politicians: own as many as possible. The political wards in Chicago are the firmament of urban life, a symbiotic constellation with the criminals and bootleggers. Because of how much is at stake, election days in Chicago are becoming more dangerous to life and limb than most natural disasters. Consequently, on July 22, McGurn experiences his second arrest, this time giving his name as James Gebardi. He is served with an indictment for conspiracy to commit vote fraud, as he has been spotted "making false canvases of voters" in the Third Precinct of the Twenty-Fifth Ward. In plainer words, he is caught intimidating voters.

Once again, McGurn calls a Capone bail bondsman, either Louis Cowan or Isaac Roderick, who immediately notifies his attorney, Ben Feldman, who in turn comes to court and bonds him out. The law is moving swiftly on this day, pressured by the city into dealing with this gangster blight on the democratic process. McGurn is whisked into a courtroom; counselor Feldman shows up just as his client appears before a special grand jury on vote fraud. McGurn is able to walk out within a couple of hours after the cagey Feldman gets the first in a series of continuances for an entire year. This will give any witnesses a chance to "change their minds." Somebody, perhaps McGurn himself, gets a list of the complainants; they are threatened into backing away. With no witnesses, judge William J. Lindsay files a nolle prosequi on July 15, 1927.

The events of the latter part of the summer and early fall of 1926 eventually bring McGurn and his methods to prominence in the Outfit. Capone turns to McGurn's more thorough and orchestrated tactics after a summer of mayhem that further outrages the public. This begins on the morning of August 10 in "the battle of the Standard Oil Building." Hymie Weiss's associate Schemer Drucci is attacked by four Capone gunmen during the morning rush hour at 910 South Michigan Avenue. This confrontation occurs in front of the new Standard Oil Building when the streets are crowded with people as they go to work.

The gunfight explodes, forcing everybody to dive for cover. Bullets fly all around, one nicking an office clerk in the thigh. The shooting continues for some minutes until both sides run out of ammunition. Afterward, Drucci tells the police that it was a robbery attempt to steal his pocket money, which the *Tribune* reports as being more than thirteen thousand dollars in cash.[4]

There are no serious casualties in this incident, but the average Chicagoan begins to step quicker and stay more alert. It is now apparent that the rules of the streets have changed—the gangsters are giving less consideration to innocent bystanders. Whether McGurn is involved in this incident or not, what transpired was not his style. The attack in front of an unsuspecting public is carried out so loosely that it probably embarrasses McGurn and frustrates Capone. It certainly suggests that Capone has not yet realized McGurn's professional superiority.

Later on that same evening of August 10, McGurn finally kills Louis "Big" Smith, which makes the tall ink in the press because it's the forty-second gang murder in Chicago since January 1. Quite probably Smith's demise is also related to the murder of Jules Portugese a few weeks earlier. Smith's headstrong competition with the Capone Outfit is definitely his undoing. His killing is somewhat reminiscent of the O'Banion handshake, with a cleverness to the setup that indicates McGurn's strategic thoughtfulness.

Smith's murder is simple and quick, taking place on the street corner just before dusk. An acquaintance of Smith's, M. J. Passin, buttonholes the gangster as he gets out of his expensive Lincoln sedan on South Avenue. While they stand on the corner talking, an automobile that has been waiting up the street for the meeting pulls up quietly. When Passin spots the car, he quickly disappears as McGurn jumps out, takes a shooter's stance, and empties a .38 revolver into Smith. The first shot to the head kills him, but McGurn fires five more rounds, including one into the heart for good measure. Very few people mourn the passing of "Big" Smith, although there will be repercussions from law enforcement.

The Standard Oil Building fiasco and the growing body count, topped off by the Smith killing, leads to another crackdown by police. They begin immediately rousting recognizable gang members when they are spotted on the streets. Chicago police officer William Drury and his partner, John Howe, are out looking for familiar faces when they spot McGurn on the morning of August 20; they pat him down and find a loaded .38 revolver, which he does not have enough time to ditch before the two cops are upon him. Once again, he reports his name as James Gebardi. As he is carted off to the Cook County Jail, arrested on the familiar concealed-weapon violation, he has little fear for his fate. By now, it appears that agreements have been reached between Capone and many members of the judiciary.

McGurn appears before Judge Ward, represented by one of Capone's attorneys; the Chicago fix is in. The case is dismissed, and McGurn is discharged.

In a 1948 interview with columnist Frederick Othman, officer William Drury will restate the obvious after reminiscing about McGurn, claiming that he arrested twenty-two armed gangsters but only one ever went to jail, that "somebody always turned 'em loose after he nabbed 'em."[5]

By this time, McGurn is just starting to become noticed by the reporters who stake out the Criminal Courts Building, initially because they recognize his lawyers. They know that if they follow these attorneys, the path will eventually lead to a gangster in trouble. Seeking to avoid the prying eyes of the press, McGurn disappears from the courtroom, led by his lawyer, whose access to most parts of the building will allow them to dodge photographers and reporters. For the rest of his life, McGurn will do everything he can to avoid the cameras, even going so far as to hold a handkerchief to his mouth in courtrooms, avoiding staring into the lens at all costs. Because he is so boyish, he somehow seems ashamed, his eyes cast downward in a hangdog look, but he simply hates the limelight and is merely toughing it out.

For the next month, Chicago's gangs strike a fragile, delicate balance. Capone, Weiss, and thirty other gangsters agree to meet in an attempt to reach a consensus not to war with each other. The summit takes place at the Sherman House Hotel. Truly the savvy Johnny Torrio protégé, Capone considers the demand for alcohol big enough for all the Chicago factions. He pleads his case that there is plenty of business for everyone.

This is an understatement. US attorney Edwin Olson will estimate the Outfit's gross at $70 million for 1926, despite all the killings. Capone makes at least $3 million himself, although he will try to report $195,677.00 to the IRS at his future tax trial.[6] When he tells Hymie Weiss and the other gang leaders that there is enough opportunity for them all, he speaks the truth, but his comments fall on deaf ears. The amount of real hope for peace that comes out of the Sherman House wouldn't fill a shot glass.

Weiss is truly a tormented soul. He perceives himself as the knight who inherited the kingdom of his fallen ruler, O'Banion. He is compelled by his own code to show Al Capone that he represents the most formidable figure in beer running and everything else. There are reports that his terrible migraine headaches are becoming worse and more frequent. However, as with all stalwart gangsters, the very manhood of his clan has been threatened. He must not only act but must also prove himself worthy of leading the late O'Banion's troops. The pressure is on Hymie, mostly

Hymie Weiss, 1926.
CHICAGO POLICE MUG SHOT, AUTHOR'S COLLECTION

self-applied. His rather explosive behavior at the useless Sherman House meeting worries Capone. It won't be long before Weiss acts out.

It only takes a month until Hymie's erratic actions cause a shift in Capone's assassination policies. The volatile Weiss takes the offensive, making history for Chicago and the machine gun and providing a career move for Jack McGurn. The anguished North Sider does something outrageous that will raise the already escalating violence in Chicago to an entirely new level.

On September 20, the restaurant of the Hawthorne Inn, Capone's headquarters in Cicero, is packed with people finishing lunch, including Capone and his saturnine lieutenant and main bodyguard, Frankie Rio. Suddenly an automobile speeds by, heading west on Twenty-Second Street in front of the restaurant. One of its occupants fires a submachine gun into the air, a decoy move to get the curious gangsters outside.[7] In the silence that follows, Capone makes a move for the door, but Frankie Rio senses the ruse and physically pushes his boss to the floor. Seconds later, a caravan of several more automobiles slowly file by the Hawthorne Inn, each stopping in front of the hotel while North Side gunmen with submachine guns from each car systematically spray bullets at the windows of the restaurant and the neighboring storefronts.

A Capone associate, Louis Barko, is shot in the shoulder as he enters the Inn after the decoy fusillade. A tourist named Clyde Freeman, his wife, and their five-year-old son are sitting in their car in front of the hotel as the Weiss gunmen begin shooting. Bullets blow Freeman's hat off his head, strike the child in the knee, and shatter glass that explodes into Mrs. Freeman's arms and eye. From the last vehicle emerges a lone machine gunner, believed to be George Moran, who walks up to the doorway of the Inn, drops down on one knee, and fires a massive, hundred-round drum—nicknamed a century—into the lobby and the restaurant. When the drum, which is the size of a dinner plate and weighs at least twenty pounds, is empty, the shooter steps back up on the running board of the automobile as it follows the motorcade east up Twenty-Second Street, back into Chicago.[8]

This is one of the gravest attempts ever made to kill Al Capone. It is a bold headline event at the time. Coming on the heels of the Standard Oil

Building incident, people believe they've returned to an even more violent, higher-tech version of the Old West. Capone immediately responds to his adverse publicity. When told that Mrs. Freeman will need surgery to save her eye, the Big Fella insists on paying her medical expenses.

Everything suggests that at this time Jack McGurn is given his chance to take over Capone's troops. After the outrage at the Outfit's own headquarters at the Hawthorne Inn, Capone, who is nearly impossible to intimidate, is admittedly afraid of the unstable and deadly Hymie Weiss. Now he knows he must kill his North Side nemesis out of pure self-defense. Because he is intelligent, he also knows that he is standing at the brink of a public relations abyss. His men have been running around shooting up the town, and now his name is being associated with murder. Capone's loyal customers, his vast public of illegal-alcohol purchasers, are becoming nervous about the mayhem. Besides the obvious primary threat to his own life, Capone knows that this kind of behavior is terrible for business—everybody's business.

At this point, McGurn sees his opportunity for advancement. He presents his boss with a critical analysis of the current methods of operation. Based on faith in his youngest and already most successful assassin, Capone makes strategic changes; by the end of September, McGurn has been moved into a leadership role. It is probably one of the smartest decisions Capone ever makes with his personnel resources. McGurn will begin to receive larger rewards for killing the Outfit's adversaries. The number increases with time, as does his salary. For Al Capone, this is money well worth spending. McGurn proves to be a born general of assassins: he is intelligent, cautious, and as merciless as a Sicilian don.

Louise Rolfe wants to get paid to dance in the swankier cabarets. She constantly hounds the owners of the various dance lands, and as soon as one of the girls in any of the dance choruses falls ill, gets pregnant, or leaves for another job, she is among the first to audition. Meanwhile, she bounces from one man to another, seeking gold while dreaming of a career in any part of show business. While things develop, though, she is more than happy to remain at the never-ending party.

Louise is ensconced in the most creative, active milieu of jazz musicians, who seem to be making history with their music on a nightly basis. She also continues to be a member of the first American youth culture who clamors to hear the music in their homes. To answer this demand, the African American musicians record constantly, with 1926 being a prolific year for records, many of which are monumental. Louis Armstrong's Hot Five band records on the Okeh label; his megahits of the year are "Heebie Jeebies," with a scat chorus, and "Coronet Chop Suey," which reminds the world that he is not just a singing personality but one of the truly great horn players.

Young Benny Goodman, who is becoming wildly famous, records "'Deed I Do" and "He's the Last Word" on the Victor label with the Ben Pollack Orchestra. Almost overnight these become standards, requiring additional pressings. The Victor Company is truly a vanguard for jazz innovation; they also sign up Jelly Roll Morton and the Red Hot Peppers. They fill up 1926 with the ecstatic joys of the "Original Jelly-Roll Blues," "Kansas City Stomp," "The Chant," "Sidewalk Blues," "Georgia Swing," "Shoe Shiners Drag," "Dead Man Blues," "Doctor Jazz," "Wild Man Blues," and the number that Louise Rolfe prefers over all others, "Black Bottom Stomp." Whether she is performing in one of the cabarets or simply there to enjoy herself, she becomes known as Lulu Lou, the Black Bottom specialist. As soon as Jelly Roll Morton hits the ivories, accompanied by his magical banjo player, Johnny St. Cyr, Louise is a standout.

The Sunset Café, on the corner of Thirty-Fifth Street and Calumet Avenue, is an Outfit hangout, frequented by Al Capone and his lieutenants. A Capone associate, Joe Glaser, is able to talk Louis Armstrong and pianist Earl "Fatha" Hines into leaving the Dreamland Café to come over to the Sunset, which is owned by Glaser's mother. The Carol Dickerson Band enjoys tremendous turnouts, but as soon as Armstrong and Hines join them, the Sunset becomes the number-one place to be in Chicago, packed to overflowing with white swells and middle-class revelers every night.

There must be several evenings when Jack McGurn, bodyguarding Al Capone, crosses paths with the vivacious blonde Lulu Lou. In the smoky, gin-driven stratosphere of exploding jazz music and pounding drums, perhaps they eye each other from across the dance floor, yet they still move in separate orbits, both enjoying what the other loves. Neither is wanting for company, but their time grows nearer with every muted slide of the snaky, seductive trombones.

16

I'm Not Afraid of His Words, I'm Afraid of What He Can Do

1926

It becomes immediately apparent that mistakes and chaos are no longer part of the gang operations under McGurn's leadership. As ill planned as the attacks of the Capone Outfit have been that summer, the assassination of Hymie Weiss on October 11 will prove quite the opposite. Al Capone's methods seem to change dramatically; in retrospect, the best evidence of McGurn's leadership in Weiss's murder, besides the fact that he is suspected by the police, is the killing itself.[1]

McGurn's signature style surfaces for the first time. There will no longer be Keystone Kop antics in the populated streets of Chicago, at least not by Capone's people. The stealthy McGurn favors reconnaissance, strategic planning, and patience. The tales he was told as a boy regarding the ambush techniques of the Sicilian outlaws are his combat manual. The concrete and steel canyons of the city are his craggy mountain passes. His philosophy, borrowed from the clever, shadowlike Sicilian assassins, is to watch, learn, get in, and get out. Just as he no doubt learned as a child, he will be a scorpion in his enemy's shoe.

It takes McGurn exactly three weeks to kill Hymie Weiss after the shoot-'em-up outside the Hawthorne Inn galvanizes Capone. When Weiss is killed, the elements of a military strategy glare off the front pages, contrasting with the insane shootings of the previous summer. It is abundantly clear that somebody different, a person with orderly intelligence, has engineered the scenario. This will remain Jack McGurn's signature, not a nickel left in a dead hand, a newspaper reporter's myth that will be repeated often enough to be construed as truth.[2] His methodology will become well-known in Chicago and then familiar to the world in the next several years.

In his operation to murder Hymie Weiss, McGurn favors a subtle form of reconnaissance and stealthy infiltration into the North Side killing area that lies north of Madison Street, the heart of enemy territory for Capone men. Weiss's headquarters are on the second floor of the building at 738 North State Street, which still houses Schofield's, the flower shop of the departed North Side gang leader Dean O'Banion. It is across the street from Holy Name Cathedral. Weiss, ever O'Banion's protégé, keeps his offices and consequently the headquarters of the gang above where the Irish gangster had fallen. Typical of what will eventually be recognizable as McGurn's style, Weiss's murder is planned right under the target's nose.

McGurn rents two rooms to serve as observation posts—they are machine gun nests facilitated by innocent-appearing advance people. On October 3, a young, pretty blonde woman, giving her name as Mrs. Theodore Schultz, rents a third-floor front-room apartment on West Superior Street. Her windows overlook both the front and rear entrances of the flower shop across the street. That same day, a young man who gives his name as Oscar Lundin rents a room at 740 North State Street, next door to Schofield's. It is the last available space in the rooming house, a back bedroom. When Lundin takes the room from the building manager, he also reserves the front bedroom on the second floor, overlooking State Street, "should it become vacant."[3]

Capone is afraid of Weiss, and for good reason. Weiss is quick on the trigger, eccentric, and personal; his intensity and utter fearlessness are unsettling to the Big Fella. However, Capone is smart and more interested in good business, which depends on good public relations. Having learned from Johnny Torrio that negotiation should always be attempted, Capone tries to take the high road.

On Monday, October 4, there is an emergency attempt at a peace treaty at the Morrison Hotel. From all accounts, Weiss, crazy-eyed and raging, makes demands that nobody else, especially Capone, will agree to. He refuses any treaties unless Capone will give up for execution the Murder Twins, Anselmi and Scalise, to answer for Dean O'Banion's killing.[4] In that room, where Weiss supposedly refuses even to sit down with his enemies, Capone is able to see clearly that Weiss will never stop until one of them is dead. As everyone carefully leaves, backing out of the Morrison, Weiss is now destined to be put on the spot, having ensured his doom.

Later that afternoon, after the fateful meeting, the management of the building on State Street "unexpectedly" changes hands.[5] The very next day, just as unexpectedly, the front room on the second floor is vacated; the new manager, Anna Rotariu, lets Oscar Lundin move in. The finesse of this operation is in its unmistakable quiet. Nobody sees any gangsters; the new manager merely kicks out a roomer. Lundin pays a week's rent in advance, stays for one day, then vanishes. Two different men, who have been seen visiting Lundin by the previous manager, move in.

Not long after this, Mrs. Schultz also moves out of the Superior Street apartment; she has also paid for a week's rent in advance. Two male Italian "friends" of hers now occupy the room.[6] Nobody can directly enter the neighborhood without one or the other observation post spotting them. The east side of State Street, from Holy Name Cathedral to the corner, is always in view (and in range) of "Lundin's" apartment. Both machine gun nests are established for at least three days before McGurn makes his move against Weiss on October 11.

As the Capone shooters patiently wait and watch, Weiss finally appears at four o'clock in the afternoon, just before the rush hour. He is with his driver, Sam Peller, and his bodyguard, Paddy Murray. They have been in court and are returning to Schofield's. Also along for the ride are Benjamin Jacobs, a Twentieth Ward politician and private investigator, and William W. O'Brien, an ex–state's attorney and now one of the most prominent criminal lawyers in Chicago.

Peller parks the Cadillac sedan in front of Holy Name Cathedral, opposite the flower shop. The five men start across State Street. McGurn's men, who are in the apartment on Superior Street, see that Weiss is directly in the sights of the other team; their job is done. They bolt, leaving behind a shotgun and two bottles of wine, losing a perfectly "clean" weapon rather than be spotted with it as they emerge from the building. The two shooters in the State Street apartment, one of whom is McGurn, open up on Weiss and his group with a submachine gun and a shotgun.[7] There are a few people on the street, but their marksmanship is excellent, with the fusillade centered on Weiss and the four men who accompany him.

Ten bullets hit Weiss, killing him instantly; Paddy Murray, absorbing fifteen rounds, dies a few yards away. Counselor O'Brien, who is punctured by seven bullets in his arm, abdomen, and thigh, drags himself to the curb. The police arrive to find Peller, shot in the groin, begging the growing crowd for help. Jacobs has been hit in the leg. The two killers run down the back stairs of the building, climb out a window, and escape into the alley. The Thompson submachine gun that McGurn uses is later found on top of a dog kennel one block south of Superior Street.

When police enter the State Street room after the shooting, they find the floor littered with spent .45-caliber automatic cartridges that have been ejected from the Thompson gun. There are also three spent shotgun cartridges, two chairs by the bay window, and a large pile of cigarette butts where the two shooters patiently waited for Weiss to appear. It was simple to rain down bullets; at least thirty of the fired rounds passed through bodies.

Such precision becomes another of McGurn's signatures, an impressive accuracy with the hard-to-control submachine gun.[8] This remains consistent in every shooting where he uses the Thompson, although in reality he much prefers to use a .32- or .38-caliber revolver when he kills. Even though the Weiss murder is only the sixth shooting so far where the automatic weapon is used, the frightening gun begins growing a legend of its own. Around the country, Weiss's shooting is particularly exciting because of the Thompson, raising headlines such as MACHINE GUN USED IN THE CHICAGO FIGHT TO RULE BOOZE TRAFFIC and the even more dramatic DEATH DEALING INSTRUMENT USED IN VICINITY OF HOLY NAME CATHEDRAL.[9]

Chicago Police Chief Collins reacts with great vigor, putting seven hundred officers on gangster patrol in squad cars. The headlines scream

SHOOT TO KILL ORDERS ISSUED FOR GANGLAND, making people all over the country imagine that the streets of Chicago are constantly blazing with machine gun fire. Collins, not a man with guile, admits that he is "putting officers in every part of the city in the hope that they might run into a gangster killing in progress, which, according to him, is the only way the murderers can be found."[10]

This crime is particularly shocking because it occurs across the street from the cathedral, which is perhaps the second most sacrosanct building in Chicago, next to the old water tower on Michigan Avenue that survived the Great Fire. Chicagoans are shocked to find that there are machine gun bullet holes in the façade of the church. Therefore, because the Weiss killing is so successful and the public relations so bad, Al Capone decides to talk frankly to the press, to run damage interference by himself. He candidly admits to being the bootlegging chief that he is, unabashedly discussing the rigors of the dangerous business. He tells reporters that he wants to see gang murder in Chicago end, stating, in his most diplomatic Torrio style, "because there is enough business for all of us without killing each other like animals in the street." He adds, "I don't want to die in the street punctured by machine gun fire."[11] When he says this, he is no doubt visualizing being pulled to the floor as the caravan of North Side shooters began their attack in Cicero. He knows full well that his chances of not being machine-gunned are much better now that McGurn has eliminated the incendiary Hymie Weiss.

The Weiss murder also turns a corner for the beer wars of 1926. Attempts are made at peace between the Chicago gangs, leading to a treaty forged in a meeting at the Sherman Hotel on October 21, which is attended by thirty gang leaders. Although tenuous at best, the ceasefire will last into the New Year. McGurn's black magic is already effective as Chicago begins to realize the consequences of challenging Al Capone, engendering a new amount of respect and fear for his boss.

Despite the period of relative tranquility that follows the Weiss murder, one of the stranger acts of violence occurs on November 28, when Theodore "Tony the Greek" Anton—Capone's close friend since 1923— disappears. Apparently on the report of a witness, police begin dragging the Des Plaines River west of Chicago for Tony the Greek's body in the first week of December.[12] Anton is an ex-pugilist, a Cicero restaurateur, and a hotel owner—he owns the Anton Hotel on Twenty-Second Street, in the heart of downtown Cicero, as well as the Hawthorne Hotel next door. Both are Capone headquarters.

Fred D. Pasley's 1930 biography, *Al Capone*—which has always been considered a public relations presentation sanctioned by Al himself—states that when Anton goes missing, the Big Fella stays up all night in Anton's restaurant, sobbing like a baby.[13] The immediate police theory is that Anton has been taken for a ride by rival gangs.[14] But obviously something is not right about everybody's dubious story concerning this event, leaving a gigantic question mark in the frozen pre-Christmas air.

Also before Christmas, legendary singer Bing Crosby opens at the Tivoli Theater with his partner Alton Rinker, billed as "Two Boys and a Piano." In his youth, Crosby is already a dedicated drinker, and he goes on a bender, visiting various Chicago speakeasies. In his authorized 1975 autobiography, *Bing*, he will claim that he passes out in a hotel room that is shot up by gangsters while he remains unconscious. He will note that he has been drinking heavily with Jack McGurn, although he has little memory of the evening. When he wakes up and is told what transpired, he is shocked. McGurn will never forget his raucous revelry with "Der Bingle," whom he will now regard as a pal and drinking buddy.[15]

Her hair dyed blonde and her eyebrows finely tweezed into pencil-thin lines, Louise continues to sleep until noon, dancing and drinking her nights away. This is all paid for by various young men and with continuing subsidies from her father. She is the quintessential baby doll, her hips and dancer's legs perfect, although she complains about having thick ankles. She has the dreams of a gold digger, and she'll continue to play all the angles until she meets the right man.

She sees most of the silent films, reads every Hollywood magazine, and is hypnotized by the it girls, like Clara Bow and Mary Pickford. They are American royalty. She's learned from Harold Boex what she doesn't want—a life without glamour. Why else has she been made so pretty? She always expected she'd ultimately be famous, but at twenty-one, she also contemplates the virtues of another marriage and being taken care of by a strong man with lots of money.

At her tender age, Louise has an intuitive understanding of males and how to manipulate most of them. She is now the perfect example of Chicago haute couture, spending much of her money on elegant, revealing outfits. She is constantly burning like a rocket in the night, eager and predatory. She makes the most of the party, out-dancing, out-drinking, and out-flirting every young woman and most young men.

The aspiring actress and model Lulu Lou seems to be searching underneath her continuous revelry. She wants something different in a partner, something special. As she encounters one fellow after another, quickly bored with most of them, she remains desirous of some dynamic, powerful prince. Her hunger for performance and public recognition, and her penchant for overindulgence, makes her one of the more familiar personalities in Chicago's cabarets and cafés. However, so far, no man has appeared who can truly captivate her.

17

Aren't You Ashamed of What You Did?

1927

The New Year sours quickly when the body of Theodore Anton is discovered in a shallow, lime-filled grave near Calumet City on January 5.[1] He is identified by his diamond-studded belt buckle—a gift from Al Capone—which is initialed TA. The official word is that he is the victim of a gang assassination, having been snatched cleanly off the streets of Cicero. However, things are not quite what they seem.

According to several historians, including Capone biographer John Kobler, North Side gang members grabbed Anton from in front of the Hawthorne Inn and killed him.[2] This seems highly unlikely, especially after Hymie Weiss had shot up the hotel in September of the previous year. Since then, Capone has heavily armed security men posted all over the block, in every store and on every corner. It would take a highly trained, elite team of operatives to walk into Cicero and abduct anybody, let alone one of its most famous proprietors. These are not talents that belong to the North Siders.

A later theory of Anton's death, circulated in the *Daily News* in 1943, is that Capone killed Anton in a drunken rage because Anton insulted him. This same story reappears in 1947. In 1989, a witness who saw two of Capone's men beat Anton to death comes forward. In an interview with Chicago historian and gangster expert Michael Yore Graham, Dr. Jerome Nachtman will claim to have seen two thugs attack Anton. Nachtman played piano in several of Capone's Cicero establishments to pay for dental school.[3] While he was "browsing where he shouldn't have been," Capone-era historian Mark Levell was able to access the Chicago police records through a friend on the force. The reports indicate that Jack McGurn and another Capone bodyguard literally beat Anton to death with their fists. Young Nachtman, then in his early twenties, describes McGurn to the police. But being bright, he also declines to testify against anyone, which is why he will be able to live a long life and retire an old man with interesting stories.

If indeed this account is true, it certainly reestablishes the level of frightening volatility in Al Capone and the tremendous brutality on demand from McGurn. Perhaps because Anton had been a boxer, McGurn was encouraged by Capone to fight the older man when things got out of hand. Whatever the scenario, Anton is found with a bullet in his head and his body badly beaten.

Events continue to get even uglier in the winter of 1927. Capone's efforts to replace Mike Merlo have led to Sicilian bloodshed that still continues to infuse his cause célèbre with one murder after another. Capone's man Tony Lombardo finally "wins" the presidency, beating Joey Aiello—the great friend and business associate of the Genna brothers. After the Gennas have been dealt with and their man Samoots Amatuna, who has also tried to capture the Unione, is eliminated, Capone has finally been able to help put Lombardo in office. Joey Aiello, already full of venom for the killings of the Gennas, is so enraged that he offers fifty thousand dollars to anybody who will kill Capone, the Napolitano interloper. This is perhaps the least intelligent murder-for-hire contract in history. Aiello's offer brings hungry professional killers to Chicago, but the Capone intelligence network is outstanding—Jack McGurn is always waiting for them, always at least one step ahead.

There is a new need for reliable manpower in the face of such a threat, and the "graduating class of 1927" of the 42 Gang provides an excellent candidate. It is probably during the early spring when twenty-year-old Antonino Leonardo Accardo is brought into the Capone Outfit, sponsored by Jack McGurn. Young Accardo is driving trucks full of alcohol collected from the multitude of neighborhood stills to a central distribution center. That he has been arrested eight times for disorderly conduct suggests he is a brutal, prodigious pummeler and not a fun guy. The word is out to bring in these ripened apples from the satellite gangs, and Accardo is one of the first to be moved up to the Outfit.

Accardo was raised in the Patch and has grown a fierce reputation since he first joined the gangs in 1923. According to William F. Roemer, the FBI agent who will watch Accardo for thirty of his later years, young Tony has handled everything, including burglaries, hijackings, armed robberies, muggings, sluggings, and car thefts.[4]

Accardo's forte, his personal idiom, is the baseball bat. He prefers the equalization of the Neanderthal-style cudgel on the street. Many writers and reporters have traditionally given kudos to Al Capone for nicknaming him Joe Batters. More probably, Accardo, whose parents are Sicilian, earns the name from McGurn, who refers to his young protégé as a *battiri*, the Sicilian word for "one who strikes." It begins as a private joke among the Sicilians in the Outfit. Soon he is known as "a real Joe Battiri," which becomes Joe Batters to Capone.

Two propitious events take place in April that prove to be a boon for Al Capone. On April 4, detective Daniel Healy shoots to death North Sider Schemer Drucci as they sit in a Chicago squad car, saving Jack McGurn the trouble but costing him his assassination fee. Drucci had been picked up in a pre–mayoral election sweep ordered by Police Chief Collins.

On the heels of Schemer's timely demise, William Hale "Big Bill" Thompson upsets reformist Mayor Dever on April 5. Thompson is aided tremendously by the bootleggers, especially Capone, who donates a large sum of money to the campaign. Dever, who has been mayor of Chicago since 1923, leaves the city open for the anti-Prohibitionist Thompson and his administration, which will be far more than friendly to the Outfit, producing a new standard of political corruption.

In the spring, summer, and early autumn of 1927, to protect his boss, McGurn does some of his most efficient work. He displays a brilliant combination of precision murder and excellent gang intelligence. This is made easier since Joey Aiello's idiotic open-murder contract has the Outfit completely forewarned. McGurn and his men kill at least three assassins who have come to Chicago to eliminate Al Capone. Apparently, McGurn takes it as a personal affront that anyone would come into Al's town to try to execute him.

Whenever any of the bodies of the five are found, it is immediately obvious that McGurn has given them the "buckwheats," a slow and painful death.[5] However, this is not totally personal anger on McGurn's part, the way it probably was with the Genna men who killed his stepfather. These amateurs are in town to kill the Big Fella, and there is information to be extracted at all costs, as well as a message to Joey Aiello and anyone else who would attempt to assassinate Al Capone.

Imported killer Anthony Torchio from New York is the first would-be Capone assassin to die—he is shot to death hours after he arrives in Chicago to kill Capone and collect his fifty thousand dollars. His body is discovered by police on May 25. Apparently his plan is to sneak into town from a train at Dearborn Station, wearing "laborer's clothes." Despite this attempt at subterfuge, McGurn's spotters identify him. Although he avoids the tell-

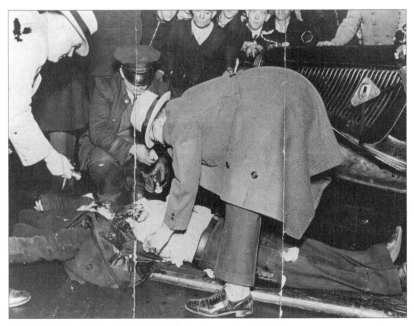

The body of would-be Capone assassin Anthony Torchio, 1927.
PHOTOGRAPH BY ANTHONY BERARDI, AUTHOR'S COLLECTION

tale double-breasted suit and fancy fedora of the well-dressed gangster, his costume doesn't work and something gives him away—perhaps he smells too good, or he is wearing shiny, expensive shoes. Something sets off the alarm for McGurn's spotters. He walks out of the station, and later his body is found at DeKoven and Des Plaines Streets, shot five times.[6] Chicago police suspect McGurn, aided by Murder Twin John Scalise.[7]

Detective squads are now constantly out on the streets, looking for the usual suspects as the bodies begin appearing. On June 6, less than two weeks after Torchio's corpse is found, two police officers recognize McGurn on the street. They frisk him and find a loaded .32 Smith & Wesson revolver, once again arresting him on the now familiar concealed weapons charge. He appears before his old pal, judge William Fetzer. Handsome Ben Feldman arrives and pronounces as usual on McGurn's behalf. Either the arresting officers fail to show up to testify or Feldman makes some tricky maneuver that includes a financial understanding. Fetzer dismisses the case and discharges McGurn.

It is somewhat surprising how Fetzer can allow McGurn to walk on the same violation on which he had been convicted in 1925. This is another example of Capone's invasive influence in law enforcement and the criminal courts. Years later Virgil Peterson, ex–FBI agent and longtime executive director of the Chicago Crime Commission, will claim that a majority of Chicago policemen are either corrupted and are on Capone's payroll or they are so intimidated by the police officials who are beholden to Capone and his political pals that it is impossible for them to do their jobs.[8] This revelation also pertains especially to the state's attorneys and the judiciary.

McGurn starts to feel invulnerable from what seems like infinite power, because he gets careless at the end of June. He and Capone gunner Orchel "Rocco" Degrazia are spotted with three other men kidnapping a part-time bartender named Dominic Cinderella. Police claim Cinderella is a member of a Chicago auto-theft ring operating between Chicago and Milwaukee, but he has apparently made the grave error of allying himself with Joey Aiello.

On the beautiful Sunday of July 17, members of a family outing are horrified when Cinderella's body washes up on the shore of the canal near

Calumet City. He has been sewn into a large burlap sack, doubled at the waist with his feet and hands bound with wire. His face is covered with a handkerchief thoroughly wrapped by adhesive tape. The cause of death is strangulation; he has been tortured for information and given the buckwheats. He is identified by his automobile license, which is found in his pocket.[9]

At least one witness identifies McGurn and Degrazia as two of the men who grabbed Cinderella five days before he is murdered. They are arrested and arraigned as suspects in the killing on August 2.[10] McGurn, in a new burst of imagination, humorously tells the police he is a saloon proprietor, although the detectives and officers immediately recognize him from his recent, regular exposure to the system. The small, slender, cherubic-featured lad with Valentino hair and flowered neckties is becoming a far-too-familiar face to fool anybody.

McGurn is immediately bonded out, spending no time in the lockup in the Cook County Jail until his hearing before the always-sympathetic Judge Fetzer. Capone's legal machine proves its mettle as McGurn's appearance gets scheduled for August 10. Between August 2 and August 10, the witness recants or disappears, no doubt after being suitably threatened. Since detectives cannot manage to tie Degrazia and McGurn to the Cinderella murder, benevolent Judge Fetzer decides to file a nolle prosequi. McGurn and Degrazia take the Chicago stroll, that joyful journey out of one more impotent, sullied courtroom.[11]

The joys of summer continue on the golf course; Capone is also crazy for the links, although his abilities are comically limited. The local golf pro, William "Willie" J. Harrison, has taught gangsters and politicians to play golf for many years. He is an excellent golfer and an even better instructor. Impressed with McGurn's abilities, he offers vital lessons while the Outfit boys play the Burnham Woods Golf Course. Willie operates a famous speakeasy on West State Street in Calumet City that is popular with politicos, businessmen, and mobsters. He is a rather outrageous womanizer, who once lured a young girl up to his room at the Savoy Hotel on State Street. When he made his advances, the terrified teenager, realizing she was in way over her head, jumped out of the second-story window to escape. Willie avoided prosecution by paying the girl and her

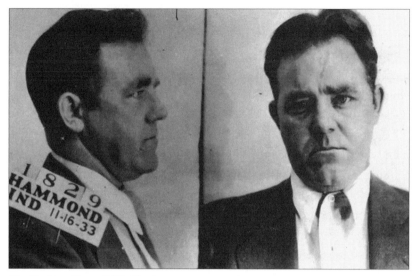

The Outfit golf pro, Willie Harrison, 1927. COLLECTION OF RICK MATTIX

parents a princely sum that he will continue to complain about for many years, evoking many a laugh from his listeners.[12]

A wonderful eyewitness description of Jack McGurn during the summer of 1927 is recorded by Milton "Mezz" Mezzrow, the famous Chicago jazz musician. Mezzrow leads the jazz band at the Arrowhead Inn in Burnham, which Capone owns. The band is often quartered in rooms at the inn. As Mezzrow tells it,

> One day we were called out to the backyard, where we saw some men putting up a large circus tent. . . . When we went inside the tent we saw barrels of beer being lined up in long rows and a large ice-box being built off to one side . . . a man named Jack, one of Capone's lieutenants, came along. He gave us a brace and bit, a box of sticks like the butcher uses to peg meat with, and some galvanized pails. Then he yelled, "One of you guys drill holes in these barrel plugs and let three-quarters of a pail run out of each barrel. Then another guy plugs up each hole with these here wooden sticks, to stop the beer from running out." That cat was stronger than Samson after a raw steak dinner. He would roll

a barrel over so the plug was facing up, then break off the meat stick and place a new plug over the old one. With one mighty swing of a big wooden sledgehammer he would drive the new plug all the way in, forcing the old one clean into the barrel. In all the time I understudied at this spiking routine, I never saw Jack take a second swing at a plug.[13]

Louise spends 1927 in a state of reverie. She dances in a couple of cabarets on the North Side, like the New Rendezvous and the popular Green Mill. She still passionately wants to be in the movies and no doubt is contemplating another pilgrimage to Los Angeles. Further inspiring her are the many famous people who come through Chicago to entertain. Louise still craves the nightlife and the illusory glamour of the overheated, boozed-up revelers at their neverending party. She still burns with the desire to perform; she also seems, however, to be somewhat practical, dedicated in her search for men who can help her in any way.[14] There are rumors that a Chicago producer has decided to get her either a job in a film or a stage role. In the 1980s, Louise herself allegedly will tell her pal Nancy Miller that she'd had someone influential "interested" in her, but this opportunity will never materialize.[15]

It is a year of serpentine, trombone-rich jungle music with jumping rhythms. Bandleader Paul Whiteman and his enormous orchestra are allegedly "as big as the New York Yankees." For the Fourth of July, Whiteman appears at the Chicago Theater with an ensemble of thirty-three musicians playing a total of 125 instruments. Blowing coronet and trumpet is Bix Beiderbecke, who receives a standing ovation after his solo in "Riverboat Shuffle." This is a particularly magnetic concert, the kind that appeals to the music lover Al Capone. Probably Louise and McGurn both attend, in their final year of parallel play, with McGurn guarding the Boss. Capone rarely misses the most highly touted musical events.

For Louise, it is a time like no other. Similar to her future counterparts in the 1960s, she makes sure she is in with the in crowd, showing up at the hottest venues and hobnobbing with high-profile people who have money. Lulu Lou is the bee's knees, a red-hot mama still continuously out on the town. For her, 1927 is a blur of great music, rivers of alcohol, and endless chains of cigarettes. In December, Duke Ellington records the monumental "Black and Tan Fantasy," which becomes a huge seller, especially in Chicago. After all, it is the pinnacle moment for the black-and-tan cafés, which are the favorite haunts of hip white aficionados such as Jack McGurn and Louise Rolfe.

18

Sometimes Cat and Mouse Dance Together

1927

As summer progresses into autumn, the last contract killer to try for Joey Aiello's bounty on Al Capone is Sam Valente from Cleveland; he is shot down in September. All five mercenaries have lasted less than a week. Any honest Chicago police officers or detectives are definitely considering McGurn by now. In an age-old tradition in Chicago, even though he's never been convicted of anything except carrying a concealed weapon, they will continue to arrest him on suspicion of almost anything. They will hold him as long as they can and attempt to interrogate him, while street patrols and detectives try vainly to find witnesses who are brave or stupid enough to testify against him. Then, after they've inconvenienced him as much as they can, they let him go. It becomes a familiar scenario.

In any of the photographs that are taken of McGurn in police custody, he is very unhappy and unable to look at the camera. The photos of the various gangsters and gang bosses are often sneering or even laughing at the cops. However, the truly tough guys always seem to be particularly mortified at their captivity; there's nothing for them to smile about. In McGurn's eyes is an unmistakable message that gets projected out to the photographer, the cops, the jailors, the judges, and ultimately to history.

The corpse of would-be Capone assassin Sam Valente, 1927. PHOTOGRAPH BY ANTHONY BERARDI, AUTHOR'S COLLECTION

McGurn begins to feel the pressure as he is being eagerly awaited on the streets by police as well as assorted North Side gunmen. He cannot venture anywhere unarmed, so he's damned either way. If he leaves his weapon at home, he risks being defenseless; if he carries a gun, he risks arrest on concealed weapons charges. This must make him mourn for his lost anonymity. On September 19, detectives are literally competing to find McGurn. They spot him coming out of a club after drinking and dancing and eagerly descend on him. He is angry at the harassment, mumbling a few epithets at the bulls. He is a generous spender, and after a night out he has only pocket change left. He's dressed in a beautifully tailored three-piece suit, and they arrest him for disorderly conduct because he's able to ditch his gun. Most of the time he is extremely courteous to everyone in the system, but when he perceives he is being singled out and abused, he displays an unsettling, piercing toughness.

McGurn and, of course, a Capone lawyer appear before judge Peter H. Schwaba. McGurn's lawyer efficiently convinces Schwaba that his client is a victim of police harassment, money or favors are exchanged, and the charges are once again dismissed.

At this point Jack McGurn has become a steady source of employment for the cops in the city as well as an important meal ticket for the Capone attorneys. He is also a lovely source of extra income for the bent members of the judiciary. All signify a pinnacle of corruption in the legal system to which Capone and all his mentors before him have contributed. Despite this, the men who take their integrity with seriousness do not stop, even with the heavily unbalanced odds. Less than a month goes by until McGurn is once again stopped by police on October 7. He is frisked, discovered armed, and arrested on his fourth concealed-weapons charge.

An unhappy McGurn mug shot, 1927.
COLLECTION OF JOHN BINDER

Of course, the fates (or the state's attorneys in Capone's pocket) make sure that he appears before Judge Fetzer, who slaps him on the wrist and essentially lets him walk. Either Fetzer is being paid off or he is "softly" complying, because he can always be counted on to rule favorably. He hands out a six-month probation to McGurn. Given McGurn's history of disdain for the process, there is undoubtedly a probation officer who is also thrilled to benefit from a mutual understanding, because there are no records attached to the probation report.

In 1950, Judge Lyle will recall that the police have been bringing in McGurn for lurking near fresh killings since as far back as 1924. Up to this time, it has been a revolving-door experience for the gangster, who must be again starting to entertain the illusion of invulnerability.[1] He seems completely undaunted by his usual suspect status.

After being convicted on October 7, McGurn keeps his head down for a month, playing golf while the weather is still warm enough. During the tenuous gang truces he frequents the Green Mill, the speakeasy and cabaret at 4802 North Broadway, enthusiastically working his way through the girls in the dance chorus. To further assuage any guilt that he might have about his wife, Helen, he prefers blonde, milk-skinned women, as if a part of him keeps Sicilian mothers in some sacred, untouchable place.

No doubt McGurn is extremely cautious when he's at the Green Mill, which is in North Side territory. A Moran gang hangout, the Wigwam, is only a couple of blocks away.

For decades to come, journalists and writers will insinuate that McGurn possessed a piece of the Mill, along with the alleged owner, Danny Cohen. This turns out to be patently untrue. Not only is McGurn not a partner, but it is more likely that Danny Cohen is a front man for the real owner, North Sider Ted Newberry, an associate of George Moran's, Capone's main competitor.

In a six-part remembrance of Prohibition, ace Tribune crime reporter James Doherty, one of the first reporters who will view the results of the St. Valentine's Day Massacre, recalls how the outrageous entrepreneurial hostess Texas Guinan moves her nightclub and show into the Green Mill in 1930. Doherty claims that Newberry has owned the Mill since 1927.2 During the truce periods there seems to be a certain subtle alliance between McGurn and Newberry because McGurn spends many an evening there. Eventually, Newberry, a many-faceted, duplicitous fellow, will escape the St. Valentine's Day Massacre and gravitate to the Capone Outfit, even getting a gift of one of Al's famous diamond-studded belt buckles. However, like Theodore Anton, that particular trophy will turn out to be a dubious reward, for in 1933 he will overstep his bounds and earn Capone's wrath.

The year 1927 contains a lull in Capone-Moran conflicts, a situation that must make McGurn feel more comfortable being north of Madison Street.3 He is an indefatigable dancer and still an aficionado of good jazz musicians. He guards Capone whenever the boss visits the Sunset Café or the Friar's Inn or any of the other popular venues. While Capone is also famous for his adoration of Italian opera, McGurn is a dedicated jazz buff, letting bodyguard Frankie Rio accompany the boss to the Chicago Civic Opera House as well as to the north woods of Wisconsin for hunting trips. McGurn never appears in the photographs of the Capone brothers and their associates with their field weapons and the deer they've bagged. He is a strictly urban denizen, with absolutely no inclination for roughing it.

The comic entertainer at the Green Mill is "Smiling" Joe E. Lewis, a vaudeville comedian and singer with an extremely energetic and hilariously vulgar act. He was born Joseph Klewan on the Lower East Side of New York. Like McGurn, he is a legendary womanizer, thus ending up as another rooster in McGurn's yard. Even though Lewis is loud and has a humorous face with comical features, he is a dedicated drinker and a constant wolf, always on the make. He is gangland's favorite comedian, also considering himself tough because he is a World War I veteran. He and McGurn cannot help but overlap in their activities, and apparently

McGurn, for many reasons, grows to detest Lewis, who is obnoxious and completely irritates him.

Lewis has been a big hit in 1927, especially with the Jewish population on the North Side, who laugh at his use of Yiddish slang. They are showing up at the Mill in droves. Ralph Jacobs, a well-known handball player who has sold life insurance to Lewis, brings his pretty young wife, Elsie, to see the show. They are seated at a table near Jack McGurn, who ogles Elsie Jacobs and makes a rude, suggestive comment that her husband clearly hears. Ralph Jacobs is a tough Jewish kid; one of his brothers insured the late Dean O'Banion's flower shop. Consequently the Jacobs boys know who's who in Chicago. Ralph, who has a bit of a temper himself, cannot suffer the insult to his wife. He stands up and confronts Jack McGurn.[4]

There is a nose-to-nose exchange, which leads to a little pushing and jostling. Manager Danny Cohen, who is McGurn's good friend, jumps in and pulls the gangster away, talking in his ear, telling him that Jacobs is a stand-up guy and reminding him that this kind of behavior is bad for business. This action is apparently uncharacteristic of McGurn, who patronizes the Mill often, where there is enough blonde attrition to keep him interested in the chorus line. The girls admire his quiet machismo and his athletic dancing style; however, he does not display his most charming demeanor when he drinks too much. Fortuitously for Ralph Jacobs, whose progeny will recount this episode for the next eighty years, McGurn displays maturity, comes to his senses, and ends up apologizing to the insurance man and his wife.

There seems to be enormous tension around this time at the Green Mill, an underlying ugliness, perhaps because of the booming business accompanied by the usual greed. Ted Newberry is a very tough owner, and the undercurrents of the bootlegging gangs tend to run near each other in his establishment, although he himself remains in the background.

One thing is for certain: Joey E. Lewis is attracting record crowds.[5] People find him incredibly funny. They like his corny singing style and his excellent tenor voice. For 1927, he is making a huge salary of six hundred fifty dollars a week. The entertainment industry in Chicago is traditionally competitive, however, much like everything else even remotely connected with bootlegging. Sam Rothschild and his partner George Leiderman at the New Rendezvous Café—another popular North Side cabaret at West Diversey and Broadway—secretly approach Lewis and offer him one thousand dollars a week, plus a percent of the cover charge. The next day, the comic announces that he will not be renewing his contract, that he will be leaving the Green Mill and headlining at the New Rendezvous on November 2. According to Lewis, in his 1955 biography, *The Joker Is Wild*, McGurn, who is present and has no affection for the comedian, threatens him, telling him that he "will never live to open." Apparently Lewis doesn't believe him, writing it off. He does open at the New Rendezvous on November 2, and within a week he is once again a smash hit, even bigger than before.

On November 9, Lewis answers his door at the Commonwealth Hotel and three men explode into the room. They fracture his skull with the butts of their pistols. Then one man stabs Lewis three times in the jaw, almost destroying his throat and nearly severing his tongue, inflicting nine more wounds into his body. They flee, no doubt believing they have killed the comedian, but Lewis is able to stumble into the hall. A hotel clerk helps him back into his room, and the house physician is able to staunch the blood spurting from his throat. He is rushed to Columbus Hospital, where he remains in critical condition for several days. The press reports

Joe E. Lewis, six months after surviving the attack at the Commonwealth Hotel, 1927.
CHICAGO TRIBUNE

that he will be terribly disfigured and may not live. When he is first brought in, before he loses consciousness, Lewis tells police that he knows who attacked him, but he passes out before naming his assailants. Two armed policemen remain constantly stationed at his bedside in case the gangsters who did this try to finish their botched job.

At first, the press blames the heinous event on a "bitter fight between rival cabarets for Lewis's services," but they also imply that "jealousy over a love affair" might have prompted the attack. Allegedly, Lewis has had a relationship with a blonde chorus girl named Gloria, whom Jack McGurn is now seeing.[6]

Miraculously, Lewis lives. Eventually he even learns to speak and perform again, taking ten years to regain his former success, although acute alcoholism is another of his major obstacles. According to the comedian in his biography, *The Joker Is Wild*, Capone buttonholes him two years later, saying, "Why the hell didn't you come to me when you had your trouble? I'd have straightened things out." He then gives Lewis an envelope with fifty thousand dollars, offering to put him back on top in Chicago entertainment, to which Lewis allegedly responds, "No dice."[7] Corroborative evidence to Lewis's claims will never materialize, especially since he co-writes his biography in an alcoholic haze in 1955, after Jack McGurn and Al Capone are long dead and cannot refute the story.

Some historians and authors, such as Capone biographer Robert Schoenberg, also believe there is reason to doubt that McGurn personally attacked Lewis.[8] The violence itself doesn't fit McGurn's usual profile; he is never known to use a knife, and he isn't remotely coy about killing. Neither is it his style to send somebody to do that for him. Moreover, it is more likely that McGurn isn't the wronged party; Lewis makes a dangerous enemy in Ted Newberry, the real owner of the Green Mill. McGurn may tell Lewis "You'll never live to open" because he knows Ted Newberry to also be a vicious killer. In fact, McGurn's words, if Lewis's quote is accurate, may be a matter-of-fact admonition and warning rather than a threat. It certainly stands to reason that Jack McGurn is not an enforcer for Ted Newberry, who is closely allied with Moran and the North Siders, but the best evidence that McGurn is not one of Lewis's attackers is that Lewis survives.

In his book, Lewis and his biographer, Art Cohn, record a completely false reiteration of McGurn's life and the death of his stepfather. It is as fanciful and untrue as anything that will ever be written about Jack McGurn. Lewis also claims that his protector is a North Side gangster named John Fogarty, who guards him after repeated threats by telephone, such as, "Don't be a sucker, Joe. You better be back at the Green Mill tonight or else." In reality, Fogarty is allied with Ted Newberry, who owns the Mill. Lewis seems to have mixed up his gangster pal's allegiances.

Perhaps it is the serious skull fracture that has clouded his brain and destroyed his memory after the attack, because none of the facts regarding the deadly episode seem to match up. The one truth that does emerge from Lewis's recount is his quotation of Danny Cohen's words, spoken on behalf of the silent owner Ted Newberry: "McGurn hasn't a nickel in my place. . . . McGurn is just a customer."[9]

As the holiday season approaches, the Capone Outfit has a shocking $100 million in gross receipts for 1927. To celebrate, the Big Fella decides to take a veritable troop of his friends on a rather elaborate hunting trip in the north woods of Wisconsin. After Thanksgiving, on what will become a well-publicized shopping spree, Capone spends five thousand dollars at Marshall Field's on the latest fashions and gear. McGurn is conspicuously absent. The greenest thing McGurn—a street kid from Brooklyn—has ever seen is a golf course or a palm tree in Florida. He prefers the three-piece suit and big-city comforts to taking on the great outdoors with Al and the boys, killing men and never animals.

As 1927 recedes into history, the Capone Outfit enjoys a pinnacle of enormous success that promises even greater rewards in the future. Jack McGurn has prevented his friend Snorky from becoming a victim, but with the press and the honest minority of the justice system becoming increasingly focused on Capone, the forces are gathering in opposition. This includes Moran's North Siders, who want their larger piece of bootlegging and racketeering. While Capone and his organization celebrate their fortunes, their adversaries and enemies wonder how they can reverse the powerful Outfit hold on Chicago.

19

We'll Come Back Later

1928

As 1928 begins, the first few weeks contain lots of fireworks and bombings against North Side properties owned by gangsters Zuta, Bertsche, and Skidmore. McGurn attends orgiastic New Year's parties from the week before Christmas through the first week of February. Perhaps half the time he participates; the other half he stands watch and guards Capone, who sometimes gets out of control. Being the boss, Capone tends to lead in the hardcore revelry, which provides many ugly mornings after legendary, all-night excess.

With hostilities with the North Siders continuing, Capone makes himself more available to reporters and ruminates in the press about not being able to have peaceful dinners with his family, mourning for a safer, less dangerous legitimacy. He complains about always having to look over his shoulder and never being able to stand in front of windows. He gets sloppy and sentimental, even singing opera. To the public who follow his interviews in the papers, his public relations façade makes him appear to be a pretty decent fellow and even a victim of his own success.

This particular New Year's Eve, Capone, McGurn, and twenty others go to the ornate Granada Café on Sheridan Road, near Loyola University. It ends up being quite an amazing evening for race history in Chicago when Guy Lombardo and his orchestra shock the city by inviting Louis Armstrong onto the bandstand to pepper up their dance music. Until that moment, the only African American faces in that far North Side neighborhood belonged to servants.

However, there is business to be taken care of as the New Year arrives. It is a perfect time, with everyone distracted by the revelry. Shortly after midnight, the murder team of Jack McGurn and Johnny Armando begins 1928 with a bang. Early that morning, police suspect that McGurn and Armando kill twenty-five-year-old Frank "Dutch" Carpenter, a cohort of gangster Danny Stanton, and dump his body onto a pile of plowed snow at Ogden Avenue and Polk Street. A heavy length of wire is wrapped around his neck. The echoes of the New Year's revelers haven't even faded when the first gangland murder of the infant year gets chalked up.

Carpenter, who owns a seedy, violence-prone dive on West Madison Street, is on McGurn's short list. Consequently, McGurn makes sure that Dutch gets set up like a bowling pin. The overly confident and clueless Carpenter has escorted one Peggy Brown to the Radio Inn on New Year's Eve. Police will find her phone number written on a scrap of paper in his pocket after his death, an excellent indication that she is not his girlfriend or was even known to him previously.

Apparently Peggy is the decoy trap for Carpenter, luring him to the Radio Inn for their New Year's date. Eventually she disappears, perhaps suggesting she is bound for the powder room. She makes a phone call, and soon Armando and McGurn are waiting behind the bar partition for the clueless Carpenter, who is extremely drunk and stupidly showing off his wad of a thousand dollars. There are some very tough people at the Radio Inn this New Year's Eve, including a thug named Eugene Marshall, who was held as a suspect in the murder of a police officer in 1923. The official story, after Dutch Carpenter vanishes, is that he is robbed and shot, which is McGurn's design.

When they eventually investigate Dutch Carpenter's last evening, the police find bullet holes in the ceiling and blood spattered near the back door.[1] Outside in the snow are tire tracks from the automobile that is backed up to the entrance, into which Carpenter's body is thrown and driven away. Peggy Brown claims she was drunk and remembers nothing. The police immediately buttonhole any potential witnesses. They apparently have good reasons to suspect Armando and McGurn. They assume

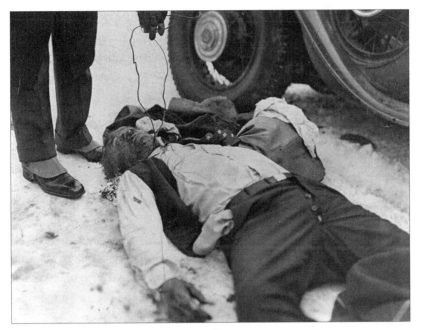

A terrible way for Dutch Carpenter to begin the New Year, 1928.
PHOTOGRAPH BY ANTHONY BERARDI, AUTHOR'S COLLECTION

McGurn to have used a .32 revolver and Armando a .38-caliber, long slide automatic, both of which they have recovered.[2]

Finding a courageous witness in a Chicago cabaret on New Year's Eve who is willing to testify will prove to be impossible. Nobody at the Radio Inn will be brave enough to stay the course and finger Jack McGurn or his petite buddy Armando. There will be no attempt at justice for Dutch Carpenter, who initiates the brand-new 1928 with his unwilling sacrifice.

It doesn't take long for McGurn to check off number two on his New Year's short list. He and an accomplice, perhaps Armando, shoot down twenty-six-year-old Isadore "Nigger" Goldberg, another well-known lieutenant of Jack Zuta, on February 14, Valentine's Day. McGurn always seems to hover close to the great abyss, doing his best work on this holiday for sweethearts. In exactly one year, he will help to put a permanent blight on the popular Catholic saint's commemorative day.

Goldberg is a tough Jewish hoodlum. There is no suitable explanation for his most unfortunate nickname, although it is possible that he has a swarthy complexion and tight, wiry hair. Another theory is that he is quite friendly with African American musicians and spends time with them. He is involved in gambling on the West Side, associated with Jack Zuta and his partners Barney Bertsche and William Skidmore. Goldberg has been part of direct incursions into Capone territory.

Goldberg is walking up Harrison Street near Racine Avenue when witnesses see a closely curtained sedan pull up to the curb. The passenger door opens and McGurn emerges, letting loose with a .38-caliber revolver, which is eventually recovered.[3] However, uncharacteristic of McGurn's close-range marksmanship abilities, Goldberg doesn't die immediately. He is taken gravely wounded but still conscious to Bridewell Hospital. Chief of detectives Michael Grady and Daniel Lynch, the familiar captain of the Maxwell Street police station, try to get Goldberg to reveal who shot him. Goldberg, who is dying, remains a tough guy; he plays by the familiar gangster rules. He looks at the congregated police officials and stenographer, struggling to get through his final performance: "Two fellows, both strangers to me, stopped me and asked me for a match," rasps Goldberg. "'Sorry, I haven't one.' I told them as politely as I knew how, and then for no reason at all, one of the chaps outs with his rod and begins throwing slugs at me."[4]

Goldberg descends into a coma soon after cracking wise, eventually dying on February 17. Police suggest that Goldberg's murder may signal an outbreak of a new gamblers' war, which is true because Capone has his men installing slot machines all over the North and West Sides. McGurn is involved in this, and despite it being too close to the wrong side of town, he has moved his wife, Helen, and their little daughter, Josephine, into a suite at the McCormick Hotel at Ontario and Rush Streets. They are living there as the Johnson family. It is from there that he is also running the expansion of Outfit gambling.

Not even a month goes by before McGurn is sent to dispatch 1928's third transgressor. He allegedly kills Joseph Calebreise on March 6. With him are John Scalise, the tall Murder Twin with the "lazy" eye (which never affects his aim), and Joseph "Hop Toad" Guinta.[5] Calebreise has been a muscle for the North Side bootleggers since he was first arrested in 1923 with a loaded revolver, claiming he was a business agent for the

Meat Cutters Union.⁶ Probably a Genna employee originally, Calebreise has become associated closely with Jack Zuta, rising to priority status on McGurn's list. After Calebreise is gunned down, the word is immediately out on the street that another man has fallen; retribution is in the wind blowing off the lake. Consequently, McGurn has become a priority himself on somebody else's short list.

The next evening, on March 7, McGurn is lounging with Capone button Nick Mastro in the McCormick Hotel Smoke Shop at 638 North Rush Street, conversing with the owner, Joseph Etao. Mastro claims he is a real estate operator, but the real estate he's selling is extremely limited acreage with a coin slot and a handle. He and McGurn have been working together near the fringes of the Near North Side territory, delivering Capone pinball and slot machines to various businesses. Somebody from the North Side gang who is passing by the McCormick spots them and makes a phone call to George Moran. Minutes later, a sedan pulls up outside, discharging three men, one with a submachine gun who begins firing into the doorway. Mastro is shot in the lung and arm. McGurn's reflexes save his life as he ducks against a wall for protection; however, two bullets hit him in the right lung and right shoulder. Mastro and McGurn both go down, badly wounded. The shooter backs away, covered by one of his partners, who brandishes an automatic pistol.

It has long been thought that the gunmen are Moran's henchmen Frank and Pete Gusenberg in their second attempt to kill McGurn. The press immediately claims William Clark and ex-fireman William Davern, both Moran gang members, were also identified. As assassins, they are apparently not the sharpest of stilettos; they seem to get very little practice with their weapons. They jump back into the car and speed away.⁷

Mastro, badly wounded, staggers into the lobby, where he encounters the resident physician, Dr. Robert Lamb, whom he asks to help him. The self-righteous Lamb does not feel disposed to extend his Hippocratic oath to gangsters who have been shot in his hotel, advising Mastro to go to a hospital. A few minutes later, a bellman grabs Lamb and drags him to room 906, where a man is supposedly bleeding to death. Lamb finds McGurn there, lying on the floor. "I'm Jack McGurn," he tells the doctor. "But around here, I'm known as Johnson. See if you can't do something for me." Lamb sees how serious the wounds are and calls for an ambulance, which takes McGurn and Mastro to Alexian Brothers Hospital. The triple Roman arches at the entrance of that hospital still welcome everybody, even gangsters.

Upon his arrival, McGurn, weak from loss of blood and in terrible pain, swears at police who try to interrogate him, insisting they allow him to call his lawyer. He eventually passes out and is wheeled into surgery in the emergency operating room, where he is successfully repaired.

All the newspapers tend to be characteristically dramatic, announcing that his survival is highly doubtful. He remains in a critical state for a couple of days, until his athletic body prevails and he turns the corner. His mother and his stepbrother Anthony faithfully stay by him.

Three days later, as the reporters and photographers crowd around his bed, McGurn tells them that he's been shot before, saying, "I'll take care of things myself when I get out." He also says he knows who shot him.[8] He puts the message out that if anybody thinks the shooting is going to stop, they should certainly reconsider. In accordance with Judge Lyle's new strategy, supposedly effective against gangsters who have no legal source of income, police charge McGurn and Mastro with vagrancy and disorderly conduct, even though they are obviously the victims.

With the Gusenbergs now openly gunning for him, McGurn makes no effort to pay his bond as long as they keep him in the hospital, accompanied by two police guards. The photograph of him in his hospital bed, being tended to by a male nurse, appears on the back page of the *Tribune* and the *American*. His face is even more pathetically innocent than

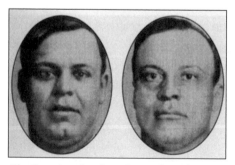

The Gusenberg brothers, Pete and Frank, 1928.

usual, with his furry eyebrows reaching up toward each other like the steeple of a cathedral. With the covers pulled up under his chin, he looks like a lost little boy. People who see this photo will find it extremely difficult to believe that he is a merciless killer.

The United Press spreads the news: GANGLAND BREAKS LOOSE AGAIN: MCGURN IS SHOT. The country is told that he is gravely wounded near the heart and that he will die.[9] They identify him as "chief lieutenant of 'Scarface' Al Capone's forces." Whoever provides the reportage for the United Press desk in Chicago hears McGurn repeatedly cursing after being asked questions by the police. He is lung-shot and his consciousness is flickering, but his plight captures the rather limited imagination of the reporter, who indulges in a tad of pulp fiction himself as he describes the shooting, which he did not personally witness: "McGurn leaped from the lounge and tried to flatten himself against the wall. But the stream of machine gun bullets halted him. He jerked two revolvers from under his coat, but collapsed."[10]

In a typical instant mythology of details, with impossible color poured into the event, it becomes easy to see how the excitement of the moment can, with a bit of added drama, capture the imagination of the reading public. In actuality, McGurn is found with two .45 automatic handguns, not revolvers.[11] The reporters, depending upon when they arrive at the scene, interview different people. Not surprisingly, because a machine gun has been utilized in the attack, witnesses hesitate to get involved; statements from the same person change as he realizes that civic duty might illuminate him as a perfect target.

Two days later, on March 9, the Associated Press announces that Chicago police are trying to trace a shipment of six Thompson submachine guns that "mysteriously disappeared." They were ordered by the Mexican American Company at 10 South LaSalle Street and were shipped to a West Taylor Street warehouse, where they vanished. Police claim that one of those weapons may have been used in the attack on McGurn and Mastro. With reporters clamoring to talk to McGurn, he gives them his standard line, but with the life coming back into him, he sounds more animated, his sense of humor having returned. The reporters record his every word: "McGurn, lying near death at a hospital, has persisted in his refusal to name his assailants. 'I know who plugged me,' he said. 'But that's my business. I'll attend to this myself—if I ever get up.'"[12]

His words and especially his attitude will inspire the ersatz cinema gangsters. James Cagney, George Raft, and Edward G. Robinson will continually attempt to reproduce Jack McGurn's seemingly indomitable spirit and edgy demeanor. The gangster code will become part of American society as the ethic of silence becomes accepted; nature abhors a vacuum and apparently a stool pigeon as well.

The resilient McGurn is out of the hospital and out of jail two weeks later, after Capone lawyers furnish his bond money. He spends the next three months recuperating and staying out of the limelight as well as the line of fire. Because of his extensive shoulder wound, he cannot properly fire a gun, and because of the incisions in his lung, he cannot torque his body to swing a golf club. His excellent, athletic physical condition still allows him to come back, but gunshots wounds from a .45-caliber bullet rarely ever heal completely, even flesh wounds, which tend to get infected and remain scarred and problematic. McGurn's wounds are deep, chewing up muscle, tendons, and a small part of his lung.

There is very little doubt that the men who tried to kill him have a great deal to worry about.

In this incredible year, the music in Chicago has reached a sublime epitome. Certainly Louise seizes the opportunity to attend the Savoy Ballroom to hear Louis Armstrong, who is now widely regarded everywhere. Chicagoans love the new records that Armstrong has made of "Struttin'" and "West End Blues," written by King Oliver. All the serious music fans love the Savoy orchestra. Fred Robinson plays a classy, mournful trombone, with Jimmy Strong on the clarinet and Earl Hines attacking the ivories. Especially notable is the drummer, Zutty Singleton, who drives the whole show from underneath with his rhythms. Jazz music has never been better or more exciting. It underscores the accelerated pulse of Chicago, drawing the youth to worship at the stage.

Many will say that 1928 is the last great year for Chicago jazz. *The Jazz Singer*, the first film with sound, opened the fall of the previous year and is beginning to change the meaning of entertainment in Chicago and the world. But, for the moment, the birth of jazz and its formidable exponents still drive the very lifeblood of Louise Rolfe, Jack McGurn, and their urban realm. The syncopation of Zutty Singleton's drums and the ever-present symphony of gangster gunfire add to the pounding cadences of a metropolis in which life speeds by like a locomotive.

With innovative music, bootleg booze, and the ongoing atmosphere of a great, unending party, 1928 is a hallmark for the post–World War I decade. Al Capone, happy days (they won't be this happy for a long time), and widespread giddiness inhabit the city, ignoring Prohibition. The pervasive stink of the Union Stock Yards is nothing compared to the pollution and subjugation of law enforcement and the justice system. This is truly a remarkable time of tuxedoes, blood, and social rebellion. Louise Rolfe and Jack McGurn are in their heyday. Chicago is their adult playground, capturing the imagination and wonderment of the more mundane hinterlands of America where the ordinary, workaday citizens read daily accounts in the newspapers about the city that never sleeps or even shuts its eyes.

It is an extremely special time, unlike any other moment in history. Despite the love that will soon enter their lives, things will in many ways never be better for either Jack or Louise.

20

Do You Know Who I Am?

1928

It is spring, and Jack McGurn has arrived in the popular culture of 1928 Chicago. The hungry, ever-vigilant press loves him. As David Ruth notes in *Inventing the Public Enemy*, the reporters "gloried in the exploits of men who seemed willing to try anything, no matter how daring, and almost always succeeded."[1]

This is why the average subscriber to any of the Chicago papers seems to automatically have the most interest in the fiercest competitors. The efforts and battles of the underworld are like a bizarre new sport, monitored and annotated daily, with the players who survive becoming recognizable and infamous.

Beginning in the local press at this time, there are subtle image-making tendencies and exaggerations regarding the gangsters. The *Daily News* and the *Chicago American*, William Randolph Hearst's paper, have almost no sympathy for any of the mobsters; they are tersely condemned in every article.[2] This certainly establishes support for Prohibition and absolute enforcement of the laws, perhaps also compounding the general feeling of hypocrisy. Oddly, the more liberal, tabloid-type Chicago rags seem to take a tougher line on crime, even though there is hardly a newsman or reporter who doesn't blithely drink alcohol, often to excess.

On the other hand, the *Chicago Tribune* is quite dedicated to its continuing story arc on McGurn, suggesting that the gangster's wounding is a reprisal for the almost fatal stabbing of Joey Lewis a few months before, helping to expand the mythology of that horrible episode.[3] *Tribune* reporters are also tying McGurn into the Capone Outfit as a "gambling chief" with the claim that he's been running the games at the North Clark Street den of Capone associate Louis Barsotti. On the same afternoon, the *Daily News* has him "invading" the North Side with Capone's "shock troops, planting slot machines everywhere."

Surprisingly, the famously conservative *Tribune* also notes that McGurn is "one of the most courageous of the lieutenants of Alphonse Capone." Just that platitude alone indicates a form of admiration and perhaps even a growing affection for Chicago's most usual suspect. In its inimitable way, the *Tribune* uses headlines to declare a "gaming war," which, like the "beer war," demands its soldiers. This seems to imply that since it is a war, it must have its armies, casualties, winners, losers, and heroes. The most Republican newspaper in Chicago seems to be making McGurn almost heroic, waxing lyrical about his survival in the gangster trenches.

At this point, it is obvious that Capone and McGurn sell lots of newspapers. Some of the editors and writers sense that a few dynamic gangsters like McGurn have begun to appear "creative," as if they are exercising their freedom of expression, an esteemed American property. This is especially exploitable in 1928, when so many other dynamic people put these virtues to honest use.

It is not difficult to see how an uneducated immigrant like McGurn, challenging America's biggest structures, such as law enforcement and the justice system, can capture the imagination of the public and the reporters. Ruth, in *Inventing the Public Enemy*, eruditely points out that "gangland's chroniclers offer a reconciliation of the values of efficiency and individualism that might otherwise seem at odds."[4] This certainly helps to explain the appeal of men like Jack McGurn, who to the provincial pioneers of the Midwest experience must stand out as a paragon of efficiency. It's almost as if he's the necessary sheriff of the other bad guys. After all, the work ethic is vitally important to both the farmers and the urban dwellers of Illinois; clearly, unlike the tainted police departments, Jack McGurn gets the job done.

The Capone Outfit runs like a machine due to Al's superior administrative and personnel skills. He has surrounded himself with the toughest, smartest men he can find. He is, for the most part, an equal opportunity employer. His organization contains a vital core of gangsters who represent an impressive division of labor and talent, albeit brutal. It is already evident to the whole country that the violence in Chicago seems to be more out of control than anywhere else, almost exhibiting a life of its own. It is the most scintillating, titillating news. The ever-illuminating fires of the press feed on blood and death like they are sustenance. One can almost smell the scent of gunpowder on every front page.

On Friday evening, March 9, Chicago state's attorney Robert E. Crowe gives a memorable election speech in a church in Wilmette, one of Chicago's wealthiest and most conservative northern suburbs. He reminds his audience that there are thirteen cities in the United States that have worse crime statistics than Chicago, including Washington, D.C. "But their newspapers do not advertise their crime," says Crowe. "They advertise Chicago's."

The constantly campaigning and politically astute Crowe is there in upscale Wilmette to raise donations. Although the people in the farther northern suburbs can't cast votes in Chicago, most of them have their places of work and privately owned businesses in the city. They do live in Cook County, and so their deepest financial interests are affected by Chicagoland crime. Many of them belong to private country clubs that have the finest golf courses, where some of them even enjoy playing golf with a gangster or two. Many people will claim to have played with Jack McGurn, who loves to take the swells for money.

Crowe's words still resonate today. The best places to find 1920s United Press and Associated Press feeds, which are the least influenced by Chicago politics, are in small-town newspapers all over America. In the 1920s, reportage of Chicago criminals appears everywhere, keeping anyone who can read abreast of the current electrifying details. To the country, and eventually to the rest of the world, the gangster wars in Chicago are like a great ongoing piece of pulp fiction. However, unlike the penny dreadfuls and dime novels of the turn of the century, the exciting events in Chicago are real. Al Capone and Jack McGurn start to become infamous celebrities, spreading to the furthest reaches of America, already larger than life.

Now that it is once again election season in Chicago, all the various interests are being "represented." The primary is held on April 10 with sluggings, dynamite, and lots of arrests. It will be referred to as the Pineapple Primary because so many bombs and grenades are thrown throughout the battling wards, including an explosion at the home of Robert Crowe's opponent for the office of state's attorney. There is a lot at stake in any Chicago or Cook County election, especially for the Capone Outfit. McGurn is extremely busy on this day as he does some "campaigning" with Johnny Armando, an escapade that will come back and bite him. The accompanying negative publicity is the simple cost of doing business for the gangs. But their vilification will not be issued from the people; Chicago voters tend to have an extremely short memory if they still desire a drink.

On April 17, McGurn and Nick Mastro appear before judge Emanuel Eller at the Chicago Avenue court regarding their charges after the attack at the McCormick Hotel. Apparently the proper business has been done to "settle" their problem. McGurn's lawyer dramatically recalls how seriously his client was wounded. Even if the usual fix wasn't already in, his impassioned plea is enough to shame the judge into not victimizing his client further. The charges of vagrancy and disorderly conduct are dropped. McGurn avoids the reporters and photographers as usual and gets into his new 1928 Model L Lincoln sedan. Distinctive with its greyhound hood ornament, it can outrun most police cars. Relieved, McGurn heads for the comfort of his family.[5]

At a stop sign on Morgan Street, in his mother's neighborhood, a large touring car with four men and two machine guns pulls up alongside him and begins firing. McGurn ducks, grabs a gun from the glove box, jumps out of the car, and runs into the doorway of 525 Morgan Street. He reportedly is able to return fire, although it is far more likely that he simply goes to ground, knowing he can't best machine guns with his revolver. Even McGurn isn't that courageous, and he's certainly not that foolhardy.

A frantic call to the Des Plaines Street police station reports an ongoing gun battle. Minutes later lieutenant William O'Neil and sergeant Fred

Joiner arrive at the intersection of Morgan and Harrison Streets; they find McGurn's beautiful new Lincoln sedan empty and riddled with bullet holes, with his registration card in the glove box.[6] Once again, McGurn, unharmed, has escaped the unsuccessful North Siders and probably the two Gusenbergs. However, there is little doubt that he has definitely had enough of being a target; now it is simply a matter of time before he will retaliate.

McGurn's life and liberty are now constantly in danger: he is a priority on two different lists. The North Siders have committed to killing him as much for survival as any other reason. The police also have their eyes out, expecting McGurn to make a move at any time, which is why they raid his apartment in the Guyon Hotel at Crawford Avenue and Washington Boulevard on May 14, coming up with an impressive weapons cache that surprises nobody. They find a Thompson submachine gun loaded with a clip of fifty dumdum bullets, notched on the tips to expand once inside the targeted body. They also grab two Colt .45 automatic pistols and several more boxes of ammunition.

McGurn claims the weapons are for protection, announcing that he is no longer a gangster and has nothing to do with his old friends since his recent grave wounding. The cops and reporters almost double over when he tells them that he has decided to become a real estate dealer.[7] This is something that Capone has claimed as well, which also gets a good laugh when he says it. Isn't a Thompson gun standard issue to all Chicago real estate agents? When McGurn is brought in under arrest for vagrancy and disorderly conduct, Deputy Police Commissioner O'Connor, acting like he's Wyatt Earp in Tombstone, contemptuously tells him, "Get out of town."

McGurn is immediately bailed out; however, the last thing he does is leave town because he must return to court to answer the charges on May 31. His lawyers eat up the unwarranted police raid, a nice amount of greenbacks no doubt change hands, and a satisfied Judge McCarthy discharges McGurn once again.

McGurn plays golf for much of June, frequently accompanying Capone on the course at Burnham Woods. It almost seems like things might settle down until the middle of July, when the word goes out in the New York newspapers that Jack McGurn is being sought for question-

Cubs player Gabby Hartnett autographing a baseball for Sonny and Al Capone at Comiskey Park. *CHICAGO TRIBUNE* ARCHIVES

ing in the murder of Frankie Yale. Consequently, McGurn disappears for a few weeks, perhaps guarding Capone in one of the Outfit retreats in Michigan or Indiana, where the Big Fella goes to escape the heat of the city as well as the heat of the law.

During this time, it is also reported that McGurn is being hunted to appear before a special grand jury concerning the shootings that took place on the day of the most recent election. On August 10, police captain John Stege takes it upon himself personally to arrest McGurn as a driver of one of the cars in the killing of African American politician Octavius Granady, who had the hubris to challenge Twentieth Ward boss Morris Eller for the committeeman's post. McGurn is released after promising Stege that he will appear at the grand jury quiz about the Pineapple Primary confrontations.

Later that month, during a crosstown baseball game between the Chicago Cubs and the Chicago White Sox, McGurn and several of the

A closeup showing McGurn
with his hand on his gun.
CHICAGO TRIBUNE ARCHIVES

Capone lieutenants surround Capone in the front rows of the box seats at Comiskey Park. In a famous photograph, Cubs star Gabby Hartnett is signing an autograph for Albert Francis ("Sonny"), Al's son. Sitting next to Sonny is politician Roland Libonatti. McGurn is directly behind the Boss. Somebody, perhaps the peanut vendor, is far too close to the retinue, and as the picture is snapped, the photographer captures McGurn with his hand protectively on his gun inside his suit jacket. He is the only one of the Outfit boys who is paying attention to the possibility of a threat to his pal Snorky—McGurn is always on the job.

21

When Love Knocks, Be Sure to Answer

1928

It is August in Chicago, which means heat layered upon humidity. These are aptly named the dog days, when a canine won't even move from the shade. The lake feeds the city with a cloying steambath, piquantly scented with the airborne aromas of the Union Stock Yards, depending on which way the winds are blowing. On these tremendously hot days, the air doesn't move the stink of the animals, which becomes more and more pervasive as every hot spell endures. Even the jazz clubs are a bit more thinned out, because few folks can enjoy dancing in such discomfort.

Still, people prowl the streets as the party continues. A "cold one" usually means weak beer "needled" with alcohol. Ceiling fans in the clubs suffice for air-conditioning, a technology on the near horizon but not yet present. Antiperspirants are weak and the spreading sweat stain is accepted by the stalwart August dancers in Chicago. It is an earthy, slow-motion period that Chicagoans either adore or abhor, a time that will be mercifully fleeting. However, when it's ninety degrees Fahrenheit with 90 percent humidity, it seems like the eighth month lasts forever.

Along with the weather, the beer wars and gang battles are simmering toward a boil. Capone is insinuating himself day by day into the labor unions, especially the powerful Master Cleaners and Dyers Association

Union, where the Outfit has installed their man, John G. Clay, as president. Moreover, North Sider George Moran and his men also believe in the vision of labor racketeering. They visualize rivers of gold in the other unions, including the closely related Cleaners and Dyers Union, the Laundry and Dyehouse Chauffeurs, and the Drivers and Helpers Union. The 1929 Chicago phone directory shows hundreds of cleaners and laundries in every part of the metropolis. Once a union is taken over, "dues" can be collected from the employees, prices for services can be controlled, and cash can be skimmed. The physical plants can be dually used to hide any number of criminal endeavors, including prostitution and gambling. Perhaps most important, gangsters can appear to have legitimate jobs at every level, from workers to union officials. Their names are listed on union rosters.

This portends that an even more complex battle is brewing. The beer, the rackets, the unions, the gambling, the entire substream of underworld activities have an ominous, prevolcanic tension. Chicago is entrenched in the grip of a political-criminal conspiracy so pervasive that it bleeds into every corner of the city. There is a growing fear on the streets of the New Jerusalem; the corruption is taken for granted because it's everywhere. At the same time that the culture of the music and fascinating revelry has peaked, the city's underworld has formed its battle lines. Jack McGurn is the general of the much larger army.

With personal recollections of McGurn during this period being extremely rare, one of the few real ones is recounted by Roy Erickson, who worked as a busboy at Texas Guinan's Frolics Café at Twenty-Second Street and Michigan Avenue. Erickson remembers vividly the gangsters who frequent the Frolics, including Ralph Smith and Dennis Cooney, who run Capone brothels. Al Capone, his brother Ralph, and various members of the Outfit often dine at the Frolics, where all patrons are greeted by the vivacious brunette Guinan, who calls out, "Hello, sucker!"[1] Jack McGurn and Frankie Rio are usually the bodyguards in attendance. According to Erickson, McGurn often has a "small guitar case" next to him, which is quietly placed under the table next to his leg. The waiters and other employees are taught to simply ignore this and forget anything they see.

One evening, Erickson, who is eighteen years old, accidentally spills some soup on Jack McGurn as he is clearing the table. Erickson is immediately frozen with fear, struck dumb and motionless. McGurn sees the alarm in the young waiter's face, smiles, and says, "That's all right, kid—don't worry about it." Erickson will never forget those words. At the table with McGurn are Al and Ralph Capone and Curly Humphreys.[2]

It is easy to understand why McGurn brings a camouflaged machine gun into public places. Besides protecting the Big Fella, he is living the edgy life of a marked man. He is young but certainly not the "boy" he is described as being, which is why the lagniappe of love can still penetrate the convoluted world in which he is embroiled. If jazzman Mezz Mezzrow was right in 1927 and McGurn is as strong as Samson, his might will prove useless, as he is about to meet his Delilah.

Louise Rolfe, the prototype of 1920s hellions and baby dolls, is still living the hedonistic existence of a gold digger, getting away with anything and everything because she is an adorable, desirable brat. She wants a bad boy with money and the brass to make her feel special, but she is not expecting who is actually around the corner. She is about to meet her Jack. Their lives, conducted in such close proximity with the pounding beats of the jazz revolution, has placed them on converging paths, bringing them together and depositing them in a veritable crucible of history.

Wandering through a maze in the shape of the streets of Chicago, Louise Rolfe and Jack McGurn finally meet sometime around the second week of August 1928, possibly at the New Rendezvous Café. Wherever the location, they suddenly recognize each other from across a crowded dance floor at one of the Chicago nightspots.[3] It is certainly lust at first sight, and their personal chemistry is a mixture of perfection.

McGurn is a handsome, twenty-six-year-old Sicilian, dangerous and incredibly self-confident, a very bad boy. He is a marvelous dancer, treated deferentially by the club owner and everyone else who knows who he is. He is everything that Louise wants; his animal magnetism is undeniable. Louise is a twenty-two-year-old Kewpie doll minx, cute as a button, the best dancer in the place, adorable from blonde hair to painted toes, from wicked blue eyes to rouged knees. Even though she is an obvious temptress, she has a fresh look and a delectable smile. She is everything McGurn wants, an erotic physical match to his demanding libido, the exact, pro-scribed opposite of his wife, Helen. In short order, lust will blossom into love. They are both each other's unexpected surprise.

The fireworks go off. They enter each other's lives in an accelerated fashion. Jack probably goes with Louise to a movie, something he is cer-tainly not fond of doing because it's hard for him to sit still for an hour and a half. It is also because he feels like a sitting duck in a dark theater, plus he frequently requires a cigarette.[4] Louise no doubt accompanies McGurn to a prizefight, which is once again legal in Chicago, or to one of the week-long bicycle races on which he is allegedly so fond of betting. Certainly they visit one of the horse or dog racetracks. They eat voraciously like lovers do, and dance like there's no tomorrow, perfectly complementing each other physically in the best cabarets. McGurn is never afraid to spend too much money, and he certainly impresses Louise as being a well-heeled fellow.

Meanwhile, as Jack and Louise get to know each other, the Aiellos and the North Siders import a New York killer known as "Little Augie" Pisano, who with his partner guns down Unione Siciliana president Tony Lombardo at Madison and Dearborn Streets on September 7. Capone's man Lombardo is walking with his two bodyguards, Joseph Ferraro and Joseph Lolordo. The two shooters are waiting inside the vestibule of the Raklios Restaurant. When Lombardo and his boys approach, the assassins open fire with .45-caliber revolvers, fatally wounding Ferraro and blowing off most of Tony Lombardo's head.[5] Lolordo gives chase to the killers but is arrested by police, while the gunmen get away.

Capone once again loses his control of the Unione, but only momen-tarily. He is able to help install Pasqualino "Patsy" Lolordo, bodyguard Joseph's brother, as president, a move that will only cause more bloodshed in the ongoing war to capture the coveted organization.

While these events take place, Jack and Louise fuse together in their mutual heat, moving into room 854 of the Lexington Hotel on September 13, 1928, under the names Mr. and Mrs. George McManus. Louise stays there in Capone land, but Jack puts on a show of living elsewhere with Helen and Josephine. This arrangement will continue until December 22. With his new love tucked away in the Lexington, sleeping all day and waking in time to shop and party, McGurn conducts business as usual. After all, many men do some of their best work when inspired by love.

Early on the morning of November 14, McGurn allegedly shoots the forty-year-old ex-fireman William Davern, who was suspected in the March 7 McCormick Hotel attack. He is found at Rush Street and Austin Avenue. The son of a Chicago police sergeant, Davern is gut shot and bleeding profusely at the foot of the firebox he has accessed to summon help. He has been shot in the C&O Diner on Rush Street, a known gangster hangout.[6] He is loaded into an automobile and thrown out a few blocks away, regains consciousness, and has the presence of mind to use the firebox telephone before loss of blood prevents him from speaking.[7] Firemen take him to Henrotin Hospital, which is becoming another American capital of gunshot wounds.

Davern is a North Sider living on Brompton Place. He is involved in gambling or bootlegging, his allegiance certainly to the North Side Moran gang. There are witnesses at the diner, but when called upon to 'fess up, they all claim ignorance; they know better. Firearms forensics also suggest McGurn.[8] When questioned by patrolman Paul Gholson, the mortally wounded Davern refuses to talk and incriminate himself. Soon he is no longer able to speak. He loses his gallant, silent fight on December 30 and is buried in Mount Carmel Cemetery.[9]

The police recover the gun, another .32-caliber revolver. Because Davern is able to survive six weeks, although mostly in a coma, it is at this point when McGurn realizes that the .32 bullet is not lethal enough. It is the last time he will use it. He has remained incredibly lucky, coming far too close to leaving his targets alive too many times. From now on, he will carry .38 revolvers or .45 automatics, relying on devastating notched bullets called dumdums, which are hollow and expand upon hitting their target. Despite this, in the near future, with all that firepower and caution, one more man will still be able to crawl away before dying.

A week after McGurn shoots Davern, the Moran gang launches a violent takeover of the Cleaners and Dyers Union. Just before Thanksgiving, they kill Capone's man John G. Clay, the puppet executive director.[10] He is gunned down in his union office, allegedly by North Sider Frank Foster. This event will end up as precipitous as Hymie Weiss's shoot-'em-up of the Hawthorne Hotel. The murder of Clay and the direct challenge to the Capone Outfit's union activities is a stunning attack on the domain of Curly Humphreys, who is carefully orchestrating the Outfit invasions of the richest unions. There is no doubt that Humphreys will convince Capone to draw a line in the sand in retaliation.

Capone assuages Humphreys and issues a reprisal for the killing of Clay. Al Capone may be a gangster, but petty street crimes like robbery and jack rolling are not what he's about. He is a provider and a subjugator. With labor racketeering scheduled to grow exponentially in the immediate future, this new confrontation with Moran over the unions is ultimately the weight that tips the scale. Capone realizes with perfect clarity that a devastating blow must be dealt to the North Side organization. There are several theories as to the time and location of the meeting where it is decided to make a definitive move against George Moran. In their book, *The St. Valentine's Day Massacre*, William J. Helmer and Arthur J. Bilek recall how Byron Bolton, allegedly a massacre accomplice, declared that the killings were planned at a meeting as early as October or November 1928, in a lodge at Cranberry Lake in northwest Wisconsin.[11] Yet another idea, proffered by Capone biographer Laurence Bergreen, is that McGurn asked Capone's permission to retaliate in early 1929, which probably meant January.[12]

One thing seems certain: the modus operandi of the massacre fits McGurn's signature scenario, enacted with patience and precision. It is most certainly his design. There is no doubt that he owes retribution to the Gusenbergs, who have to die if the spine of the Moran gang is to be broken. Unfortunately, McGurn, who would relish killing his sworn enemies, knows how difficult it will be to get near them in their neighborhood without being spotted and immediately shot down.

However the scheming goes, McGurn meets with all his chosen men, and his dictates are followed to the letter, as always. Whenever the initial planning session occurs, whether it is early in December or January, McGurn invents a creatively devised revenge for his failed assassins and the core of the Moran gang.

While the attack on Moran is scheduled and the assault is being prepared, McGurn also realizes that he is tired of sneaking around with Louise. He confronts his wife, Helen, confessing that he loves someone else and that he is leaving her and their daughter. With the deed done, on December 22 he and Louise board the Seminole Limited train for Miami, where they spend some quality time in a luxurious Pullman sleeping car. As their journeys for the next five weeks will later be excruciatingly chronicled by the state's attorney's investigators, a complete record of their comings and goings exists, including love notes written on the train by Louise to Jack.

When they arrive in Miami, they acquire an automobile and register at the Dallas Park Hotel as Mr. and Mrs. Jack McGurn. Capone and several of the boys have preceded them and are at Al's estate on Palm Island, where there will be parties, golf, and lots of typically hedonistic recreation.

In the meantime, back in Chicago, the mice are playing while the big cat and his killers are away. While Capone and McGurn are enjoying Florida, George Moran truly earns his hated nickname, Bugs, and makes a crazy power play that will prove volcanic and deadly to his organization. He installs his man Albert Weinshank as president of the Cleaners and Dyers Union a few days after the New Year. The coup is highly reminiscent of Samoots Amatuna's fatal grab for the Unione Siciliana, drawing the same volatile reaction from Al Capone. Moran obviously doesn't sense or admit to himself that he is outmanned, outgunned, and outmaneuvered. By stupidly planting his flag in Capone's second-favorite union, he will precipitate the beginning of the end for his own gang and ultimately for Al Capone as well.

On the same day that Weinshank steals the union, Jack and Louise leave the Dallas Park Hotel and rent a house at 453 NW Third Street in Miami. A couple of days later, Louise displays her legendary driving skills and is arrested for speeding. McGurn pays her bail and then her fine when she is found guilty. It is very likely at that moment when McGurn, who can hardly afford to be stopped by police anywhere, begins telling his new love, "I'll drive, honey."

Almost simultaneously, more things are blowing up in Chicago. Joey Aiello, who is as strong as a fox and as smart as a bull, has been hiding out of town after his failure to kill Al Capone with his fifty-thousand-dollar open contract in 1927. Aware that the Big Fella is in Miami, he returns to the city to regain control of the Unione Siciliana. He visits interim Unione president Patsy Lolordo in his lavish home on West North Avenue. As soon as their meeting is over and Aiello leaves, North Siders Pete Gusenberg, Albert Kachellek ("James Clark"), and Frank Foster arrive and put eleven shots into Lolordo, dropping two of their three Smith & Wesson .38 special revolvers at the scene.[13] The Unione is once again leaderless and primed for a takeover. This reckless coup is ultimately transparent, putting Joey Aiello right back at the very top of Capone and McGurn's short list. Capone, who loved Lolordo, is heartsick and beyond furious.

With Patsy Lolordo dead, Capone doesn't hesitate for a minute. From Miami he makes sure that twenty-six-year-old Joseph Guinta is installed as president of the Unione Siciliana. Guinta, a Capone driver and muscle, dresses like a dandy and has a reputation as a hyperactive dancer, which has gained him the unusual nickname of Hop Toad. He is a close friend of Murder Twin John Scalise. Since the death of Mike Merlo, the Unione presidency has already proved absolute doom for anybody who would assume it—but rather than seeing this as the suicide mission that it must be, Guinta becomes inebriated with the potential power. He sets the stage for another round of violence that surrounds the tragedy-prone Sicilian organization. Reports from Chicago reach Capone that another cartel is forming within its ranks that are directly against his interests.

Lovebirds McGurn and Rolfe return to Chicago on January 24, 1929. They register at the LaSalle Hotel as Mr. and Mrs. Vincent D'Oro, Havana, Cuba, in room 1113. They only stay one night, apparently deciding that Chicago is too inhospitable. There are certainly mitigating factors in their spontaneous exodus after having just arrived. It may have to do with McGurn's family situation, and it also may be connected to how hot he is, still being sought by the Gusenbergs and being rousted by the police whenever he is spotted on the street.

Whatever has transpired, it is another severe winter in Chicago, and the fact that he and Louise can play golf in the warm sun convinces them to run back south. The very next day, Jack and Louise get back on the Seminole Limited and travel to Jacksonville, Florida, in compartment B, car 257. In Jacksonville they apparently aren't happy with the hotels, or they simply can't get into one that pleases them. They go back to the train station and recheck their baggage, continuing on to St. Augustine, where they buy tickets for Biloxi, Mississippi. They actually pass back through Jacksonville on the same evening they had arrived. They reach Biloxi on January 26. This time they register at the Edgewater Gulf Hotel as Mr. and Mrs. Vincent D'Oro of the Congress Hotel, Chicago.

Unfortunately, a particularly sharp hotel porter sees a label on their luggage that says Jack McGurn, not the name under which he has registered. The hotel manager consequently summons McGurn and asks for money up front as well as references. McGurn is enraged at this and at his abominable luck. He remains obstinate, putting off the hotel authorities, refusing to check out. On January 29, the manager loses his patience and kicks them out. That afternoon, McGurn once more purchases train tickets—this time on the Panama Limited back to Chicago. He regains at least some of his luck when they are able to board, even though it is the very height of travel and tourist season and the train is fully occupied.

Back in town, at 10:44 in the morning of January 30, Jack and Louise check into the Stevens Hotel, room 2313-A, once again posing as Mr. and Mrs. Vincent D'Oro but from Havana, Cuba. They probably aren't fooling anybody, but no hotel clerk is willing to call the bluff of Jack McGurn.

The gangster is particularly picky about their accommodations, finding the room unsatisfactory because it doesn't have a good-enough view of Lake Michigan. They end up instead in room 1919-A on the nineteenth floor, a love nest that will certainly embarrass the Stevens family, who are so proud of their new hotel. McGurn makes a concerted effort not to be seen; he has Louise pay all the hotel bills with cash. The "Golds from Cuba" settle in, and when they do leave their room, it is always by a back stairway. None of the elevator operators will be able to identify them.

While Jack and Louise enjoy each other, the decimating invasion of the Moran gang grows nearer day by day.

PART III

Massacre

22

Who Looks for a Quarrel
Finds a Quarrel

1929

Jack McGurn, killer of killers, has experienced the *fulmini*, the legend-ary lightning bolt. Louise seems flawless to the enraptured McGurn, aside from the fact that she is a dangerous and homicidal driver. He loves her kittenish act, her lustful honesty, and the way she's excited by his power. She knows exactly what she wants and exactly what she'll get. He also loves the fact that she makes every one of her needs known. Unlike with his wife, he can envision playing golf with her when he is old and too rich to work—if he lives.

Love notwithstanding, in February, McGurn redefines criminal mur-der, not just in Chicago but all over the world. After the St. Valentine's Day Massacre, he will remain under the law enforcement microscope for the remainder of his existence. Of all the things he did or may have done, planning the massacre will remain the biggest part of his legacy. The modus operandi will be a combination of his previous assassinations but with a creative new twist. It will prove so effective that it will reset the standards for urban violence—but it will also get away from him, causing the collateral damage that he had always managed to avoid.

Researching the St. Valentine's Day killings is a complicated chal-lenge. There are so many accounts to scrutinize in order to get all the known details, several of which will always remain a mystery. Historians have always agreed on some things concerning the event: men dressed as policemen, in the employment of Al Capone, execute seven men associated with George "Bugs" Moran's North Side gang. Moran and Capone have been adversaries since 1924. Capone has helped to kill O'Banion and Weiss, Moran's closest friends. To this day, every Capone biographer believes that Jack McGurn planned the massacre. Whether he was one of the assassins himself is a matter of continuing debate.

William Roemer, the FBI agent in Chicago, will listen to mob conversations on wiretap tapes for years. Roemer will claim he heard Tony Accardo reminisce about being one of the killers at the massacre with Jack McGurn.[1] Regardless of whether he did the actual shooting, the signature style is McGurn's: there is stealthy infiltration into the Clark Street neighborhood, precise planning, and precision killing.

The massacre is designed somewhat similarly to the Hymie Weiss killing in that the groundwork and preparation are completed long before the actual shooting. In January, a month before the murders, a polite young man, who claims he is a cabdriver named Morrison, rents a room at Mrs. Michael Doody's boarding house at 2119 North Clark Street. He insists on a front room that overlooks the street. McGurn installs him there before leaving for Florida with Louise. In her statement to police on February 18, Mrs. Doody will tell the police investigators that Morrison arrives every morning about nine and that a half hour later, two other men show up with brown paper bags, presumably containing their lunch. They leave around 3:30 in the afternoon. Mrs. Doody will identify them later from photographs as brothers Harry and Phil Keywell, members of Detroit's Purple Gang. Both men will furnish alibis for Valentine's Day and will never be prosecuted for the shootings.

In a statement to police patrolmen Connelley and Devane of the Thirty-Sixth District police station, Mrs. Minnie Arvidson describes the renting of the second observation post. On January 27, two more young men rent a back room as well as a front room overlooking the street at 2139 North Clark Street, in Mrs. Arvidson's rooming house.[2] Both Mrs. Doody's and Mrs. Arvidson's rooms on Clark Street afford excellent views of the front door of SMC Cartage Company, where Moran maintains his delivery vehicles for his bootlegging enterprise. However, this time they are simply acting as lookouts; the killing will be done by others.

The two men at Mrs. Arvidson's also claim they are cab drivers, asking if there is a garage available in the alley behind the apartment building where they can park their automobiles. Apparently McGurn's original thought is to keep the two cars used in the attack literally across the street, but there are no garage spaces available. Both men will eventually occupy only the front room, claiming they can't afford to pay for both. Allegedly they are Byron Bolton and Jimmy "The Swede" Morand ("McCrussen").[3] Bolton will accidentally leave a bottle of prescription medication with his name behind, and he will eventually confess his role to the FBI a few years down the line when he is finally arrested.

The duo at Arvidson's and the other two men at Mrs. Doody's will immediately disappear after the gunfire starts. One thing is for certain: McGurn has made sure that all four lookouts are completely unrecognizable to anyone in the area and especially to the Moran gang members. This is why he hires four fresh faces; it is the same reason he will use a group of imported shooters.

McGurn invents a ruse that will lure George Moran and his men to the garage on the morning of Valentine's Day. Many writers and reporters conjecture that the bait is a truckload of allegedly hijacked Capone booze that is offered up for sale to the North Siders. The only evidence countering that idea is that none of the men killed in the garage are suitably dressed to unload dirty wooden crates of whiskey: six of them are found dead in three-piece business suits. Somehow McGurn is able to create some type of urgency so that Moran and his lieutenants will definitely be on the premises at SMC Cartage, waiting for a truck to deliver something.

Shortly after 10:00 AM on the morning of February 14, 1929, the two spotters at Mrs. Arvidson's watch as various Moran gang members walk in the front door. Eventually they see someone entering the garage whom they allegedly think is George Moran himself—he turns out to be Albert Weinshank, the new president of the Cleaners and Dyers Union. From a distance, Weinshank physically resembles Moran. Since the temperature is fifteen degrees Fahrenheit and there is light snow filling the air, Weinshank has his fedora pulled down to cover his face and his calf-length overcoat bundled around him. The spotters call a pay phone in a garage near Capone killer Rocco Degrazia's apartment and the Circus Café, where double teams of killers are waiting.

Two men in stolen Chicago police uniforms immediately get into a black Cadillac, which is driven by a third who is dressed like a civilian. The automobile is fitted to resemble a Chicago police car, with the traditional gong alarm mounted on the side. A second automobile that also looks like a police vehicle—either a Peerless or a Cadillac—starts out for Clark Street at the same time, with a driver and two men in long overcoats who are posing as police detectives. A truck, which will be the main diversion, starts out for Clark Street. The car with the two phony detectives pulls into the parking area in the alley behind the garage; the car with the uniformed men pulls up to the curb on Clark Street in front of SMC Cartage. The two "police officers" get out and quickly enter the front door. They are armed with police-type shotguns.

As the decoy delivery truck arrives at the garage door in the alley, the two "detectives" waiting in the parking area get out. They wait for the truck to honk its horn. When a Moran man inside pulls open the double garage doors to let the truck in, the two phony detectives wait for a signal to enter the garage. A teenage witness, George Brichet, fortuitously happens to be standing in the alley and, unnoticed, sees the scene unfold.[4]

After the Moran men open the garage doors, they are surprised to see the two uniformed officers who have entered the front door from Clark Street with their shotguns. The "cops" announce themselves and line up the seven men in the garage against the side brick wall. The Moran men are probably not that worried, since the police in the district have been paid for years to leave them alone. They must assume that it's either some kind of shakedown for more money or that the two officers are out of their neighborhood and don't know the rules. They simply stand facing the wall, their backs to the cops, one of whom whistles out the signal for the remaining two killers in detective mufti to enter through the open garage door.

Five of the seven men against the wall constitute the basic core of the Moran gang. Frank and Pete Gusenberg are Moran's main killers, the perennial would-be assassins of Jack McGurn. Albert Kachellek ("James

Clark") is also a gunman. Albert R. Weinshank is the implanted Cleaners Union president and owner of a speakeasy, the Alcazar Club, at 4207 Broadway. Adam Heyer ("Frank Schneider") is part-owner of dog-racing track Fairview Kennels. The garage is leased in his name.

The sixth man is the luckless John May, an ex-safecracker turned mechanic. He lives in an impoverished neighborhood on West Madison Street. Both of the St. Christopher medallions hanging from his neck will be deformed by machine gunfire.

The last man is Dr. Reinhart Schwimmer, a gangster wannabe who lives in the Parkway Hotel, where his neighbor is George Moran. Schwimmer has two ex-wives hounding him for alimony and child support, yet he basically lives off his wealthy mother.

Missing from the garage are the boss, George Moran, and his lieutenants Frank Foster, Willie Marks, Leo Mongoven, and Ted Newberry, who will all live because they are late or perhaps because one of them is a secret Capone informer who has helped with the setup.[5] Ted Newberry will end up working for McGurn, and he will be given the Capone "medal of honor," that diamond-encrusted horseshoe belt buckle with his initials.

The two killers who now enter carry Thompson submachine guns under their long overcoats. Although seventy of the spent bullets will be examined for forensics, Tom Loftus, the first real police officer who will arrive on the scene after the shooting, estimates that there are about a hundred spent casings.[6]

At this point, there are two possible scenarios of the massacre. The traditional belief is that Jack McGurn, unseen by any witnesses, has left Louise sleeping in their room at the Stevens Hotel and is leading the operation in civilian clothes. He is accompanied by a partner, perhaps Tony Accardo, and a driver.[7] They are the men who emerge from the parked automobile in the alley. There are many knowledgeable Capone-era researchers who find it impossible to believe that McGurn would ever let somebody else kill his archenemies, the Gusenbergs.

There are at least eight back stairways leading to side entrances to the Stevens Hotel where McGurn can leave without being seen. A waiting automobile can pick him up at one of several relatively secluded places, including three streets and at least as many alleyways. It is extremely possible for him to be with his men near the Circus Café within fifteen minutes as they wait for the call from either one of the observation posts. If he is in the "detective" car in the alley behind SMC Cartage, perhaps with his hat down over his eyes, he has only to walk a few feet to enter the rear of the garage, remaining unrecognized.

The second scenario, which is offered by William J. Helmer and Arthur J. Bilek in their book, *The St. Valentine's Day Massacre*, is that McGurn is far too hot and well-known to even get near the garage on Clark Street, which is a claim the gangster himself will make to the police after the massacre, although he certainly would never admit the truth.

Helmer and Bilek's theory, strongly based on the recollections of Georgette Winkeler, widow of Capone gangster Gus Winkeler, is that her husband, Fred "Shotgun" Goetz, Raymond "Crane-Neck" Nugent, and Fred "Killer" Burke did the actual shooting. In their version of the massacre, Jack McGurn remains in bed with Louise at the Stevens while others do his bidding. This is contemporary scholarship, well researched, and has quite a lot of supportive evidence. Georgette Winkeler's memoirs, which were kept on file with the FBI and were eventually published in a crime magazine years later, may correctly finger exactly the right men, the group that Helmer and Bilek call "the American Boys," because they were not Italian and most of them came from St. Louis.

Regardless of whether McGurn himself takes part in the shooting or not, his design is simple and brilliantly effective, although the attack gets out of control because of the huge number of bodies. With the murders of three nonessential and noncombatant individuals, the death toll becomes stunning. Quite probably, McGurn has no idea how many men will be in the garage. The two men with the Thompsons open up and mow down all seven victims.

McGurn's plan to gain access to the men in the garage in the guise of police raiders is based on a technique utilized by the gangs in St. Louis. He assumes Moran's men, especially the Gusenbergs, will be armed but that they will do nothing if the fake cops have the drop on them, which is exactly what happens. The two uniformed "cops" are no doubt from out of town, with faces that are unknown to everyone in the garage. As soon as the seven Moran men are facing the wall, the two killers enter from the garage door.

The two machine gunners walk right in, stand in front of the phony cops, and begin firing from a few feet away, sweeping the seven men three times. The first volley is fired into their lower backs, upper shoulders, necks, and heads. The empty .45 cartridges from the Thompsons spew out of the ejection ports in fountains of brass, landing all over the garage floor. The victims' hands are still raised in the air as they fall. Pete Gusenberg collapses into a chair in the corner; the other six drop to the concrete.

Forensics and a re-creation by the investigators will show that the machine gunners then squat and sweep the victims' heads, emptying the magazines of their guns; some of the bullets puncture the victims' upturned feet. Two of the fallen, Schwimmer and May, are apparently still twitching, because they are shot again at close range with a coup de grâce from the uniformed fake police with shotguns. The spent shotgun cartridges are found on the floor.

Both machine gunners give their empty, smoking Thompsons to the driver of the diversionary truck, who pulls out of the alley and speeds away, followed by the ersatz detective car that is waiting in the parking area. The two "cops" in uniforms point their shotguns at the machine gunners, who proceed out the front door onto Clark Street, putting their hands in the air as if they are being arrested by the two "officers" following them. At 10:30, Josephine Morin, who lives on the third floor at 2125 North Clark Street, looks out her front window and sees two men with their hands up enter the curtained Cadillac, which seems incredibly odd. She is the first of many witnesses to give confusing testimony.

As soon as all four of the men get into the Cadillac, joining the fifth, who has remained in the car, they speed south on Clark Street. This is seen by several witnesses. The entire operation takes four to five minutes from beginning to end. The killers are in the garage for only three minutes.

The seven bullet-riddled men in the garage are mute witnesses to who really pulls the triggers. Contemporary forensic reexaminations may imply that Frank and Pete Gusenberg have turned toward their attackers, perhaps suggesting that somebody calls their names before the shooting starts. If McGurn is one of the machine gunners, it is plausible that he lets the brothers realize he is there before he kills them. Considering McGurn's urge for retribution, it makes perfect sense that he would want the Gusenbergs to know he is on the other end of the gun. Just as likely, everybody in the garage dies because the American Boys can't leave anyone alive as a witness. This is the case whether McGurn is there or not—however, this time there is collateral damage because three of the dead are there by accident.

When Tom Loftus, the first real policeman, enters the garage, he finds Frank Gusenberg barely alive, trying to crawl out. Gusenberg has twenty-two bullet wounds; life is slipping from him. He survives for nearly three hours in Alexian Brothers Hospital at 1200 Belden Avenue, ironically in the same room where McGurn had been brought after the Gusenbergs shot him the year before in the McCormick Hotel.[8]

The only temporary survivor in the garage is Highball, an Alsatian shepherd, who never stops howling until police eventually untie him and take him away. Later reports suggest that Highball becomes the eighth victim of the massacre when he is euthanized, too traumatized to remain a pet after being adopted by one of the police officers.[9]

As soon as the alarm goes out, police, reporters, photographers such as Tony Berardi, and many officials, including Judge Lyle, rush to the scene. *Chicago Evening American* reporter Willis O'Rourke walks away from the slaughter, claiming with the blackest humor, "I've got more brains on my feet than I have in my head."[10]

The savagery of the executions, with the formidable number of seven victims, makes headlines internationally for several days. There isn't an American, European, Scandinavian, or Asian newspaper that doesn't put the Chicago horror on its front page. It is one of the most-written-about crimes of the twentieth century, or, as Capone biographer Laurence Bergreen puts it, "Machine Gun Jack McGurn's failed attempt to assassinate 'Bugs' Moran turned into the biggest story ever to come out of Chicago in the 1920s."[11]

At the onset, gangland bloodlust and revenge defines the hideous assault, but there appear to be more subcutaneous motives. Within a few days, reporters and investigators will begin to recognize a connection to Capone's labor racketeering, as the Chicago Cleaners and Dyers Union

Crowds form outside the massacre garage on Valentine's Day.
PHOTOGRAPH BY ANTHONY BERARDI, AUTHOR'S COLLECTION

appears to be quite relevant to the St.Valentine's Day Massacre. This is still an overlooked factor that has been mostly ignored against the more romantic vengeful passions of the Moran and Capone gangs. It is more probable that the massacre is not simply about gang hatred or the beer wars—it is one of the first salvos in a new war to utilize the unions to supplement and finally replace the income from bootlegging. Regardless, the massacre will signify eventual doom for the contentious North Sider interests. In a few months, George Moran's organization will all but disappear, leaving the Outfit as the dominant criminal power in Chicago.

In retrospect, the dawning of the criminal invasion of legitimate labor appears to have a much greater role in the extermination of the North Siders. Thomas Donnelly, president of R. R. Donnelly and Sons, the largest printing company in Chicago, runs an open shop and hates unions. He gives a propitiously timed address to an Employers' Association dinner group a couple of weeks before the St. Valentine's Day Massacre. He announces, "The racketeer is a man who poses as a member of the labor union. Most of them are not connected with legitimate unions. They are thugs and murderers who attempt to organize, not the working men and themselves, but the employers into organizations by force, and from these organizations levy tribute."[12]

One of Donnelly's examples of the most compromised unions is the laundries.

Capone, the man of the street, knows that the real wealth of kings comes from the people. Since his days with the late Frankie Yale in Brooklyn, he has already adopted this as a master plan. There are two hundred different unions by 1929, and according to the state's attorney's office, ninety-one are controlled by racketeers.[13] Capone learns about usurping laundry unions from Yale, who has engaged in such activity in Brooklyn since before World War I. It is an education for everybody, and Yale continues to expand these interests into the 1920s with growing success. At first, Yale extorts one hundred fifty dollars a week from laundry and cleaning establishments to help prevent union organizers from coming into their businesses. When all of the laundries and cleaning establishments in Brooklyn are subscribers, Yale re-creates his own union, which works in an almost feudal manner to collect a dollar a week from all employees. If they don't pay up, they are fired, beaten, or even killed. Yale's union is not a champion of betterment for the laundry worker but rather a method of extortion on a large scale. It is Frankie Yale's model that inspires Capone's plan for the Cleaners and Dyers in Chicago.

Because George Moran surprisingly has the same vision, he isn't going to hand the laundries over to Al Capone on a silver platter. The fact that Albert Weinshank is one of the seven men slain the next month in the St. Valentine's Day Massacre may suggest that he is one of the principal reasons for the timing of the attack on the Clark Street garage.

It has been the traditional opinion of many who have written about the massacre that the shooting is ultimately a failure because McGurn is not able to kill Moran that day. This detail adds to the horror of the crime, because the perpetrators don't even accomplish their primary goal. But perhaps the execution of Capone's adversary, George Moran, is not the prime motive for the slayings. In order to regain control of the union, Capone must eliminate Weinshank. When the spotters at Mrs. Arvidson's rooming house call in the attack, it is conceivable that they know the man they see entering the garage is Albert Weinshank and not George Moran. Regardless, regaining control of the union by killing Albert Weinshank is a direct result of the massacre.

The Chicago police and state's attorneys' investigators immediately know there is a union connection to the massacre, and they say so. They are convinced there are men allied with the Clay organization—meaning Capone—"who would have committed the seven killings if they were sure they were exterminating the killers of Clay." The *Tribune* reporter who records that quote also wonders how Jack McGurn, ex-prizefighter and known criminal, is affiliated with Clay's Cleaners and Dyers Union, where his name has been found on employee lists as a member.[14]

Of course, McGurn never labors honestly, and the police know that this is the Outfit's effective way to "legitimize" scores of Capone employees by getting them on payroll lists. It is a gambit that is probably designed to avoid the scrutiny of the Internal Revenue Service, which is already hard at work trying to indict Capone and several of his main lieutenants, including his brother Ralph, Jack Guzik, and Frank Nitti.

Others also believe the unions are behind the killings. After the massacre, the Employers' Association, which is virulently antilabor, releases a pamphlet called *It's a Racket!* on Chicago labor racketeering and a dramatic account of the ongoing war for the cleaning and laundry industry in the city. The authors, Gordon L. Hostetter and Thomas Quinn Beesley, describe the victims of the massacre as "seven racketeers." The *Tribune* immediately expands that idea with its headline, which reads KILLINGS LAID TO UNION WAR. The article states that the cause for the massacre is somehow rooted in the struggle for the Cleaners and Dyers Union.

Still, this concept is not good enough for the press. The entire involvement in the unions takes a backseat in the wake of the far more interesting epic of the Capone-Moran battles. It could very well be that this first hypothesis by the press is quite accurate. Moreover, the Cleaners and Dyers Union will suspiciously resurface in 1936 in events surrounding Jack McGurn.

23

The Wicked Man

1929

As soon as the massacre is reported, the police begin hunting for the usual suspects. Chicago law enforcement is especially outraged that police uniforms have been used by the killers. It only takes a few hours for McGurn's name to be mentioned on the list of those sought by police. He has been under suspicion from the minute Frank Gusenberg, dying of machine gun bullet wounds, is found crawling away from his six dead companions. With mayhem on the streets, and with police shaking down every known gangster, McGurn is still safely secluded in the Stevens Hotel with Louise Rolfe.

Jack and Louise are having much more fun at the Stevens than they did on any train. The Stevens is advertised as the world's greatest hotel, which will remain true for the next couple of years (it later becomes a Hilton hotel). It is a massive structure that occupies the entire block on Michigan Avenue between Seventh and Eighth Streets, a twenty-five-story fortress with three thousand rooms, each with a luxury bathroom. It is essentially a small city within the city, with banquet halls, restaurants, and a massive hotel switchboard staffed with seventy-five operators, enough for a town of twenty-five thousand people. The barbershop has twenty-seven chairs.[1]

This is where Jack and Louise are cuddling, eating from room-service trays, and enjoying what any couple would consider a honeymoon. Apparently there are days that go by when they hardly leave their room. Rarely has someone enjoyed the establishment of an alibi more. After the massacre, as police hunt for McGurn everywhere, the couple remains in the Stevens for two weeks, occasionally venturing out stealthily in the evenings to see a movie or visit the theater. They use the side entrances of the vast hotel, avoiding the scrutiny of the Stevens employees. None of the staff can recall seeing them enter or leave—an ignorance that may be prompted by abject fear. The lovebirds have most of their meals served in their room and get every edition of the morning and afternoon newspapers.[2]

When police finally discover them, the prosecutors investigating the seven murders are completely humiliated to learn that their "special headquarters" in the Stevens Hotel is three floors above where McGurn and Louise have been cohabitating. This is an auspicious beginning to an investigation that will cast a polluted shadow for the next eighty years.

When someone at the Stevens finally admits to the police that he believes McGurn is in the hotel, deputy commissioner John Stege, lieutenant William Cusick, and sergeant John Mangan immediately plan a raid on the room where the couple is holed up on the evening of February 27. For good reason, they are extremely cautious when it comes to approaching or confronting Jack McGurn. They actually wait until the couple calls down for room service. They dress a police officer as a waiter and stand outside while Louise answers the door, expecting the delivery of dinner. The "waiter" is followed by the law enforcement retinue as they rush in, guns drawn. They find McGurn in a dressing gown. He makes no move toward his two pistols on the bureau. Louise is wearing a slip. They allow her to put on her clothes and fur coat after they examine everything for weapons. They let McGurn throw on his suit, after which they handcuff the unhappy couple and haul them to the detective bureau.

McGurn is immediately placed in a lineup, referred to as a "show up" in the 1920s. He is positively identified as one of the men at the massacre by at least two witnesses; they pick him out of a group of twenty other men. Both people state they have no doubt that McGurn is one of the killers. One witness is an unidentified woman who rides horseback in Lincoln Park, and the other is George Brichet, the newsboy who saw more than anybody as he watched the car in the alley, then ran around to Clark

Street to view the phony cops and their phony prisoners exit the building. Both witnesses are hustled away and ensconced in a downtown hotel for protection, but too many eyes have already seen them and can identify them. They will ultimately claim forgetfulness and be useless to the case.

The massacre is such an enormous event that it naturally brings out some pathetic characters who desperately want to be a part of the crime. A particularly strange allegation is made by a North Side dentist named Lowell Tacker on February 22. Tacker's office is at 2530 North Clark Street, three blocks from the SMC garage. The dentist is discovered mumbling and incoherent in Detroit by police officers. When he is taken to police headquarters, he regains his senses and claims he was abducted by four gangsters as he was walking near his residence at the Sheridan Surf Hotel. Tacker, described as "trembling from exhaustion and fear," is attended to by a physician at the Hampden Court police station in Detroit. He is allowed to call the Chicago police, telling them, "Four men were in the car, and I'm sure that one was Jack McGurn."[3]

Tacker tells a wild tale of being forced into an automobile where one of the men is holding a machine gun. Supposedly he is struck with a black-jack and is thrown onto the floor of the backseat, where he is bound with rope. "They drove on, all night, in silence. No one said a word," details Tacker. When they reach Detroit, the dentist claims he is thrown out of the car, where he is found wandering the streets. At first, the local police announce that Tacker's story is proof that Detroit's Purple Gang, Capone allies led by the brutal Bernstein brothers, was involved in the massacre. The dentist is driven back to Chicago with great fanfare. Initially it appears that he is offering a tremendous break in the Valentine killings. The excitement in the state's attorney's office is palpable.

As it turns out, Tacker, who has perhaps been imbibing too much of his own laughing gas, had approached the Chicago detectives immediately after the massacre, swearing that he pulled a tooth from a man who fit the description of Jack McGurn.[4] They showed him pictures of various suspects, and Tacker identified the man who had been in his chair. To everyone's dismay, Chief Egan quickly explains the truth about the dentist's bizarre story: "We checked up and found out that the man whose picture he picked out was in jail and had been for some time."[5]

Meanwhile, in captivity, McGurn seems nonchalant and exchanges banter with the detectives, who begin to grill him about anything and everything. They ask him about the abduction of the dentist, to which McGurn discerningly reasons, "I never saw him and never kidnapped him. He probably got lit up and ran away for a night with some Jane and had to fix up a yarn for his wife." They ask him if he committed the massacre in the garage, to which McGurn answers, "No." They ask him who did do it. He shrugs. "Aw, a squad of cops probably. They probably had been doing business with Moran and found things getting hot and had to bump 'em all off." This infuriates the police. State's attorney Harry Ditchburne asks him if he's been in the SMC garage, to which McGurn answers, "I don't know anything about the garage. I'd never have been able to get inside it alive. The Gusenbergs would have shot me down the minute they saw me."

With Louise causing a stir of excitement in another room, Lieutenant Cusick asks McGurn who she is. He answers, "She's my wife." Cusick spits back at him, "She must have bleached her hair wonderfully well, as your wife has black hair and black eyes." McGurn, laid naked on this particular subject since Helen Gebardi has already been questioned by the detectives, looks annoyed and spits back, "Aw, suit yourself."

After several hours of intermittent interrogation, Commissioner Stege has McGurn thrown into an empty cell where he is forced to spend the night. He uses his elegant suit vest for a pillow and his overcoat as a blanket—the ultimate indignity to one so meticulous about his clothes.

Police and investigators are also searching for Capone gunner Rocco Fanelli, who quietly walks into a police station the next morning and gives himself up, asking if anybody wants to talk to him.[6] With both heralded suspects being arrested within a dozen hours, the halls of the criminal courts are exploding with reporters, publicity seekers, lawyers, cops, and detectives. The flash pans are going off and leaving black smoke marks on the lower expanses of the ceiling as photographers try to capture anything they can by holding the cameras above their heads. They catch nothing of Fanelli or McGurn, who are braced by dozens of uniformed cops. Everyone who isn't a police officer is screaming out questions, creating a din that fills the stone halls as they usher the two gangsters of the hour to another, larger interrogation room.

Louise posing as captain John Stege watches her antics, 1929.

The fastidious McGurn, who has slept in his clothes, looks vaguely rumpled but still manages to joke with State's Attorney Ditchburne, telling him, "You didn't look so well last night. You fluttered around like you had the jeebies." He does his best to smooth out his creased trousers and jacket, and then he faces the photographers, telling them, "Make me look swell. Going to take my girlfriend's picture, too?" They once again ask him who she is, to which he replies slyly, "Oh, just a little lady I been helping out. The cabarets aren't doing much business now, you know."

The cops are beyond gleeful, but it all seems too easy. Even though McGurn is arrested on suspicion of murder, the state's attorney is worried about the lack of evidence and has his staff working overtime. To make certain that Chicago and Cook County get a hook into McGurn, they creatively charge both Jack and Louise with a violation of the moral code because they have been found living together in the Stevens Hotel.[7]

From a holding cell in the detective bureau at the South State Street station, Louise Rolfe tastes her second delicious hint of true fame, Chicago-style. She is also delighted to pose for the *Daily News* photographer, as if getting arrested in conjunction with the St. Valentine's Day Massacre is the obvious way to end up with some free composites for her "Lulu Lou" portfolio.

Brought into an interrogation room, Louise happily manipulates the reporters, balancing her innocent baby doll looks with an unabashed lewdness. She loves to shock people, and the reporters love her, eating up her attitude. She tells them, "Of course Jack had nothing to do with the massacre. He was in bed—all night and until noon." She constantly pats her unnaturally yellow-gold waves, incessantly chain-smokes cigarettes, lighting one off another, and seductively tells the men who surround her in the depressing bowels of the Cook County Jail, "When you're with Jack, you're never bored."[8]

The topic of discussion soon turns to Louise. She explains that she dropped out of Senn High School: "You see, I just had to complete training for my degree as a model." The reporters love this, especially when she gives out her address and phone number. This revelation eventually causes her mother, Mabel, to run from her apartment, leaving the maid, Frances Connors, alone to care for little Bonita.[9]

The *Tribune* anoints her the Blonde Alibi, which immediately makes her a media star, although she detests the term and reproaches anyone who calls her that. To Louise May's dismay, the name will follow her for all of time.[10] She has no difficulty telling dozens of reporters from every Chicago newspaper that her Jack is innocent, repeating that he had been in bed with her when the massacre took place, which in itself shocks modest people everywhere.

The papers, via the Associated Press feeds from Chicago, herald the identification of the "ace of Chicago gangster killers" in front-page headlines, second only to the much less interesting announcement that President Hoover has completed his cabinet. There are claims by the Chicago police that McGurn had the motive in the massacre for shooting the Gusenberg brothers and that the two witnesses who saw him have all but nailed the case shut.[11]

David Stansbury, the assistant state's attorney in charge of investigating the massacre, declares the affair solved with the arrest of McGurn and the surrender of Rocco Fanelli. Chicago cannot believe its good fortune when Stansbury confidently tells the reporters, "The crime has now been solved. There is no question about it. The prisoner [McGurn] has been viewed by witnesses who declare positively that he is one of the killers. I also know the motive—and have known it for two days."[12]

Stansbury's premature announcement will go down in Chicago history as the speediest nonsolving of a major crime ever. The bluster and confidence of the callow public servants who are not on the Capone payroll will quickly fade as Stansbury and everyone else realize how well planned the massacre was. Of course, it is easy to see how ravenous the press is for anything that can seem as though it restores order in the brutalized city of Chicago. The papers pick up everything, even printing that McGurn learned to wield a machine gun during World War I. But McGurn never served in the armed forces, and neither did the Thompson submachine gun, which won't see its first official military duty until World War II.

On March 1 and 2, Louise and McGurn appear before judge Peter H. Schwaba in what will be several months of hearings.[13] The papers certainly do not neglect fashion reportage whenever Louise appears in public. They call her the Blonde Beauty and Lulu Lou, which must make her happy because it is her stage name. The moniker Lulu is also a colloquial term in the 1920s, meaning "nutty." After her increasing exposure to the bemused reporters, this name begins to fit her. There is always a complete rundown of her ensemble in the papers. After she is brought in from the Stevens Hotel, the Associated Press makes sure that readers are aware that Louise is wearing a dress of black crepe with a modest white lace collar and touches of white at the wrists. She is wearing her squirrel-fur coat and a pair of expensive duff slippers "kicked niftily from swinging feet." She constantly toys with a waist-length necklace of imitation pearls. They describe her as "modish, sophisticated, slender, and bejeweled."[14]

The press pool, packing the room to the brim and beyond, is amused and entertained by Louise. She demurely crosses her ankles, displaying a slender gold ankle bracelet. She delights the boys by casting off a comedic, Sophie Tucker–like remark: "It's got my name on it so they can't lose me." She is inventing "gun-moll chic" as she goes along. It will eventually be reflected in movies from Hollywood as female stars attempt to mirror Louise's combination of great style and practiced ennui.

The Blonde Alibi in all her glory, 1929.
CHICAGO DAILY NEWS NEGATIVE COLLECTION, DN0087576

One of the Associated Press reporters expresses his impression that, although Louise has a daughter, she is not the "mother type." He claims that Louise seems to talk frankly with the assembled crowd of newsmen but that she is "spoofing," or having them on. This is an understatement—she puts on a dilly of an act, telling them that she is of French, English, and even Indian descent, going into "elaborate" detail. She talks nonstop until the writers start truly paying attention to what she is saying, at which time she laughs contemptuously at them. One of them compliments her on her nerve, to which she bitterly replies, "No nerves," holding up her once-finely-groomed fingertips to show them that her polished red nails are bitten to the quick.

At this point she is so enigmatically charming that the Associated Press writer betrays his own opinion: "Yet with her sophistication her expertness in the artifices of makeup, her complete complacence and even bored demeanor, there is about this 22-year-old woman a touch of a wistfulness that is not so alien to motherhood after all." Then he writes something that undoubtedly thrills Louise: "Her attitudes as she sits or stands reflect in their suggestion of artistry her training as a model."

Many of the photographers present remember Louise from prior encounters. One of them had posed her for her corset ad when she was a teenager. Another recalls her from a fashion show in which she was a model under her alternate name, Lulu Lou. Still another had photographed her when she killed Frank Lasley with her father's automobile back in 1921. She is constantly handling her blonde curls, which are in disarray. One of the photographers asks her, "Didn't you have time to pick up some hairpins?" Louise smiles, explaining, "Say, when those cops came in I thought they were waiters! We ordered some dinner brought up to us. The waiter knocked. I let him in and turned away to go to the bureau. I was fixing my hair when I heard Jack say hello to someone, and when I looked there were about nine other waiters in the room. But only the first one had the tray."[15]

This gets a great laugh from her doting male audience. Thoroughly enjoying herself, Louise cannot help but naturally seek to shock. In a statement that will raise the moralistic hackles on the necks of the justice system and that will come back to haunt her, she unabashedly announces that she and Jack are not married. This leaves the press to confirm that "there is no attempt at pretense from 'Lulu Lou.'"[16]

A few hours later, Louise is charged with disorderly conduct (for lack of anything better), which is an indication that the police feel no need to keep her in jail. However, the state's attorney will hardly let her off the hook. Lulu Lou walks out into the March sunshine, leaving her Jack inside the stone walls. She knows this is just the beginning.

24

This Doesn't Suffice to Remove All Suspicions

1929

On March 2, Jack McGurn and Rocco Fanelli are each charged with seven counts of first-degree murder, one for each of the massacre victims. Immediately afterward, Assistant State's Attorney Stansbury does everything but grab a megaphone like a crooner—he once again crawls out onto the public relations limb, announcing confidently that both McGurn and Fanelli "were members of the execution squad." He adds, "We've smashed their alibis, and within 30 days we'll be ready to go to trial."[1]

Two days later, the investigators who are out in the neighborhoods of Chicago gathering actual evidence saw off the limb Stansbury is hanging on. As public pressure mounts and details become a bit clearer, everything changes overnight. On March 5, Stansbury essentially retracts almost everything he has previously said. Now the state's attorney's investigation team is certain that McGurn and Fanelli were not the killers, but they maintain that McGurn was present and directed the shooting. They still cannot allow themselves to believe that McGurn would not have been there, so now they have him conducting the gunners like the maestro in an orchestra. They confidently announce that Joe Lolardo, Fred "Killer"

Burke, and James Ray were the gunners on St. Valentine's Day and that they were accompanied by two other unknown men.

David Stansbury tells the reporters that Ray—the alias for Gus Winkeler—and Burke wore the police uniforms. According to the verbose Stansbury, Joey Lolardo was given the "honor" of avenging his brother Pasquelino, who, after briefly serving as the interim president of the Unione Siciliana, was shot down in January by the Moran gang.[2] Nothing could be further from the truth concerning Lolardo.

But McGurn is also far from being off the hook. The excitable and impetuous David Stansbury notwithstanding, most of the press has a sense of Chicago gangster justice by now. The reporters who work the city streets and the crime beat tend to believe that Jack McGurn must have been present at the shooting of his dire enemies, the Gusenbergs. Since there were at least five assassins and two are still unknown, the police as well as the public still believe McGurn is one of those unnamed. Louise, somewhat convincing despite her luminous eccentricity, is too suspicious a personality for the basic citizen to wholeheartedly believe. Mothers see right through her; fathers feel a horror that their daughters could become like her. Common sense and a basic understanding of loyalty still suggest that the Blonde Alibi is covering for her man.

On Sunday, March 10, Hearst-owned papers all over the country run a Chicago-fed biographical retrospective on Jack McGurn, with the caption HIDE-AND-SEEK TERROR OF THE WISTFUL BOY GANGSTER. The article includes a photograph from the *Chicago American* of baby-faced McGurn lying wounded in the hospital from the Gusenbergs' attempt on him in 1928. The "wistful" look on his face is certainly enhanced by the fact that he has devastating .45-caliber wounds in his lung and shoulder.[3] In terms of public opinion, reminding people that McGurn was shot first by the Gusenbergs only helps convince the ad hoc court of public opinion that he must have been one of their slayers.

Within a week, both Jack and Louise have been regarded as "wistful" by reporters who are scrutinizing them. This is somewhat extraordinary, for it represents a dimension not usually present in the gangsters and their molls who make the papers. Their combination of youth and penchant for performing, though more subdued in McGurn, and their perceived life weariness seem to reach out to the pathos in even the most hard-boiled city-desk reporters.

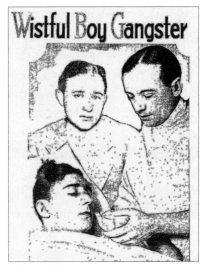

Wistful Boy Gangster

The two lovebirds, so animated and contrary, represent the single greatest source of entertainment for Americans in 1929: the real-world newsprint saga. Even though radio is incrementally taking over every day, the newspaper is still the definitive form of communication and entertainment. Americans live by the black ink of the tall headlines. The height and width of the type

The wistful McGurn, 1929.
CHICAGO AMERICAN ARCHIVES

denote the excitement and gravity of the news. There is tremendous sensitivity to screaming headlines, which radio and television will eventually supplant with the human voice.

Simply stated, Jack and Louise are likable. They capture the public's interest. They are instantly notorious celebrities of the fascinating variety, representing their wild generation and shocking everyone else. They are also solid gold for the newspapers. Despite the long, formidable list of literature published in 1929, including Ernest Hemingway's *A Farewell to Arms*, Sinclair Lewis's *Dodsworth*, Thomas Wolfe's *Look Homeward, Angel*, and Virginia Woolf's *A Room of One's Own*, more Americans will continue to follow the real-life soap opera of Jack and Louise than will ever read those masterworks. Ironically, this ends up being the exact opposite of what Jack McGurn wants or needs, which is to remain elusive and hidden in the shadows. With this notoriety comes searing scrutiny.

The black cloud descends further upon McGurn on March 11 as New York police detectives claim he has been identified as a suspect in the 1928 killing of Frankie Yale. With Yale having reneged on his bootlegging agreements with the Chicago Outfit, Capone sent several of his boys to execute his early mentor and longtime business associate on July 1. Hearst's *New York Herald and Examiner* announces that while conferring with Chicago investigators about the St. Valentine's Day Massacre, police are able to tag Jack McGurn, Louis Campagna, Mike Barnes, and Jack Perry as Yale's killers. Jack Perry is yet another alias for Gus Winkeler, and Mike Barnes is actually Fred "Shotgun" Goetz.

New York detectives traced several phone calls made from Yale's neighborhood in Brooklyn to Capone people in Chicago before the shooting.[4] The calls emanate from Louis Campagna's mother's apartment. Campagna telephones his girlfriend, Irene Dorsey, and Goetz also calls his wife in Chicago. These acts of sheer stupidity will leave a solid trail. Upon hearing this news, Capone becomes infuriated with Campagna, Winkeler, and Goetz, who has a university degree and certainly should know better.[5]

Now, in addition to being a suspect in the massacre, McGurn is reported to be the killer in another notorious gang slaying—one more suggestive piece of evidence that he also has complicity in the Valentine's Day murders. This news further aids public opinion that he is to blame. After all, he has been showing up under arrest since 1925, usually armed with a weapon. He is the most obvious player in the gangster shoot-outs, and with all that publicity, common sense dictates that he must be guilty.

Not since the Jack the Ripper murders in London has a big-city law enforcement system so desperately needed solid arrests. The mayhem and inner-office jockeying in the state's attorney's organization arrives at the point where outside aid becomes necessary. Before March ends, they reach out for technological help. The coroner of Cook County, Dr. Herman N. Bundesen, sends to Major Calvin Goddard, the brilliant father of forensic ballistics, the Thompson submachine gun that McGurn allegedly used to kill Hymie Weiss.

On April 1, Bundesen sends a seven-page letter to Goddard with a record of whom the police accuse in many dozens of gang killings for the last four years.[6] This document, in tandem with the Chicago Police Department, includes a list of every gangster suspected in murders from 1924 up to the Valentine's Day massacre. It signifies the dawn of a new day in forensics, especially ballistics, for law enforcement all over the world. Bundesen is the true post-Victorian gentleman, almost sounding as if he is from Scotland Yard: "My Dear Major: The machine gun sent you on Saturday is one alleged to have been used in the killing of Hymie Weiss."[7]

Also accompanying the letter is a different list of the gang-related murders since 1923 and the men suspected of committing them, on which Coroner Bundesen has annotated in ink the disposition of many of the weapons used as well as their manufacture and caliber. At the bottom of the final page, which is Bundesen's reiteration of a special fourteen-name "hot list," he writes a personal note to Goddard:

> Major: In the killings above the men whose names are shown under "Examine guns of" are particularly suspected of the specific killing. Take especial care for a tie-up in these. Herman N. Bundesen.

He draws an arrow to the last victim on the list, Dominic Aiello, who is the brother of Capone enemy Joey Aiello, killed on July 19, 1928, with a .32 Smith & Wesson revolver and a Thompson submachine gun. He draws another arrow to McGurn's name. Major Goddard, living in Manhattan, becomes extremely curious about Jack McGurn.

Bundesen has been sending all the gangs' guns as well as the recovered spent bullets to Goddard in his laboratory on Thirtieth Street in New York. From 1923 up to Valentine's Day 1929, this letter with its lists attempts to help Goddard begin to connect suspects with weapons. This is the best and only composite document that names, murder by murder, the men whom the Chicago police and the coroner's office suspect for all the gangland killings. Jack McGurn is suspected in sixteen murders:

1. Orazio "The Scourge" Tropea, February 15, 1926

2. Vito Bascone, February 21, 1926

3. Ecola "The Eagle" Baldelli (with the help of Armando), February 23, 1926

4. Joe Calebreise, March 6, 1926 (John Scalise and Joe "Hop Toad" Guinta also suspected)

5–6. Joseph Staglia and Jeffrey Marks, March 17, 1926 ("Klondike" O'Donnell also suspected)

7–9. William McSwiggin, James Doherty, and Thomas Duffy,
April 27, 1926 (Al Capone and Louis "Little New York" Campagna also suspected)

10. Jules Portugese, July 14, 1926

11. Louis "Big" Smith, August 10, 1926

12. Theodore "Tony the Greek" Anton, January 6, 1927

13. Anthony Torchio, January 6, 1927 (John Scalise also suspected)

14. Frank "Dutch" Carpenter, January 1, 1928 (Johnny Armando
also suspected)

15. Isadore "Nigger" Goldberg, February 17, 1928

16. William Davern, December 30, 1928

During April, May, June, and July, Jack and Louise appear before judge
Francis Borelli. They are grilled over and over by State's Attorney Root,
who is having rough sailing, to say the least. The prosecution is trying to
deal with a virulent case of "Chicago amnesia." Apparently the two witnesses who have initially identified McGurn as being present at the massacre are having grave second thoughts. Either they have been reached or,
when they realize whom they are being asked to testify against, they get
cold feet, both being the effective result of fear and common sense that
overrides their civic responsibility. Consequently, McGurn's lawyers are
able to bond him out on April 18, with the proviso that he appear at all
subsequent hearings.

During the hearing of the coroner's jury on April 20, a gun dealer
named Edward Weidner testifies that he sold two Thompson submachine
guns to a gun inventor and dealer named Vincent Daniels, who in turn
sold them both to Jack McGurn and Pete Gusenberg. One of the weapons
is found in Frank Gusenberg's closet. One of McGurn's defense attorneys
makes a thin reference to self-defense, and police chief William Shoemaker, who is looking rather impotent, feels the need to get his licks in.

He clarifies the reality about the Thompson guns: "Anybody that buys a machine gun is buying it for the purpose of murdering somebody."[8]

As the coroner's hearings continue into May, the authorities look for any kind of evidence. Gun dealer and sports-store owner Peter Von Frantzius, a skinny, ferret-faced little fellow, will spend a lot of time being questioned about machine guns. As the weeks progress, Chicago law enforcement becomes increasingly more desperate. Coroner Herman Bundesen reportedly is willing to get up in the middle of the night to hear someone being questioned if any new lead develops.

A particularly interesting report comes from Bundesen on May 2. A farmer in Rockford, Illinois, identifies a photograph of Fred Burke as one of the men he had seen practicing with a machine gun on an island in the Rock River, several miles south of Rockford. This allegedly occurs just prior to the massacre. Burke's picture previously has been identified by witnesses on the day of the massacre as the "handsome" man wearing a Chicago police uniform. A nationwide search for Burke has been in progress since February. What is particularly interesting is that the same Rockford witness also identifies another man as having been with Burke. He is apparently positive when police show him a photograph of Jack McGurn.[9]

The farmer never shows up to finger McGurn or Burke in court, joining the long list of people who are cowed by the gangsters. Although, to be fair, it's a wonder that anyone who draws breath would call in with evidence about the massacre. Still, the farmer's sighting and identification is incredibly stimulating to almost any argument, putting McGurn and Burke together with a Thompson or two, perhaps after bringing the guns up from St. Louis.

It is a tempting vision—the two snorky gangsters in their gorgeous clothes, out in a frozen Illinois field in their fashionable shoes, with their new Thompson guns, plinking away with short bursts to get in a little practice before the main event. However, when Fred Burke is finally captured, the Thompson that was used in the massacre is recovered from his home. Calvin Goddard will also determine that the same gun was used in the fatal attack on New Yorker Frankie Yale, indicating that the weapon was in the hands of Capone's men long before the alleged Rockford incident.

While the hysteria over the massacre has raged in Chicago, Unione Siciliana president "Hop Toad" Guinta has made some extremely bad choices in selecting his own allies. He makes a fatal pact with Capone's nemesis, the intellectually challenged Joey Aiello. John Scalise and Albert Anselmi have also decided that they are more powerful than Al Capone and join in the plot. Reports reach Capone that the three traitors, Guinta and the Murder Twins, have accepted an offer from Aiello to seize the Unione and assassinate him in a coup d'état. But Capone, respectful of their combined threat, keeps the outrage under wraps until he can react with a personal answer to the betrayal.

On May 7, Scalise, Anselmi, and Guinta are invited to a special dinner that includes large amounts of wine and brandy. This infamous last supper takes place at the Plantation, a roadhouse and casino near Hammond, Indiana. In a slow build to postgustatory violence, Capone works himself up to the point where his boys are afraid he's having a heart attack. In the fashion of his killer Tony "Joe Batters" Accardo, the Big Fella takes a baseball bat to the three sated, inebriated, and unsuspecting conspirators while they are held at gunpoint. McGurn and several other loyal Outfit lieutenants hold each one of them while Capone puts the buckwheats to them with the Louisville Slugger. After the hideous beatings, at least three guns are emptied into the already half-dead trio. Their bodies are discovered the next day near a rock quarry in Indiana, a secluded spot named Spooner's Nook.

A few days later, Capone takes the train to New Jersey and attends a gangster summit conference at the President Hotel in Atlantic City. McGurn is far too hot and embroiled in hearings, so Frankie Rio and two other bodyguards accompany the Big Fella to the East Coast. Also with them is Frank Nitti and money man Jack Guzik.

Many notable gang leaders are there from Chicago and the East Coast, including infamous New York prime minister of the underworld Frank Costello, the ultimate boss of Meyer Lansky, Charlie "Lucky" Luciano, and Dutch Schultz. Johnny Torrio is present as an "emeritus" consultant. Abe Bernstein represents Detroit's Purple Gang, Max "Boo Boo" Hoff comes in from Philadelphia, and Abner "Longey" Zwillman acts as host because he runs most of the crime in New Jersey, his territory. This is an unprecedented gathering of criminal leaders, a combined, core enclave that has been formed to vanguard future interests. One of the most important items on the agenda is how to deal with the massive adverse reactions to the seven killings in Chicago, which are having ramifications throughout the country.

The congregated powers of American crime heatedly voice complaints about Capone, Valentine's Day, and all the murders in Chicago. Whatever the general opinions are in the conference, Big Al is definitely in the doghouse. Nobody is happy with the way things are going in his town. Apparently the wholesale opinion is that Al needs to take himself out of things. Perhaps the Big Fella is even beginning to fear for his life. Consequently, Capone leaves the summit. On May 17, he gets off the Chicago-bound Broadway Limited in Philadelphia, where he and Frankie Rio are spotted and arrested by detectives for their concealed weapons. Both men are carrying .38 revolvers.

Many historians have felt that Capone seizes this opportunity to take a small, enforced "vacation" in Philadelphia's Holmesburg Prison, after judge John E. Walsh sentences him and Frankie Rio to a year for concealed weapons. It isn't supposed to be a year, but the good judge apparently isn't in on the "plan" and lays down a serious penalty, something that would never happen in Chicago. What is supposed to be ninety days is now a devastating amount of real time. Capone must run his challenged empire from a prison cell, although he and Rio are provided with anything they need, including the warden's telephone, lobster dinners, and Oriental rugs. Holmesburg is a horrible Victorian-style fortress, but Capone and Rio are treated more like hotel guests.

Not so good for Jack McGurn is that back in Chicago, the interim chairman of the Outfit is Frank Nitti, who seems not to have much affection for Capone's favorite boy. They have reportedly never seen eye to eye, and this will turn out to have grave implications in the future.

25

Mind Test

1929

In the second hot week of August 1929, Chicago chief of detectives William O'Connor issues an order that all prisoners must be subjected to mental tests after their arrest. This appears to be a progressive idea to establish whether mental illness is the cause for so many criminals running around shooting each other. The testing is really more of a public relations ploy to deal with the tremendous pressures on Chicago law enforcement from the press and the public since the massacre. Everybody's trying to look busy in the light of the stalemated investigation, especially the Chicago police.

Chief O'Connor has been considering this for a while, having read about the studies by renowned alienist (psychiatrist) M. Hickson, who has worked with other big-city police departments.[1] O'Connor ends up hiring Hickson's associate, clinical psychologist Dr. Gilbert P. Pond, to conduct his own battery of tests, consisting of a patient history; a testing of reflexes, emotions, and "mentality"; and an oral and a written exam.[2] The prospect of this to an educated person might prove interesting; to most of those arrested, it approaches a form of torture.

Jack McGurn is the first man arrested after the test policy becomes effective. He is scheduled to appear before judge Emanuel Eller on a writ of habeas corpus regarding the murder of Dominic Cinderella back in 1927. Since the massacre, detectives and the state's attorney's investigators are still trying to dig up anything they can find, old or new, on McGurn. His court date is August 16, but on that morning he is spotted by the ever-vigilant policeman (now a sergeant) William Drury, who rousts him and finds a pistol. Drury arrests him for the firearm, and as soon as he arrives at Cook County Jail, detectives gleefully haul him off to an interrogation room to be tested by Drs. Hickson and Pond's female assistant, psychologist Lorne Keller.

McGurn is cranky as he's deposited in the small room with the young woman, whose intimidating weapon is a fountain pen. The cops and detectives elbow each other and jockey for position on the other side of the glass window. They block the press as more reporters learn about McGurn's fate and begin arriving down the hallways. Anything involving Jack McGurn now creates an instant reaction from anyone in the building. Everything he does becomes instant news.

Dr. Keller begins by asking her subject the simplest of core questions, the very ones he consistently lies about. In a situation like this, he will usually tell the cops or the press anything that strikes his whim, making up names and addresses and cracking wise with his offhanded, machine gun delivery. But Lorne Keller's self-assured, calm, probing interrogation has immediately produced a reaction in him that nobody will ever see again: Jack McGurn is visibly nervous and even perspiring.

Simultaneously, the Cinderella case is called; a bailiff informs the judge that McGurn is elsewhere, being administered the sanity test. The irate Eller quickly sends deputies to fetch McGurn. They burst through the clot of onlookers and into the testing room, picking up McGurn by his armpits and gliding him back down the halls to court. He is visibly relieved to escape the testing. He's an artful shadow and an able dodger most of the time, but trapped in that tiny office with the smart young woman has taken him down a notch or two, reducing him to an uncharacteristic victim.

McGurn finally reaches the courtroom, angry and complaining that he was waylaid. Judge Eller is also in an ugly mood and tersely speeds things along. McGurn's attorney, as usual, is prepared with a strong, confident attack. He is able to competently challenge the weak case, and, in addition, a witness who identified McGurn near the Cinderella kidnapping spot has surprisingly not shown up, a development that makes Judge Eller act even angrier. Acting is exactly what it may be, considering that McGurn has traditionally "supported" the judge's father, Morris, in several elections. Eller is ultimately "forced" to release McGurn on lack of evidence in the killing of Dominic Cinderella.

During the course of the hearing, McGurn errs by once again communicating his displeasure with the sanity test. Eller also senses something no judge has yet found in McGurn: the dapper gangster seems afraid. Eller, whose sense of humor has a sadistic edginess, sees his opportunity for a bit of torment. Smiling for the first time that morning, Eller instructs the detectives that McGurn should immediately be taken to finish the sanity examination.

Sergeants William Drury and Joseph Connelly, who have constantly watched McGurn's revolving-door antics of evasion and escape from successful prosecution, get to witness his extreme discomfort at Dr. Keller and her test. These veterans, who have seen McGurn skip off so many times before, thoroughly enjoy themselves as they watch him sweat out the invasive, laborious, and thoroughly intimidating examination.

The rumor of the gangster's uncharacteristic fear also catches the ears of the reporters, who once again congregate outside the small room. Watching McGurn from behind a glass window, Drury is quoted as saying, "If he isn't nutty now, he soon will be." Afterward, Dr. Keller tells reporters, "There is something wrong with McGurn. I haven't decided what; maybe it was only that he was scared." The newspapers in Chicago seem thrilled that something was able to shake up Machine Gun Jack McGurn.

William Drury, the oft-utilized and virtuous cop, will become a future crime columnist. Drury, who has the ethics of a boy scout and who will be murdered twenty years later, writes in his diary about his encounters with McGurn. Drury's historian and next-door neighbor, Thomas DiGanci, possesses the original journal in which Drury excitedly records the experience, recalling his role in the psychological profiling that so unnerves Jack McGurn: "On August 16th I arrested the notorious Jack McGurn in front of 30 No. Dearborn St.—searched him and found a .45 Cal. Automatic with machine gun bullets in it in his belt, the weapon cocked with the safety off. This in line with Chief O'Connor's new plan to send all known

Hoodlums through the psychological test as conducted by the well-known alienist M. Hickson. Jack was the first to take the test and as a result I made the headlines in the past three or four months."[3]

At this point Drury, who will never take a dime as a police officer from anyone other than the City of Chicago, expresses how beneficial it has become for him to dog the high-profile McGurn: "I have become one of the best known police-men on the Dept. through the medium of newspaper publicity. The October issue of *Police* ran my photo and nominated me to their hall of fame. There is a rumor to the effect that the sergeants list will soon be posted. Here's hoping for the best and preparing for the worst."

The best will indeed occur: Bill Drury will become a detective sergeant, a hero, a staunch antimob crusader, and much more before his career is prematurely ended. He will be shotgunned to death on September 25, 1950, sitting in his garage in his parked automobile. This will take place hours before the Kefauver Crime Hearings in the US Senate. It is assumed that Drury has damning information on corrupt Chicago police officers and perhaps members of the Outfit. His column in the *Tribune* is akin to "having a big mouth" to the Accardo administration of the Chicago mob. He has tormented Tony Accardo since 1926 by repeatedly arresting him and McGurn with an almost proprietary frequency, but it is most likely that cops on the Outfit payroll do him in.

The psychological testing of gangsters will begin to be thwarted after McGurn's harrowing experience. He warns his comrades to enlist their lawyers to avoid this horror. South Side killer Frank McErlane is arrested, but his attorney obtains a writ against the psychologists. McErlane was the first killer to use a Thompson submachine gun in Chicago. Capone biographer Robert Schoenberg humorously claims, "If he was no psychopath, neither was Jack the Ripper."[4]

Chicago's most honest cop, William Drury, 1929.

South Side gangster John "Dingbat" Oberta actually goes to the extent of paying a private psychiatrist to issue him a certificate of mental health, which he carries with him at all times in case he is arrested and which he produces when he comes to court for a hearing. Chief O'Connor, frustrated, outwitted, and tired of appearing like a dupe, gives up the testing program.

On October 24, the downward-spiraling New York Stock Exchange of Black Thursday sounds the first harbinger that the euphoric party of the Roaring Twenties will soon be over. To the dismay of Americans, five days later, an even more catastrophic downturn on Black Tuesday announces the end of economic prosperity in the United States for a very long time. The collapse of the great bull market continues unceasingly for the next four weeks; like a rapidly growing hurricane, the Great Depression is coming on, invading the entire country and ultimately the rest of the world.

On November 1, with the nation reeling as if it has been beaten, Jack and Louise are handed the judicial version of the buckwheats. Frustrated by McGurn's alibi for the Valentine's massacre as well as a lack of evidence, state's attorney Daniel Anderson charges both of them with white slavery and violation of the Mann Act.[5] It is a last-ditch effort to get McGurn because the unmarried couple had traveled to Florida the previous year. It is legally far-fetched and will ultimately prove to be laughable, but it's the only thing the law can think of to put Jack McGurn in jail.[6]

The 1909 Mann Act was originally called "The White Slave Traffic Act" in Congress when Chicago representative James R. Mann introduced the bill. It was inspired by the interstate prostitution trade that fed the old Levee district in the heart of the city, reflective of the tragedies of young immigrant women getting conscripted off the street and into brothels. The bill followed a shocking report in Congress titled "Importation and Harboring of Women for Immoral Purposes." Anyone found guilty of the White Slave Act has transported a woman or a young girl from one state into another for the "purpose of prostitution or debauchery, or for any other immoral purpose." The maximum penalty is five thousand dollars and up to five years in prison. Perhaps the most powerful result of this legislation is that the Bureau of Investigation, which will soon evolve into the FBI, is selected to track down and arrest Mann Act violators. From a small office with twenty-three agents who investigate relatively small crimes, the Mann Act will make the Bureau into "the government's most recognizable and powerful legal arm."[7] The FBI will become the national police force.

The bill greatly contributed to the eventual demolition of the Levee brothels before World War I. This is how Anderson and the honest part of the Chicago system will obtusely attempt to nail Jack McGurn for the St. Valentine's Day Massacre. They don't give it a thought that Louise Rolfe, sinful by their standards but really just McGurn's girlfriend, will be the collateral damage. It is no doubt their leftover Victorian sensibilities that make them confident that the legal system will see their moral imperative and act accordingly. Capone lawyers Nash, Ahern, and Feldman cannot help but laugh at the lack of sophistication of the state's attorney's office in trying this gambit. They tell their clients not to worry, because the government doesn't have a chance in convicting them.

But Jack McGurn, who must know better when someone tells him not to worry, is certainly quite worried. The forces gathering against him are uncharacteristically formidable, and his traditional impunity is gone for good. Even the subversive structure that Capone has created is crumbling like a house of cards. Aside from his great new love with Louise, he is standing naked before his enemies. The "wistful boy gangster" is now a pariah, as his widely distributed image becomes the face of outrageous, violent death all over the world. But even though they are coming after him with a vengeance, he will still perform as an agent of the Outfit as he prepares to battle the awesome confluence of the angry cops, reformers, and judiciary who are rapidly distancing themselves from the status quo of Capone's enormous arrangements.

26

See You Soon!

1930

A fascinating insight into Jack McGurn's activities in the first few months of 1930 will be presented by Murray L. "Curly" Humphreys in his tax-evasion trial in 1939. He will outrageously try to convince the court that his income was only five thousand dollars in 1930, which he received for "straightening out some difficulties [labor trouble] in the dry cleaning industry." His coworker in this, Humphreys will add, was Jack McGurn.[1]

This essentially means that Humphreys and McGurn reinvade and subjugate the union again. Now that the North Siders no longer control the organization of which Albert Weinshank was made president, the Outfit needs to remind everybody who is in control. McGurn is still the hot kid, an instant persuader for those who would put up any argument. He is often accompanied by Tony Accardo, who still maintains a batting average superior to either of the Chicago baseball teams.

On February 1, a duplicitous and shady private investigator named Julius Rosenheim is shot to death half a block from his home by two men with pistols. They are waiting for him, knowing of course where he'll eventually be. They simply walk up on either side of him and empty their revolvers. Twin shots to the head fell him instantly. The two killers jump into an automobile that pulls up at the curb and speeds away into the morning mist. Forty-nine-year-old Rosenheim is described by the press as "a paid exposer of gangsters," a decidedly dangerous job any time, any-

where, but particularly lethal in 1930 Chicago. Several years before, Rosenheim was an undercover spy for the state's attorney McClay Hoyne. Lately
he has informed police of the address of the headquarters of Capone bagman Jack Guzik, information that could not have pleased anybody.[2]

Rosenheim has also been sneaking around the vice resorts and gambling houses in the greater Chicago area. When he dies he has a com-
piled list of four hundred Outfit businesses. These have been given to him
by "the committee of fifteen," a bunch of religious reformers who have
declared their own crusade to abolish franchised vice. Charles E. Miner,
general director of the committee, tells police he gave the list to Rosenheim for gathering information.

If all of that is not sufficient, Rosenheim has also been hunting for
evidence for crime crusader Frank Loesch's prosecution of election crimes.
Loesch is a veteran attorney and a member of President Herbert Hoover's
Crime Commission. He is still trying to connect both Accardo and McGurn
to the slaying of Octavius Granady during the Pineapple Primary in 1928.[3]
The Chicago police almost find it amusing when they are asked by the
press whom they believe killed Rosenheim. The self-important little man
had more enemies than craters on the moon. However, FBI agent William Roemer will claim in his biography of Tony Accardo that "Accardo
and McGurn took care of Rosenheim. Offed him." Apparently this will be
made clear on federal eavesdropping tapes of Accardo far in the future.[4]

As soon as Rosenheim's body is found, the cops hit the streets in waves
to round up the usual suspects after a gang-connected killing. Three hours
after Rosenheim's death, McGurn and Tony Accardo are spotted in a taxi-
cab at Dearborn and Harrison Streets by police sergeants and constant
shadows William Drury and John Howe. Drury fearlessly yanks open
the cab's door, shouting, "Keep your hands away from your pockets," to
which McGurn replies, "Don't get excited. You will find it on the right
side."[5] He must feel a flush of anger upon seeing Howe and Drury, his
familiar nemeses.

In McGurn's belt is a .38-caliber revolver. The gun is handed over to
Calvin Goddard, the forensics firearms specialist, who has moved his laboratory from New York to the Chicago campus of Northwestern University.[6] Two days later Goddard determines that the weapon has not been

used on Rosenheim. Nevertheless, concealed weapons charges are filed against McGurn and Accardo, who are, of course, immediately bonded out after the familiar machinations of the Capone lawyers.[7]

When Accardo and McGurn are brought in, chief of detectives John Egan makes the mistake of asking McGurn a question within earshot of reporters. It will prove to be one of the classic set-ups as well as Jack McGurn's single greatest comic moment. Scores of comedians will steal it in the years to come. McGurn will get a clean laugh from everybody who hears him. "Do you know Rosenheim is dead?" asks John Egan. Without missing a beat, McGurn answers, "Dead? I didn't even know he was sick."[8]

Egan probably has to suppress a chuckle himself. He also questions both men about the shooting of taxicab-company treasurer Barney Mitchell, who was murdered a couple of days previously, but McGurn and Accardo stonewall him, demanding to see their lawyers. There are more than enough reasons to hold the two since state's attorney John Swanson recently announced he would automatically indict any gangsters who were found with concealed weapons.

Backing up Swanson is the chief justice of the municipal court, Harry Olson, who proposes a far more draconian policy and claims that gun toters should be locked up in insane asylums for life. Olson is known for beginning the policy of maximum penalties for gangsters carrying weapons. The honest components of the system ironically seem to be desperate to find a way around certain civil rights, because nothing else has proved effective. Olson indignantly announces, "The proper place for any man who walks around with a gun for no good reason should be behind the bars." He makes his case by recalling McGurn's unfortunate experience with the psychologist Keller: "Jack McGurn and others were examined at various times when in custody and found to be suffering from dementia praecox [an antiquated term for schizophrenia]. . . . If we sentence these creatures for carrying concealed weapons, the maximum penalty is one year in jail. If they were brought before a jury of laymen and found insane, they would be isolated for life."[9]

Police commissioner William Russell puts his own complaint in the form of a question: "What can we do when gangsters who are mortally wounded will not name their assailants?"

Forfeiting their bonds in Chicago Municipal Court on their gun-toting charges, McGurn and his stepbrother Anthony take a train to Florida, accompanied by Louise, who sleeps in a separate berth in case any of the constantly vigilant state's attorney's investigators are watching them. With the Mann Act charges still hovering over their heads, his lawyers have no doubt warned McGurn about exacerbating his problems. Since Capone and Frankie Rio are still in prison in Philadelphia, enjoying privileges that would make a pasha envious, several of the boys, including McGurn, are invited to relax and recreate at Al's Palm Island estate. Capone's wife, Mae, and his boy, Sonny, are in Philadelphia, avoiding the recent attempts at harassment made by the Miami police.

On March 20, Dade County sheriff M. P. Lehman and a dozen heavily armed deputies raid 93 Palm Island, where they encounter Jack McGurn; Al's brothers John and Albert Capone; Leo J. Brennan, a friend of John's from Philadelphia; and Al's caretaker, Frank Newton. The shotgun-wielding cops in western-style hats march onto the estate like an old-fashioned posse of Texas Rangers. They arrive with a warrant signed by a judge and look for liquor, which of course they find.

They arrest Frank Newton for possession of alcohol and John Capone for vagrancy because he has no money in the bathing suit he is wearing. The loyal caretaker, Newton, takes full responsibility and is eventually

The raid on Capone's Palm Island estate, 1930. *MIAMI HERALD*

Jack and Louise living it up in Miami, 1930. COLLECTION OF JOHN BINDER

fined five hundred dollars, claiming the liquor—which includes the dozen bottles in John Capone's closet—is his.

McGurn is arrested and gives his name as "James Gebhart," even though he has identification that says he's James Vincent—sometimes even he can't keep his phony monikers straight. He doesn't want Chicago to know where he is because he's slipped his bond and the police are looking everywhere for him. Capone's Miami lawyers eventually show up and get him out of jail so he can resume his vacation with Louise.

Jack and Louise have put a deposit on a beachfront house, the ultimate rose-covered cottage for two lovers accused of collaborating in white slavery. There is a golf course nearby where McGurn is trying to teach Anthony how to keep from digging huge holes in the grass. The party has begun; Jack is pouring the drinks while Louise is rewinding the Victrola again and again as Chicago's finest jazz loudly fills the fragrant Miami evening. Unfortunately, they have unknowingly moved next door to advertising mogul Albert Lasker and his close friend, the automobile broker John D. Hertz.

McGurn has a few little get-togethers, inviting some of the boys who are down in Florida with their girlfriends or wives. The dancing and drinking on the veranda and beach apparently reaches a hedonistic pitch. Lasker and Hertz are outraged. They make a few inquiries: Who is living next door? The Miami police 'fess up that the cute little couple is Machine Gun Jack McGurn and his Blonde Alibi, Louise Rolfe. By this time, Miami detectives have figured out that McGurn is on a forfeited bond and is wanted back in Chicago.

Lasker and Hertz complain bitterly to the Florida police, then to the chief of police in Chicago, demanding that McGurn be extradited back to Illinois.[10] In the meantime, somebody bends Lasker's ear about Capone Outfit justice and the extreme lengths that are undertaken to achieve it. Now wiser and fearful of Jack McGurn and Al Capone's wrath, Lasker has second thoughts, which he confesses to a Capone attorney. Upon being informed of this, Capone sends Lasker a note from the penitentiary where he is playing a lot of gin rummy with Frankie Rio. There is little doubt that Capone gets a very good laugh out of this. He responds to Lasker, saying there are no hard feelings. The Big Fella is in great humor because he's finally about to leave the Pennsylvania prison on March 16.

The Miami police follow through, having been alerted by the powerful businessmen, arresting Jack, Louise, and Anthony Gebardi on a Miami Beach golf course on April 1.[11] Dade County residents are certainly titillated by the front page of the *Miami Daily News*, which displays McGurn's mug shot. No doubt they are interested to learn that the "notorious gunner of gangland, identified as a lieutenant of Scarface Al Capone," has been attempting to live not so quietly among them.[12]

Anthony Gebardi tells Miami police he is Jack's brother "Tony McGurn." This is the first time they are arrested together, a significant indication that Anthony has made the unfortunate decision to become a protégé. Because he's the kid stepbrother, he caddies a lot for McGurn and

Jack and Anthony arrested on the golf course, 1930.

DADE COUNTY POLICE PHOTOGRAPH

Rolfe on the golf course. Anthony has movie-star good looks, with a more symmetrical nose than his stepbrother. Even as a teenager, he attracts women wherever he goes.

Louise is released, but McGurn and Anthony are held in the Dade County lockup until April 10, when McGurn's pals Sergeants Drury and Howe arrive in Florida to escort them back to Chicago. McGurn will wait out his continuance for the concealed weapons charge at home.[13] Back in the city, McGurn and Accardo are rebonded, guaranteed by Capone lawyers, and released. They will come to trial on June 2.

On April 24, Frank Loesch, the president of the Chicago Crime Commission, issues a list of the twenty-eight most prominent gangsters in Chicago, using the term "public enemies." The concept of the public enemy is invented by George A. Paddock, the Crime Commission's finance director during the late 1920s. The Crime Commission is a private crime-fighting organization formed in 1919 by the Chicago Association of Commerce. The Commission is more of a public relations booster for law enforcement, battling the gangsters through the press and from rostrums, with words and without guns. Al Capone is first on the list. Having returned to Chicago to face the music, Jack McGurn discovers that he is Public Enemy No. 5.

Whether guilty or innocent, the twenty-eight men on the list basically stand convicted in the court of public opinion. The term "public enemy" will immediately be accepted as part of popular culture, even becoming the title of a legendary movie in 1931 starring James Cagney and Jean Harlow in roles reminiscent of Jack McGurn and Louise Rolfe.

27

I'd Send You to Jail

1930

Back in Chicago and bonded out, McGurn is responsible for some unfinished family business on the Saturday of Decoration Day—later to be known as Memorial Day—weekend. The fourth Genna man suspected in the shooting of Angelo DeMory in 1923 has surfaced. Phillip Gnolfo, partner to the late "Scourge" Tropea and "Eagle" Baldelli, is spotted on the West Side with two imported killers, William Carnedo from Toledo and Joseph Flannia from New York. It is likely that they are involved in making a move on the Cleaners and Dyers Union. Curly Humphreys will also imply this at his income-tax-evasion trial in 1939.[1]

Once again, a happy confluence of motives, both business and private, are at work. McGurn has wanted to kill Gnolfo for seven years. Consequently, he plans a full-frontal assault. With four of his boys with him in the car, he spots Gnolfo driving in the Canalport district, an Italian neighborhood next to the Union Stock Yards. They chase him and open up with a Thompson, a shotgun, and two revolvers, putting nineteen bullets into the automobile and its occupants.[2] Gnolfo dies at the wheel as the car continues over the curb and into the brick façade of a church. Carnedo and Flannia are wounded, and a fourteen-year-old boy is struck by a stray bullet, one of the small handful of bystanders nicked in the gang wars. The shotgun is tossed out of the car and later recovered by the police.[3] This killing is rather spontaneous for McGurn, who is the ultimately careful planner; the opportunity presented itself, however, and the deed is done.

Since Gnolfo has a long police record as a professional extortionist and killer for the Gennas, he is simply chalked up as yet another gang casualty. Before anybody can get excited about his demise, all hell breaks loose the next day when another, smaller massacre occurs in Fox Lake, a resort near Chicago. Everyone is reminded of St. Valentine's Day and Jack McGurn. The timing and the fact that Capone allies are the victims might suggest that this is a reprisal for the Gnolfo death the day before, but it is more probably coincidental.

Fox Lake, which is about fifty miles northwest of Chicago, has become very popular with Chicagoans in the late 1920s. An inevitable muscling in of Chicago gangs culminates in a shooting late on Decoration Day. Terry Druggan and Frankie Lake, independent bootleggers who have an alliance with Capone, are pushing their beer business in the area of Fox Lake. They are being stalked by North Side gunmen, who stealthfully follow them to Manning's Restaurant and Bar. As soon as they are seated at tables in the barroom, machine gun fire from outside crashes through the south window. Three men are shot dead—gangsters Sam Peller, Mike Quirt, and Joseph Bertsche. Thompson machine guns are used by two shooters. As usual in gangland murders, the gunmen are "not seen." The only viable eyewitness, bartender Louis Capella, dives to the floor behind the bar and escapes injury.[4]

The telltale style of the shooting has the Chicago police rousting every known gangster who ventures outside, and in a profiling orgy more than two hundred men are picked up for interrogation.[5] It is reported that most of them are alien Sicilians, who are questioned by federal immigration agents in the hope they can be deported. The police intercept three cars with Capone men racing south on Clark Street, allegedly on their way to avenge their fallen allies at Fox Lake. Capone bodyguard Frank Diamond has an eight-cylinder Lincoln; he outruns the police and gets away. Izzy Andelman and "converted" North Sider Frank Foster are pulled from their cars and dragged to the detective bureau. The only information the police get from the two is that they have recently changed their allegiance from the Moran gang to being allies of Al Capone.

Police also pick up Caponites James "King of the Bombers" Belcastro and Ralph "Chink" Avino, but they don't have to look very hard for McGurn. He appears bright and early in court on the following morning, June 2, with Tony Accardo, to fight their concealed weapons charges from the February 1 arrest. They are finally set to appear before judge E. I. Frankhauser at 10:00 AM in the Criminal Courts Building. By 10:10, Capone attorney Nash has of course been granted yet another continuance, because he is engaged in another trial. McGurn is released. He darts from the building into a waiting roadster driven by Capone gunner and McGurn protégé Charles Joey, who slides over and lets McGurn take the wheel. McGurn drives east on Twenty-Sixth Street to Blue Island Avenue, where he takes a left and races northeast.

Almost instantaneously, one of the detectives makes a radio call; sergeants John Foley and William Hinkins intercept McGurn at South Robey Street and Blue Island Avenue, a location approximately four minutes from the Criminal Courts Building. McGurn actually steps on the gas and tries to elude the police car, but Foley stays with him, eventually cornering him. They arrest him on suspicion of the Fox Lake shootings. He is back in the police station by 10:30, having been loose for less than twenty minutes. The papers have a field day with the story, amused by the close scrutiny on McGurn: "At 10:30 he was in the familiar police station, giving an oral and intimate autobiography, explaining why he was here, there, and elsewhere, and, in fact, why he was anywhere at all."[6]

McGurn is subjected to several hours of questioning about the Gnolfo shooting and the Decoration Day murders. Attorney Nash is uncharacteristically thwarted most of the day in trying to have McGurn appear before a "sympathetic" judge. Consequently, McGurn spends that night in the lockup.

It all starts again the next morning. After several hours, they finally appear before judge William Schulman. Nash is finally able to wrestle a snarling McGurn away for lack of evidence, providing great entertainment to the reporters who are present. McGurn is starting to appear slightly worn down by the constant arrests, his general attitude becoming uncharacteristically reactive and more negative.

This episode is a strong acknowledgment on behalf of law enforcement that any successful machine gun killing smacks of Jack McGurn. Even though a year and a half has passed since St. Valentine's Day, such violence is now solidly McGurn's domain in most people's minds, especially that of the law. His enhanced infamy as Public Enemy No. 5 hasn't helped him in the least.

Interestingly, Sam Peller, Hymie Weiss's driver, whom McGurn had wounded in the 1926 assassination, is one of the fatalities in Fox Lake. Recently he has been associated with two Capone allies, bootleggers Terry Druggan and Frankie Lake. Peller is one more North Side gangster who has reconsidered his life and switched his loyalty to Capone. The cops are having a hard time keeping everybody's alliances straight. It is conceivable that Chicago police detectives see Peller as unfinished McGurn business. After all, in their minds, he's already shot Peller once and failed to kill him.

There seems to be a hyperconsciousness about Jack McGurn that has grown since Valentine's Day, 1929. By the time of the Fox Lake shootings, it has become the continual job of the press to remind Chicago and the world that McGurn has gotten away with murder. On the afternoon after the Fox Lake shootings, the *Chicago American* runs a three-inch evening banner that reads SEIZE JACK M'GURN.[7] The fact that he is brought in for questioning is enough to draw the tall print, as if the police have finally gotten their man.

It is already taken for granted by both the police and the public that if three people are machine-gunned, McGurn must have done it. In the current mythology of the Chicago streets he is the best-known brand. This also reflects the still frustrated and increasingly desperate measures taken by law enforcement to arrest McGurn for anything and everything.

As counselor Nash's continuances are finally depleted, McGurn goes to trial on June 23, 1930. After three days of attempts by Nash and his partner Michael Ahern to redirect the issue, McGurn is once again convicted on June 25 of carrying a concealed weapon. The reporters react and the papers run the hot story—the law has finally triumphed over Jack McGurn! United Press describes him as the "dapper gunman," and they note that he "seemed more astonished than frightened when the jury foreman pronounced the words 'Guilty as charged.'"[8] An hour later, Judge Frankhauser allows McGurn his liberty on a ten-thousand-dollar bond, which attorneys Nash and Ahern personally guarantee.[9]

The word is prematurely out, but the real outcome doesn't get printed. On July 2, McGurn's twenty-eighth birthday, the editorial page of the *Oakland Tribune* celebrates the fact that Jack McGurn has been convicted. Mostly because he is a Californian and doesn't understand the way things work in Chicago, the editor is under the mistaken impression that McGurn is safely packed away in jail, having been found guilty: "But in Chicago, it is unusual for a court to sentence known gangsters for carrying concealed weapons and it is on this charge the one [McGurn] will have to spend a year in prison." Then, with unknowingly misdirected West Coast optimism, he adds, "Heretofore, in Chicago, the courts have released gangsters almost as fast as the police have brought them in. The change is regarded as encouraging, and indicative of the results which may be obtained when the public expresses itself vigorously."[10]

Despite the admirable stoic stance and support of law-abiding citizens all over the country, the Chicago Outfit boys have their parachutes, despite any "vigorous" expressions by the public.

In Chicago, the most strident demand of its citizenry is still "Give me a drink." Capone, ever the visionary, is absorbing the more useful employees of his adversaries. Manpower is needed to keep bootleggers and the "resorts" that sell illegal alcohol—from the blind pigs that exist by the hundreds to the elegant, musical cabarets—in business. It is reported that Capone has hired Ted Newberry, ex–Moran gang member and owner of the Green Mill. The word is that Newberry and Jack McGurn are now Capone's "secretaries of war."[11]

For many reasons, it isn't surprising that Newberry ends up with Capone. He is the recipient of another one of the infamous diamond-studded Capone belt buckles. Several historians and writers have suggested this was Ted Newberry's reward for being the informer in Moran's gang, a duplicitous Capone agent next to the top of the North Side hierarchy. This would completely make sense in terms of Jack McGurn's relative comfort being at the Green Mill back in 1927, a North Side address. Newberry is a smart fellow with a coat of many colors. If he really has helped to overthrow Moran's gang, it very well might be in his nature to attempt the same thing again one day. Perhaps Newberry fancies himself a grand manipulator in the true Machiavellian sense, which, to others, is considered being a traitor. For the time being, he is a loyal Capone employee.

With so much attention being focused on him, McGurn keeps a low profile for the remainder of the summer. His absence is felt in a failed attempt to kill Jack Zuta on July 1, when shooters brutally attack Zuta in police custody. Zuta escapes and disappears, but he doesn't go far enough. He ends up in nearby Aurora, posing as a salesman named Jack Goodman. When he is finally eliminated, it is by Capone ally Danny Stanton and five others.[12] Zuta is shot down in the Lake View Hotel dance hall in Delavan, Wisconsin, on August 1 in an assassination that is described as having "machinelike precision." If it is McGurn's design, he is nowhere near the area.

There is an important, long overdue piece of business to be taken care of in the fall of 1930. Joey Aiello, still stupidly contending for the leadership of the Unione Siciliana and having failed in his death contracts on Capone, is foolishly once again back in Chicago. He is one of the last survivors of the Unione gang wars, but his grave insult to Capone has still not been dealt with. McGurn is given the order to kill Aiello, and, true to his mode of operation, he sets it up in signature fashion, just like the killings of Hymie Weiss and the St. Valentine's Day Massacre.

McGurn yet again utilizes the familiar formula of reconnaissance, planning, and incredible patience. His intelligence easily finds Aiello holed up in the home of his partner, Patsy "Presto" Prestogiacoma, at 205 North Kolmar Avenue. On October 13, a polite young man, ironically calling himself Morris Friend, rents a second-story apartment at 202 North Kolmar, across the street from Presto's front door. A walkway runs alongside Presto's apartment. Another polite young man, calling himself Henry Jacobson, rents a third-floor apartment at the rear of the building at 4518 West End Avenue, which overlooks the walkway. Apparently Aiello still knows Chicago is not a healthful place for him. To McGurn's chagrin, he never strays from the apartment until October 23, ten days after the nests have been set up.[13] This certainly taxes the patience of McGurn and whoever else is watching in the two apartments.

A taxi arrives at 8:20 on the evening of October 23, and the driver honks his horn. A few minutes later, Aiello and Presto step out the front door. The Capone shooters patiently manning the watch have not taken their eyes off the entryway for ten days. Immediately a machine gun begins firing from the window across the street. Patsy Presto ducks back into his foyer, and the cab driver, James Ruane, drops down behind his taxi. Joey Aiello doesn't have time to move an inch. He is hit by several rounds and staggers around the corner of the building to escape, but McGurn has outfoxed his target, who is met with another extremely accurate fusillade of slugs from the West End nest. He dies on the walkway with more than thirty holes in his body.[14] A few of the neighborhood residents see gunmen running from the West End apartment, but no identification or arrests are ever made.

After Aiello's signature murder, Judge Lyle, who seems to have reached a boiling point, issues vagrancy warrants in the last week of October. He includes one for McGurn, who of course fails to appear, unwilling to admit he is a vagrant. He keeps his head down throughout November and December, avoiding any confrontation with the law.

The year 1930 comes to a close with the Chicago police still hunting for the men on Lyle's trumped-up vagrant list. Ignoring all of this, Jack and Louise have once again made a sojourn to Florida, where they relax and, of course, play golf. They wisely stay away from the well-known, high-profile swanky clubs like Bayshore in Miami Beach, opting for smaller, more obscure courses where they will remain anonymous.

28

Nothing Lasts Forever

1931

By 1931, McGurn seems to be a familiar character in a theater cycle. Sergeants Drury and Howe still play their reoccurring roles as they stalk the hotels of downtown Chicago, except for Capone's headquarters at the Lexington Hotel. They frisk any known gangsters for concealed weapons. A few months back, they rousted George Moran and North Side killer Leo Mongoven in the Sherman House Hotel, for they've gotten to know all the significant players from all the gangs, not just the Caponites. They are equal opportunity arrestors. Of course, in particular they still watch for Jack McGurn and any of the other familiar Capone buttons, such as Jack White, Willie Heeney, or Harry Hochstein.

Some of the other important players in the comedy-drama are of course the judges, who, if not being paid by Capone, are keeping track of all unfinished business. This is why they keep calling upon Bill Drury and John Howe, who have both moved up to the rank of detective sergeant, to track McGurn. The straight judges trust only the straight cops, comprising a rather small fraternity sailing in a vast sea of corruption. In the fold are a handful of state's attorneys, perhaps the most belabored people in Chicago. If they are honest, they are like pit bulls, never giving up the fight. They happily send Drury and Howe, an arrangement that has become even more of a treat for the two, to arrest McGurn. He has returned to Chicago for a court appearance on February 1.

McGurn is back before judge Ross C. Hall after his attorneys are granted a new trial by the Illinois Supreme Court to fight the concealed-weapons charge.[1] Drury and Howe, McGurn's perennial predators, arrest him as he leaves the court and haul him down to the lockup. The familiar playlet traverses the halls and rooms of the courts building as photographers begin to act more like hungry paparazzi, shouting questions at McGurn as he passes by, none of which he will ever answer. The favorites: "Where were you on Valentine's Day, Jack?" and "Did you kill anybody today, Jack?" The sharp, gum-chewing, wisecracking reporters still love the quiet, innocent-faced bad boy with his constant irony. If indeed this is a piece of theater, the reporters and the photographers are the everpresent Greek chorus.

Attorneys Ahern and Nash quickly have their client released on the usual ten-thousand-dollar bond, signed by judge Abraham Shannon and approved by judge Thomas Green. McGurn returns three days later to stand before judge Frank M. Padden on February 4. This time, his attorney is James McDermott. He tries to get a dismissal on a technicality because the police officer who swore to the vagrancy warrant is absent, probably having been paid enough to cover all his Christmas expenses. McDermott is able to get McGurn a jury trial and a continuance, but not before incurring the wrath of Judge Padden. "A so-called gentleman— Mr. Lyle—signed these warrants," sneers Outfit counselor McDermott, to which Padden interrupts angrily, "Judge Lyle is a judge of this court and you see that you address him properly."[2] The frontal assault on the judiciary notwithstanding, Jack McGurn once again walks outside, free to smell the frozen February air.

It has now been a year since the Chicago Crime Commission issued its initial Public Enemies list. Apparently feeling proud and partially responsible for certain triumphs against the gangsters, the commission updates the list. Jack McGurn is still fifth, described as "Jack Demore, alias Machine Gun Jack McGurn, ace Capone gunman, currently out on bail for his pending concealed weapon and vagrancy charges."[3]

The Crime Commission rather optimistically claims the Capone Outfit is teetering on the brink of extinction, that the gang leadership has been decimated by the drive against them. Capone himself is on bail pending an appeal of a six-month sentence for contempt of federal court; his income tax issue is about to kick into high gear. Frank Nitti is already serving his eighteen-month tax-evasion sentence. Business manager Jack Guzik is out on bail pending an appeal of his five-year tax-evasion sentence at Leavenworth. Tony "Mops" Volpe is fighting deportation while he is out on bail for vagrancy. Ralph Capone is also out on bail, trying to fight his three-year sentence for tax evasion. Also out on bail for vagrancy arrests are gunmen Frankie Rio, Rocco Fanelli, Lawrence "Dago" Mangano, Frank McErlane, William Niemoth, and Edward "Spike" O'Donnell.

Explosives expert James "King of the Bombers" Belcastro is in the hospital recovering from bullet wounds afflicted by unknown assailants. His citizenship papers are reported to be revoked. North Siders Joey Aiello, Jack Zuta, and Leo Mongoven are dead. Caponite Frank Diamond is a fugitive on concealed weapon and vagrancy charges, and William "Three-Finger Jack" White is once again in the Cook County Jail charged with murdering a police officer. (White escaped scrutiny for the St. Valentine's Day Massacre because he was in jail then as well.) Because of all of this, the Crime Commission and the eager press feel able to purvey the illusion that the Outfit will soon be history.

Jack McGurn has many clouds over his head, but he seems indomitable, as if he is undaunted by anything facing him. Around St. Valentine's Day, perennially a meaningful date, he becomes a suburbanite, purchasing a house at 1114 North Kenilworth Avenue in Oak Park. A warranty deed is filed at the recorder's office. Apparently many members of the Outfit are fleeing the city environs to avoid the Chicago police and detectives who know their faces too well. The block where McGurn and Louise settle has become like an Outfit enclave, also being home to chief Capone bodyguard Frankie Rio (Public Enemy No. 4), Anthony "Mops" Volpe (Public Enemy No. 2), and bootlegger Frankie Lake, Terry Druggan's partner (Public Enemies Nos. 20 and 21, respectively).

The Kenilworth Avenue neighborhood is charming, with long, narrow lots. McGurn's acquisition is a pretty and new two-story brick house, built in 1928, on a 50-by-160-foot piece of land. Its original cost is $27,000, although the stock market crash of 1929 has slightly deflated the value. The recorder's office shows the deed as being from an Emil T. Rank and his wife, Marie, as conveyed to Vincent Gebardi and his "wife," Louise.

The conveyance of the house is made in "the consideration of the sum of ten-dollars cash, plus other goods and valuable considerations, subject to 1932 taxes."

Two trust deeds on the property are recorded on March 3, one covering a first mortgage for $23,000 held by the Oak Park Trust & Savings Bank. The second is a purchase money mortgage of $4,500, payable in monthly installments of $200. McGurn, who is obviously optimistic concerning

The McGurn house in Oak Park, present day.
AUTHOR'S COLLECTION

his employment, has agreed to pay the first mortgage off with a series of notes for $3,000 a month for six months, and then a final payment due in November for $5,000.[4]

On Thursday, April 31, police find a charred body that is believed to be gangster Mike "De Pike" Heitler in an ice house in Barrington, Illinois, in the far northwest suburbs. Pat Roche, the chief investigator for the Cook County state's attorney, issues orders for police to pick up Capone for questioning. A brave and rare raid is made on the Lexington Hotel on May 1. Capone is nowhere to be found, but police take in McGurn, Louis Russo, Frank D'Andrea, Fred Rossi, Tony Accardo, and Lawrence "Dago" Mangano. Capone lawyers race to the lockup and demand cause, which the cops, who didn't want to come home empty-handed, cannot show. Everybody walks. The reporters, upon seeing such a prestigious line of Capone men brought in, claim they have been "captured." However, their captivity is extremely short-lived.[5]

A couple of days later, with the Mann Act charge still pending against them, Jack and Louise are married. One of McGurn's lawyers, Tyrrell Richardson, highly recommends this, hoping to defuse the white-slavery issue by showing the court that these were only two lovers who eventually did the right thing. Richardson first makes sure that a quick divorce from his first wife, Helen, is pushed through for McGurn; the decree is issued by James J. Kelly of the Superior Court. During the short proceedings,

Helen reveals that they were married under the name of Gebardi and that McGurn permanently left her and his daughter on February 23, 1929.[6] The long-errant husband Harold Boex had signed off on Louise back in 1926.

Dark, beautiful, and still beloved by her former in-laws, Helen will eventually remarry, to a man named Albert LaRaviere, who will raise little Josephine. Aside from her marriage to Vincent Gebardi, Helen will lead a long and happy life, having blessedly escaped the dangerous and complex life of Jack McGurn.

Louise and Jack's marriage license is issued by Lou Hendee, Lake County clerk in Waukegan, north of Chicago. Waukegan is where couples from Cook County go to avoid publicity or to elope, where Louise traveled when she was underage and married Harold Boex. They are alone, without friends or family, but they are married by justice of the peace Walter Dow Wright. Vincent Gebardi and Miss Louise Boex are the names on the certificate, with their ages truthfully recorded as twenty-eight for Jack and twenty-four for Louise.[7]

When they return to the city, the beaming lovebirds Jack and Louise have their wedding picture taken by Anthony Berardi. They appear simply to be a romantic American couple, as the adorable blonde bride gazes lovingly at her handsome husband.

The lovebirds don't get much time for another honeymoon, for the Mann Act charge that has been hanging over them since 1929 finally comes to trial on May 26 before judge Walter C. Lindley. Now that they are legally married, McGurn's attorney Hamlin expresses his confidence that the ridiculous charge will be dropped.[8] But State's Attorney Anderson has other ideas. He senses that Hamlin has not prepared much of a case because the charges seem weak, so he goes for the throat, subpoenaing an incredible number of eighty witnesses from six different states. Sixty witnesses eventually testify. The charges are three counts of conspiracy, one for each of Jack and Louise's Florida trips in 1928. There is still tremendous pressure from the surrounding law enforcement environment to get McGurn. Any cards that can be stacked in the deck are, signifying the Chicago system's own hardball measures.

In the third of what will turn out to be an excruciatingly long three days, filled with short testimonies by bellmen, ticket agents, train por-

The lovebirds: Mr. and Mrs. Vincent Gebardi, 1931.

PHOTOGRAPH BY ANTHONY BERARDI, AUTHOR'S COLLECTION

ters, waitresses, and restaurant-counter clerks who have had their way paid to Chicago, Hamlin states, "This was just a plain, ordinary love affair. Similar ones occur often in modern life. The government chose this one couple out of a thousand for prosecution," to which Anderson unabashedly replies: "As far as Mrs. McGurn is concerned, the government is not interested; but as for McGurn himself, we are vitally interested in seeing him punished."

Obviously the entire idea of any "conspiracy" is a sham. It is basically understood that this entire legal charade is a nearly transparent, last-ditch attempt at retribution for St. Valentine's Day. It is the only way the system can effectively punish Public Enemy No. 5, Jack McGurn. Not unlike the insipid Volstead Act, it is another attempt to legislate morality. Plus, the state's attorneys fully intend to throw Louise on the fire as well. It seems as if they must put away McGurn or die trying.

Characteristically, McGurn speaks only once during the entire three-day proceedings, answering Anderson's charge that he has twice been convicted of carrying concealed weapons: "I carried guns because my father was murdered and I had received threats."

Judge Lindley, a self-righteous moralist, assures McGurn that none of this has any bearing on the Mann Act charge: "So long as we believe in the tradition of monogamous marriage, the court must find them guilty."[9] And so it does. On July 21, Lindley renders a verdict of guilty, sentencing a shocked and angry McGurn to two years in Leavenworth penitentiary on the first count, two years on the second count, and two years on the third, with five years of probation in reference to the second and third counts. Perhaps the gravest insult is that Lindley also gives Louise four months in the county jail for the same offenses.[10]

But the Capone lawyers once again work their magic; there is no instant gratification for the court this day. Pending their automatic appeals, the McGurns are immediately released on a fifteen-thousand-dollar bond. Everybody on both sides walks away unhappy, already anticipating the inevitability of future battles regarding the spurious charges. The appeal to the Seventh Circuit Court is scheduled for April 2. The press quickly announces that the law is "cleaning up Chicago," that Machine Gun Jack McGurn and his Blonde Alibi have both been found guilty of conspiring to violate the Mann Act.[11] They consider the couple doomed in another spurt of false optimism, as time will tell.

While Jack and Louise are pondering their tiring future in the courts, on June 9 another sacred profession loses its immunity from gangster guns. This murder will be almost as controversial as that of State's Attorney McSwiggin. Jake Lingle, ace *Tribune* reporter, is shot down on his way to the racetrack. He is near the stairs to the underground trains when someone walks up behind him and puts two bullets into his head. Capone is immediately suspected, although Lingle is found wearing one of Capone's highly prized belt buckles, which has on it AJL—for Alfred Jake Lingle—spelled out in diamonds. It will eventually come to light that Lingle is on the Outfit payroll. In the hysteria that follows after the murder of a member of the Fourth Estate, Jack McGurn is in court and for once isn't suspected.

During this summer, Chicago law enforcement becomes unfailingly vigilant about outstanding warrants and unfinished business where McGurn is concerned, their indignant reaction to the still unrequited Mann Act debacle. On August 6, McGurn is served to stand for his last vagrancy charge. In an elegantly prepared argument, McGurn's lawyers claim that the silly vagrancy allegation should be dropped, as the defendant is already convicted under the Mann Act. They are cleverly implying that McGurn will do his slated time in the near future.

Judge Edward Sheffler is satisfied with this and files the charge as nolle prosequi. Once again, McGurn slips out the back door. Whatever machinations, if any, take place behind the scenes that help "convince" Judge Sheffler to be lenient will never be known. At this point, one can only marvel at the Capone lawyers, who consistently save Jack McGurn from the frustrated gnashing teeth and chomping bite of the system.

The Lingle murder, with its harrowing attack on the sacred press, creates a new public relations nightmare for Al Capone. With his income-tax-evasion trial looming, he finds that his popularity is also falling. He makes the mistake of taking an ill-fated trip to suburban Evanston to attend a Northwestern University football game against Nebraska on October 3. Accompanied by McGurn and a few other of the boys, he enters Dyche Stadium after the game begins, resplendent and almost comically obvious in a royal purple suit. His tickets are for the forty-fifth row, and the entire crowd of forty thousand attendees watches the gangsters take their seats. The jeering and intermittent booing begin as soon as Capone is recognized. The more obstreperous youth shout mild epithets, something none of them would ever dare to do alone. This continues during the game. McGurn is extremely nervous, constantly looking around for anyone approaching the Big Fella.

An unhappy Al Capone giving "the look," 1931.
COLLECTION OF JOHN BINDER

Al is angry and gestures for them to leave at the end of the third period. As soon as they rise out of their seats, the chorus erupts once more and "builds to a mighty crescendo."[12] The press will note that hardly anyone in the stands refrains from adding his voice to the din and that Capone and his party walk hurriedly out the exit in an abashed state. Capone biographer Robert Schoenberg writes that a bunch of children began to follow them out, booing. Jack McGurn turns, scowls, and shakes his fist as a loyal bunch of Boy Scouts who have benefited from Capone's charitable generosity try to cheer their pal with "Yeah, Al!" They are completely drowned out by the immense, united crowd.[13]

This public humiliation is a harbinger of much worse to come. On October 6, Capone's tax trial begins. It ends on October 17 with a startling conviction. The shock wave reaches around the country with an irony that will long be remembered. The ultimate gangster boss—whose minions are gun crazy and responsible for literally hundreds of murders—is brought down by men in spectacles with leather briefcases. Their ultimate weapon is the accounting ledger.

On October 24, judge James H. Wilkerson sentences Capone to ten years in federal prison and an additional year in a county lockup. The

The Big Fella on trial for tax evasion, 1931. COLLECTION OF JOHN BINDER

judge denies bail for the pale gangster, pending appeal, sending him straight to the Cook County Jail. The Outfit has been expecting a light sentence and a steep fine. The fine is $50,000, plus $7,692.29 for the court costs, which is essentially gambling change for the Big Fella. The ten years, on the other hand, signifies the end of everything as it was and never will be again.

This is extremely bad news for Jack McGurn. He will suffer personally and—most important—professionally from Capone's downfall.

29

The Bad Intention

1932

McGurn stays under the radar of Chicago police for the winter of 1931 and the early spring of 1932. He and Louise go to Florida, play golf, and soak up the sun, living off the stacks of cash that have paid for so many lives. McGurn's skin is bronzed, and his hair even picks up sun-bleached blonde highlights. He is the type of golfer who can play thirty-six holes most days, with his sunny Sicilian genetic coding. He is lean and exceptionally fit. He and Louise are having a very good time on the links during the day, dining and dancing in the evenings. They return to Chicago reluctantly; on April 1 they move into their new home at 1114 North Kenilworth Avenue in Oak Park.

The appeal for their Mann Act conviction is slated for the next day, and it must be hanging over the lovers' heads like the hand of doom. Their lawyers have reassured them that eventually the government must back down, believing that the ruling is ridiculous and will not stand. They warn McGurn that it may have to be settled out of Illinois, where no judge in his right mind would consider Jack a white slaver or Louise a victim or prostitute, especially now that they are married.

McGurn must be incredibly nervous on the day he and Louise appear in front of the Circuit Court of Appeals, but he doesn't show it. His attorney petitions the court for a rehearing. To their dismay, judges W. M. Sparks and Evan A. Evans rule that the conviction must stand; the

McGurns are guilty of making trips to Miami; Jacksonville, Florida; and Gulfport, Mississippi, for immoral purposes. Dissenting is the third judge, Samuel Alschuler, who states the obvious: "If the party charged did not transport the woman or cause her to be transported there is no crime of conspiracy to violate the Mann Act, regardless of what else might have happened."[1]

McGurn's lawyers bond the very unhappy couple out once more, immediately filing a petition for a rehearing. Louise is seen dabbing her eyes, and McGurn holds a handkerchief to his mouth as reporters scream questions before they can escape the aggressive crowd in a taxi. Their lawyers are the best defenders in the business: tough, experienced, and certainly the best connected. They are also the best paid. They still insist that they will ultimately win a reversal of the Mann Act conviction because it is simply a desperate ploy that must deteriorate at the higher level of judiciary, but it can only happen outside of Cook County.

At this juncture in the epic process, the interminable carnival has led Jack and Louise to the final step: the Supreme Court of the United States. Regardless of McGurn's high-profile reputation as a killer, they aren't without public support. Even one of the New York papers editorializes on the matter by stating with rather strong sentiment: "The Federal Government, determined to make a showing of activity against prohibition-bred gangsters, worked up a Mann Act case against McGurn. . . . The Mann Act never was anything but an instrument of blackmail, an absurdity, a legal monstrosity . . . sending people to jail on charges having nothing to do with their real crimes, if any."[2]

Wisely, McGurn pays attention to his lawyers. They have never failed him before, but they haven't done as good a job for the Big Fella. On May 3, under the hypnotized scrutiny of the public and the press, McGurn's mentor and *commandatoru* Alphonse Capone is hauled off to Atlanta to begin serving his time for tax evasion. McGurn's greatest supporter and protector is as good as dead. This stay won't be like the trumped-up 1930 vacation in the Pennsylvania prison when Capone ran things long distance from his jail cell; Atlanta is as rough a penitentiary as America has to offer.

Capone's imprisonment essentially signifies the end of the era, although the organization will survive at the hands of Capone prodigies and eventually evolve into the modern mob. The entire justice system, including the judiciary and law enforcement, holds its collective breath as Capone chooses "the Code of the Criminal—and not the Criminal Code on the law books."[3] The Big Fella keeps his lips tightly sealed concerning the pervasive corruption in Cook County, and, as national columnist Walter Winchell will put it in 1950, "Otherwise he could have stated and proven that many of the judges on the bench and the district attorneys were on his payroll, either outright or through their party." Ever the savvy commentator on the American gangster, Winchell adds, "To blow the whistle and expose them would have been as unethical in the criminal world in which he lived—as to turn in Jack McGurn for carrying a machine gun."[4]

Besides the misery and sorrow at his beloved friend's downfall, it must be a rude awakening to McGurn that he is now walking the high wire without a net. He has never been close to Frank Nitti, who is Capone's heir apparent, although there are others who might give Nitti a run, including Curly Humphreys, Paul Ricca, and even his pal Tony Accardo, who has begun to surpass him in the organization hierarchy.

To make matters worse, adding to McGurn's abject pain, the very next day their petition for a Mann Act rehearing is denied.[5] This means that there is only one chance for freedom left for Jack and Louise: they must appeal to the US Supreme Court in Washington, D.C. Their lawyers still insist that the issue will be deemed laughable and the conviction will be reversed. They file a writ of certiorari to the US Supreme Court to be heard in the October 1932 term. Machine Gun Jack McGurn and his Blonde Alibi will be taking their travail to Washington.

For those following the battle between McGurn and the courts—and there are many—and for the newspapers doggedly updating every ruling, it appears as if Jack and Louise are now taking on the entire entity of the US government. It has turned into a David-versus-Goliath story with a lot of romance thrown in, 1920s-style. The dashing Chicago machine gun killer and his adorable sex-kitten wife will face down the stone monolith of the legal establishment, the federal judiciary. Yet whatever McGurn has done, he and Louise cannot help but appear glamorous to the already Depression-weary Americans who seem to have little affection for their government.

During June, McGurn's "pal" Bing Crosby returns to Chicago to play the Oriental Theater, this time as a huge star of stage, screen, and radio. After his first rehearsal, he is told that a case of champagne has been left for him at the backstage door. Crosby tells the stage manager to send it back because he doesn't drink champagne. The stage manager warns him against this—the gift is from Jack McGurn. Bing thinks better of it and quips, "I'd better keep it then."[6]

The next day, Crosby receives a note from McGurn, who invites him to play a round of golf. The crooner supposedly considers this for a long time. He gives in because he is a passionate golfer and country clubs aren't partial to actors, who are still regarded as less than legitimate personalities. Moreover, he assumes that McGurn has access to a good golf course. They make a date on the phone. McGurn arrives in a black limousine with two men in black hats and black overcoats. In his 1976 autobiography, Crosby will describe Jack McGurn: "He looked like a university football player and was a good-looking man. We went for miles in this limousine—I guess he had to get to a safe place. We played golf and he got me back in time for the first matinee show."[7]

Most likely they play at Evergreen Park, far from the city. Crosby never tells who shoots the better score. While he is still performing in Chicago, he keeps getting phone calls from McGurn, whom he avoids out of the fear that he is getting in too deep with an extremely dangerous fellow. Eventually, worn down by the gangster's persistence, he gives in and goes out to dinner with McGurn and Louise, whom he describes as a blonde girlfriend. Louise is completely starstruck by "Der Bingle," who is becoming one of the biggest names in show business. Crosby admits that McGurn is "a very nice guy," although he doesn't repeat the assignation, worried that he'll "get caught in the crossfire."

It is now apparent that McGurn has begun working more with his younger stepbrother, Anthony, who has graduated from being a caddie to assisting in business ventures. On August 4, police pull them over at Campbell and Lake Streets, arresting them for another McGurn innovation; they have a police radio in their automobile, which allows them to monitor the squad cars. This is the first time law enforcement is faced with this cleverness. Because this is Jack McGurn, the police charge them with seven counts, including one for having the short-wave radio, one for exhibiting fictitious license plates, one for having no city vehicle license, and one for having a dubious Oak Park vehicle tag.

The tag turns out to be authentic, but it is registered to a Frank De Vito. McGurn cracks up the courtroom by telling the judge he uses that name to keep the police from harassing him.[8] Both brothers are charged with disorderly conduct. Anthony, who was driving, is also charged for ignoring a stop sign.[9] McGurn, elegant in white flannels and a brown sport coat, greatly entertains the courtroom and tells municipal judge John F. Haas that he is a "salesman" and that he gets lonesome, thus needing the radio on his trips.

Judge Haas is apparently still playing by the old, backroom rules; he is unusually lenient, dismissing every charge but Anthony's driving through the stop sign, which carries a two-dollar fine.[10] Ironically, the *Chicago American* reports, "McGurn's younger brother Anthony is still old fashioned enough to go by his correct name, Anthony Gebardi." In reality, they are wrong: Anthony's real name is DeMory, just another example of how he has adopted McGurn's penchant for moniker confusion.[11]

Meanwhile, McGurn's activities connected with unions once again become obvious in 1932 as the underworld forays get more numerous and aggressive. The Outfit's incursions into labor are still expanding. Those resistant to subjugation are learning that to be a hero, one must be dead. On October 13, Richard J. Roberts, an official of the Teamsters Union, is gunned down outside his union headquarters. The usual dragnet goes out, and police arrest Jack McGurn and Capone button Edward Nardi at Dearborn and Washington Streets, claiming disorderly conduct. In reality, they question them on the Roberts murder. They hold McGurn in interrogation and then in jail until October 17, when he is discharged by judge Harold P. O'Connell after his lawyer gets him released with the usual sleight-of-hand maneuvers.

It is clear that the Outfit is intent on expanding into the realm of the larger unions like the Teamsters, which has pivotal influence with the Cleaners and Dyers Union. This is still the agenda planned by Curly

Humphreys, who has tremendous influence in the Outfit, although Nitti remains the front man. With Al Capone in Leavenworth and eventually Alcatraz, the control of the day-to-day business falls to Nitti.

At this point in his life, McGurn, who is certainly beginning to suffer under the stress of arrest after arrest and trial after trial, relies more on his golf game for relief from Outfit pressures. He plays as often as possible, frequently with prominent Chicagoans, including wealthy businessmen who love to brag about their experience on the links with such a well-known gangster. Occasionally he will even join threesomes in need of another player that include members of the judiciary. He is always charming and an extremely fine golfer, who often gives useful tips to his partners.

30

A Great Victory

1932

On Halloween night, Louise is once again arrested for speeding and evading an officer, who clocks her at fifty miles per hour on a residential street in Oak Park. She is pursued into neighboring River Forest by officer Russel Guy. Guy hauls her back to Oak Park and books her. She is then released on bail.[1] Of course she was drinking, and one of McGurn's lawyers gets her freed, no doubt cautioning her that she is only a week away from pleading for her very soul in front of the US Supreme Court.

Louise is more than a little stressed herself, as she and her Jack face their final chance in front of another bunch of conservative elderly men. They must be terribly worried that the fix is in and that the power of Cook County will find its logical extension in the highest court in the land. Now that Capone is in prison, with the efficacy of his support dubious at best, it must seem like the odds are heavily stacked against them. Even the judges who were paid by Capone for all those years no longer have any allegiance or memory of having been accommodating. The two are essentially on their own, completely dependent upon their attorneys.

Jack and Louise take the Baltimore & Ohio to Washington, D.C. It is certainly not lost on them that their troubles began with a train trip. In Washington, their case arrives in the docket as number 97: "Jack Gebardi, alias Jack McGurn, alias Jim Vincent D'Oro, and Louise Rolfe, Petitioners. vs. United States of America, Respondent."

Jack and Louise will now do battle with the United States, which is certainly the most intimidating of adversaries. Representing the government are Thomas D. Thatcher, the solicitor general; Nugent Dodds, an assistant attorney general; and James A. Wharton, the special assistant to the attorney general. They file a twenty-page brief in June, enumerating the three charges of conspiracy, the history of the case, and their arguments as well as citing the supposedly supportive rulings of the past.[2] However, there is one significant difference. They are good lawyers themselves, and they realize that the second count of conspiracy is particularly ludicrous now that Jack and Louise are married: "In conclusion the government contends that the judgments of the District Court and the Circuit Court of Appeals as to counts one and three should be affirmed, and reversed as to count two."

When they read this in Chicago, the law is extremely unhappy. The pressure from the judiciary in Cook County becomes a full-court press as Dwight Green, the US attorney for the Northern District of Illinois, attempts to "help the government's case," obviously alarmed that they've already given away a third of it. Assistant attorney general Seth Richardson notifies Green on September 24 that their case will be submitted to the US Supreme Court on October 10. Green sends a letter to Richardson in which he painstakingly goes over the three counts. To address the fact that Jack and Louise have married, he makes an attempt to convince Richardson that they still violated the Mann Act because they had never actually lived together:

> I might state briefly that the evidence shows that the defendant Gebardi and his real wife lived together with their child at the McCormick Hotel in 1928 . . . in September 1928, defendant Gebardi rented a room at the Lexington Hotel for Louise Rolfe, which room was rented under the name of G. McManus. The evidence shows conclusively that the defendant Gebardi did not occupy this room with her. . . . It was the theory of the prosecution that the conspiracy was entered into in order that they might have sexual intercourse without the knowledge of the real Mrs. Gebardi.[3]

On September 29, the attorney general writes Green back, asking for information that is missing regarding whether McGurn purchased the famous train tickets for the love trip to Florida. Green answers the attorney general on October 1. Amazingly, he is rather honest about the Chicagoan's shaky Mann Act gambit in his explanation of why the evidence is not available:

> This can partly be accounted for by the fact that when the case originally came to this office, it was brought to the attention of my assistant Mr. Anderson by an Assistant State's Attorney of Cook County, who advised my assistant that he did not anticipate that there would be a prosecution for violation of the Mann Act but that he desired that the two be held under bond until they could complete their investigation, when they would indict the defendant for murder in what was then known as the Valentine Massacre, at which time seven hoodlums were assassinated in a garage in the near north side of Chicago.[4]

Dwight Green is nervous; the case against McGurn is proving to be less and less viable to the government lawyers. He enlists the aid of his boss, US attorney George E. Q. Johnson, the man who helped bring Al Capone down. Johnson sends an unsolicited letter to Assistant Attorney General Dodds, who is slated to present most of the government's argument. Again there is a reminder that Jack and Louise didn't live together previous to their escapade and alleged Mann Act violation: "An examination of the record will disclose that the defendants did not live together as man and wife, nor did they live in a state of adultery prior to December 22, 1928, which is the date they left Chicago for Miami, Florida. The circumstantial evidence and the records tend to prove that they had no immoral relations previous to that date."[5]

In Washington, the big moment finally arrives. The august triumvirate begins to present their case while Louise, lovely in a cloche hat, glowers at the lone *Chicago Daily News* photographer who has followed them to Washington. Jack sits behind her in a beautifully tailored suit, his hair

An intense Louise and Jack at the Supreme Court, 1932. *CHICAGO DAILY NEWS* NEGATIVE COLLECTION, DN-0088601

smooth and shining, his hands clasped in front of him as if he is making a concerted effort to keep them where everybody can see them.

The *Daily News* photographer manages to snap a telling photo of Louise exhibiting her hard side by giving him "a look that could kill." After a couple of years of living the roller-coaster nightmare of fighting these charges and the possibility of prison, she appears to be girded for battle in the helmet of her cloche hat. She knows she has the best defense attorneys money can buy. She seems determined, angry, and, to the elder gentlemen of the Supreme Court, the paragon of "alternative lifestyles"—a prototypical gun moll and unabashed sexual libertine. And she is a stand-up gal for her Jack, no doubt about that. Moreover, since the Chicago attorneys have first brought the Mann Act charges, things have changed; Louise is now an indignant, protective American wife.

To the chagrin of the stalwart state's attorneys in Chicago, Jack and Louise McGurn's Mann Act conviction is overturned by the US Supreme Court on November 7, 1932. Justice Harlan Fiske Stone explains that, except in highly unusual cases, a woman cannot violate the Mann Act, especially if she is a willing participant. With Louise eliminated from the case, there is no one with whom Vincent Gebardi could have conspired.[6] With the aid of Capone's excellent lawyers, Machine Gun Jack McGurn has now triumphed in the US Supreme Court. The reversal ruling will stand as a warning to any future prosecutors who might try to use the Mann Act for spurious purposes.

By Thanksgiving, the press declares the Chicago gangs "decimated." Capone's money man Jack Guzik and bootleggers Frankie Lake and Terry Druggan are languishing in Leavenworth. Everyone else seems to be holding their breath and biding their time, trying to make a living. Frank Nitti, now being referred to as "The Enforcer," is making money from the dog tracks and other gambling sources. The papers have Vincent Gebardi, "Machine Gun Jack McGurn," living with Louise on a quiet suburban street in Oak Park and making a small living as a "muscle man," according to Oak Park police, who seem to be closely watching their infamous citizens.[7]

In the spring of 1933, McGurn undergoes an epiphany and contemplates a career change, curtailing his mob activities in order to reinvent himself and play tournament golf. In retrospect, one of the most interesting facets of McGurn is his golf game. Perhaps one of the reasons the important gang killings in Chicago occur in the late fall and winter is because McGurn is preoccupied with golf in the spring and summer. At this point, golf has begun to occupy the greater part of his existence, which leads the public and the press to think of him as semiretired.

He has the ability to consistently shoot in the low seventies for eighteen holes. He has been playing much more since Capone went to jail, seriously working on his game at the Evergreen Park Golf Course and Maywood Country Club. He knows how to focus his concentration on training, just as when he was a ring fighter in his youth. It has now become his dream to become a professional golfer. Golf has grown to be much more than just recreation and sport; it has become an indispensable source of sustenance.

To McGurn, it must seem like everything has transformed in Chicago, certainly not for the better. The empire the Capone Outfit has built together is on the cusp of evolutionary change. It is shrinking in one way, expanding in another. When Capone takes the train to prison, Nitti, Ricca, Humphreys, and Guzik focus their eyes on gambling and union racketeering. Enforcing their attempt to dominate various national unions, McGurn, who is far from being "retired," leads his group of tough guys. These include Tony Accardo; Charlie Gioe, another McGurn protégé; Sam "Moony" Giancana, who will rise to become the Big Fella in the 1940s; and Sam "Golf Bag" Hunt.

The newly elected mayor of Chicago, Anton Cermak, inherits the deep financial woes of the Depression, with seven hundred thousand Chicagoans out of work already. He pledges to wipe out what remains of the old Outfit and initiates a citywide anticrime drive by culling out the corrupt police officers and waging a two-fisted war against vice and gambling. There are also police raids on various political headquarters to clean out the gangster influence from the wards. Cermak is an eager beaver, taking total control of patronage and progress.

Frank Nitti is no slouch either. He has assumed the role of the Big Fella, which puts him at the pinnacle of the prosecutor's flow charts and squarely in Cermak's sights; he becomes the priority in the anticrime battles. Perhaps Cermak is a bit too eager, because rather than continuing the traditional, frustrating methodology of the old days of the twenties, he allegedly gives a signal to his now trusted police to eliminate Frank Nitti. Unlike Al Capone, Nitti makes an almost fatal error by foregoing hardened bodyguards like Jack McGurn.

Nitti installs one of his dummy businesses, the Quality Flour Company, on the fifth floor of the LaSalle-Wacker Building, a new high-rise sprouted in the heart of the Loop's financial district. On December 19, two Chicago detectives plan a raid on the office, allegedly on a tip from Mayor Cermak.[8] They are detective sergeants Harry Miller and Harry Lang, who are Prohibition veterans and as tough—and perhaps as underhanded—as most gangsters. Harry Miller is the brother of Jewish gangster Hershey Miller. Before going in, they call for support, which is provided by officers Christopher Callahan and his partner, Mike Shannon. What Callahan, Shannon, and even Miller don't know is that Lang has his own special plan for Frank Nitti.

The four cops enter the office of the flour company and round up everyone inside, including Nitti, who immediately stuffs an incriminating piece of paper into his mouth. Callahan tells him to spit it out, but Nitti keeps chewing. Callahan grabs Nitti's wrists to handcuff him. To his—and Nitti's—shock, Lang fires his .38 police special into Nitti's neck at almost point-blank range. Callahan jumps away, stunned. The wounded Nitti turns toward his attacker, and, with extreme deliberation, Lang then fires two more bullets into Nitti's torso, puncturing his shoulder, lung, and kidney. As Nitti falls into a chair, Lang fires another round at his own left arm, grazing the flesh to make it appear as if Nitti shot at him first.

Nitti is grievously wounded but survives. While the Enforcer is hospitalized, Louis Campagna, Paul Ricca, and Frankie Rio are left at the helm of the Outfit. They realize that all bets are off in terms of Mayor Cermak's campaign against them. That the fix is no longer in at City Hall will radically change the way they conduct business. Perhaps it is for the best that Nitti didn't keep McGurn close, because there certainly would have been a few dead cops instead of a wounded Nitti. Consequently, Anton Cermak has placed his foot in an Outfit bear trap. The coming New Year will bring many abrupt changes to Chicago on both sides of the law.

As soon as he is inaugurated in January 1933, President Franklin D. Roosevelt asks Congress to modify the Volstead Act to increase its permissible alcoholic content up to 3.2 percent. Not only do the politicians act with dispatch, they welcome a two-step plan to relegalize whole beer in the spring and, a few months later, wine and hard liquor.[9]

With the death knell sounded for bootlegging, it is a shaky time for the gangsters. There seems to be a redistribution of power going on as Humphreys, Ricca, Campagna, and even Accardo begin sitting at the table with Frank Nitti. They rule by committee, although the still-recovering Nitti remains the figure on the masthead to the press and the public. Chief of detectives William Shoemaker, with his indomitable hard line, publishes the new thirty-nine-name "Public Enemies" list during the second week of the year, exposing Curly Humphreys as one of the new heads of the old Capone Outfit. William "Three-Finger Jack" White is second, William "Klondike" O'Donnell is third, and Jack McGurn has moved up to fourth place. The weakened Nitti occupies the fifth spot.[10]

Even though it has now been more than three years, in the mind of the collective public, McGurn is still the favorite suspect for the St. Valentine's Day Massacre. Moreover, the fact that he is still operating in Chicago and is fourth on the list of lurking villains gives him an illusion of impunity that drives the honest cops and state's attorneys absolutely mad. His freedom is a constant reminder of their failure to get their man.

McGurn's record of revolving-door antics in the courts is now legendary. Of course, what Chicagoans must take for cleverness is really a combination of highly paid attorneys and Jack Guzik's payoff structure, which enhanced the livings of scores of judges, hundreds of officials, and thousands of cops. In actuality, a sizable part of authority in Chicago has unconsciously been keeping McGurn free.

The shift from bootlegging to union racketeering and gambling is already progressing steadily, although Nitti and the boys are still running breweries and booze. Even though the Depression has tremendously curtailed expenditures on many things, gambling seems to be something that only increases along with people's dreams. Hope springs eternal at the tables and racetracks, a reliable trait of human nature on which the Outfit counts. The year 1933 seems to be more centered on the gambling, but a growing income is derived from the subjugation of the labor unions and the working person, the ongoing vision of Curly Humphreys, who counts on another, more admirable human trait—a strong work ethic—to provide future revenues.

Jack McGurn hasn't been near a courtroom since the US Supreme Court reversal in November. He and Louise prefer to escape February in Chicago to be in Florida playing golf. Even as the post-Capone organization goes through the growth pains of transforming into a new Outfit, McGurn is apparently still necessary. The enormous Chicago World's Fair is a few months from opening, and Outfit interests are battling to grab a piece of as many concessions as possible, for money will be flowing into Chicago. Moreover, Nitti, still recovering from the police's assassination attempt, seems embroiled in what is now a personal battle with Mayor Cermak. Despite McGurn's notoriety, Nitti needs every button man he can gather, particularly because the rival Touhy gang of the Northwest suburbs is attempting to invade Outfit territories.

Perhaps to nobody's surprise in the Outfit, on February 15, Anton Cermak is shot in Miami by a Sicilian immigrant named Giuseppe Zangara, who is allegedly aiming at president-elect Franklin Roosevelt. Zangara is either the divine, serendipitous instrument of Nitti's revenge by sheer happenstance or part of a brilliant conspiracy that shines for its amazing luck. Cermak dies on March 5 after suffering from peritonitis and gangrene in his lungs.

Cermak had been approaching Roosevelt for more aid in fighting the gangsters, trying to enlist the federal government to pour more manpower into Chicago and no doubt to run interference for the inevitable retribution. His is the most propitious death Frank Nitti could ever imagine. Compounding this edginess to the situation, the justice system in Florida acts like a lynch mob, proving far more effective than the medical care administered to Cermak. It only takes authorities two weeks to charge Zangara, examine him with psychiatrists, try him, and sentence him to death. On March 20, fourteen days after Cermak passes away in the hospital, Zangara is the fortieth inmate to die in Florida's electric chair.

Several writers have made interesting cases for the Outfit's role in the shooting of Anton Cermak, suggesting that, rather than an attempt to assassinate Roosevelt, it is an Outfit hit on the Chicago mayor. In what are reminiscent of Kennedy-assassination conspiracy theories, the circumstances of the crime beg for further scrutiny, mostly because Cermak's death is so advantageous to Nitti and the Outfit. What is extremely peculiar is the fact that the shooter, Zangara, crazy or not, is silenced forever within a single month.

Oddly, McGurn is considered to have some complicity, because he is stopped on his way to Florida on the day before the assassination. On Valentine's Day, as if it were an anniversary reminder, police detectives are tipped off that there are Outfit men loitering around the Illinois Central Park Row train station. Two squads arrive to find McGurn and Capone button Harry Hochstein, who is now the Twentieth Ward committeeman, in the waiting room. Also with them are Outfit gunners "Three-Finger Jack" White and Charlie Feinberg. They admit they are ticketed for the next Florida-bound Zephyr; Hochstein claims "he is only there to see them off."

Later, at the detective bureau, as reporters crowd around McGurn in their familiar attempt to get a statement, he provides a bit of droll, comic relief as he announces, "I never get a chance to see the sun anymore."[11] All four of the men act outraged and victimized, but Charlie Feinberg gets the big laughs and the headline when he demands the detectives return his confiscated lunch bag, which contains six doughnuts. They are all released without charges, but the fact that they are headed to Miami twenty-four hours before the Cermak shooting begins to raise questions.

A contemporary theory suggests that McGurn and his team are on their way to deliver money or aid to Zangara, or possibly to kill the deranged immigrant after he shoots Cermak. In *The Outfit*, Gus Russo writes that municipal court judge John Lyle stated, "Zangara was a Mafia Killer, sent from Sicily to do a job and sworn to silence."[12]

When Cermak's stooge Lang fails to kill Nitti, he crosses the line of no return for politicians, especially from Chicago, where Outfit guns have silenced a prominent state's attorney, a well-known journalist, and a couple of judges. A corrupt mayor who attempts the heavy-handed tactics of the Outfit is certainly not immune. In addition, suspicions surface that Zangara owes a lot of money to the New York mob for gambling debts. Zangara allegedly confesses this to columnist Walter Winchell before he is executed. If indeed McGurn and his team are on their way to Miami to silence the little Sicilian after his crime, the state of Florida saves them the trouble and ends all the questions, as well as the answers.

31

I Am Innocent!

1933

In the early spring, Jack McGurn consciously decides to pull away from the Outfit, absolutely serious about transforming himself into a golf professional. He plays almost every day through the summer, mostly at the Maywood and Evergreen Park courses. He is in training and disciplined, with an enormous ability to concentrate on the present task that makes him a challenging golfer. By July, his dream of tournament play begins to seem more real, more possible. He is consistently shooting in the low seventies, with more frequent rounds hovering near or below scratch par. Louise plays with him several times a week, and her game improves greatly as well.

Keeping a low profile on the links is not enough to keep him out of the papers, even for spurious reasons. On July 17, the *Tribune* shockingly announces that McGurn has been shot while playing golf and has been carted off by the rival Touhy gang.[1] The reporters are all lined up and waiting for more news when McGurn drives up to his Oak Park home. They laugh and tell him that they thought he was dead. McGurn pauses on his steps and asks them, "Did you ever hear of a ghost shooting a sixty-six?"[2]

The Associated Press immediately sends a feed to papers all over America: "Jack McGurn wishes everyone to know he is not dead. He admitted in denying a report that he was dead, that there had been a lot of shooting, but it was only golf balls that were being hit."

During this period of attempted transformation, Jack and Louise have never seemed happier. McGurn still has to be very cautious when driving around Chicago; the cops will always pull him over and search for weapons if they recognize him. The satisfying feeling of being disciplined, of being in training, must make him feel hopeful and even successful. He continues to venture out on the course at Maywood Country Club, where many of the Chicago mobsters play, enjoying the recognition and comradeship. But golfing at Maywood is becoming more of a social occasion. He does his intense practice at the Evergreen Park course, where he can constantly work on correcting the flaws in his game. He is completely dedicated, with stepbrother Anthony acting as his caddy. His intensity of focus is impressive.

McGurn's further curtailing of his Outfit activities in order to play golf must make Frank Nitti happier as well. The slow shift from bootlegging to the other rackets is much easier without the flamboyant figures of the 1920s around. Curly Humphreys, Paul Ricca, and the boys are dressing down and even driving less expensive automobiles. Unlike the Capone years, their vision is to avoid press confrontation and all police, many of whom can no longer be counted on for "support." It is certainly not like the old days.

It isn't simply athletic talents that cause Jack McGurn to consider changing his life. Perhaps it is also love that inspires him to want to be more. For reasons unknown to anyone but Jack and Louise, their hearts seem to lead them onto this completely different path. Maybe part of this is a yearning for some kind of redemption. McGurn has essentially been in combat since 1923. Like a weary warrior who returns home, he suddenly desires to effect a dramatic change in his life. Although he is the most cold-blooded of killers, perhaps time, maturity, and his love for Louise have caused him to seek a more noble existence. No matter what reasons are compelling him, McGurn has reached a point where his haunted outlaw life no longer seems to appeal to him in the same manner as it has in the past.

Louise, despite her narcissism and penchant for pampering, has amazingly put up with an incredible amount of aggravation to be with her man. She also seems to desire a different kind of fame in the professional golf world and not the newspapers. Her fuse has been burning at both ends; the realities of jails, attorneys, and public vilification no longer hold any kind of romance. The dirt and grime of the justice system has become a constant nightmare. Together, they have positioned themselves to escape their insidious pasts, to wrangle their way out of the briar patch and quicksand. Morals or lack thereof notwithstanding, it seems they have composed a dream and with it hope for a radically different future. They both must suspect that this arrives a day late and a dollar short, but between the two of them, they have invented this new, lofty vision.

If Jack McGurn is ever to be admired, it is certainly for his ability to pursue an athletic goal. He came extremely far in a relatively short time as a boxer; as a golfer, he seems confident enough to throw himself into the profession at the highest level. Fighting in the ring as a teenager takes an unusual amount of courage, but golf is an amazing, demanding art in which prowess exists in a much more exalted realm.

This is the era of Bobby Jones, Tommy Armour, and Walter Hagen, men who are pioneering the birth of an enormously popular sport and form of recreation. That McGurn has the talent is obvious, but more illuminating is his ability to commit to and pursue such a worthy goal. This is his nature, an unexpected confluence of professional assassin and athlete. He is the warrior archetype, requiring no purity of the soul to pursue the ultimate success. Nevertheless, achieving championship status may demand a state of grace that eludes killers. The fledgling Professional Golf Association and myriad country clubs that are part of the explosive American interest in golf are not the French Foreign Legion, immediately forgiving of anyone's past. The movers and shakers, such as Bobby Jones, the ultimate conservative Southern gentleman, would no doubt have a hard time accepting Machine Gun Jack McGurn into their fold.

In August 1933, McGurn plays in the first qualifying round of the Western Open Golf Tournament at Olympia Fields Country Club in the far South Chicago suburbs. He looks the part—an athletic, dapper young man of thirty-one. After lying about his identity for all of his adult life, he is ready to claim a real place for himself. He is completely certain that this is the beginning of his great second chance. He is prepared to say good-bye to murder and mayhem forever, to once again become Vincent Gebardi, this time a legitimate professional golfer. He will lay his past to rest and bring honor, fame, and hopefully fortune to his family. He knows he can do it and feels confident that he will be able to reinvent himself completely, and Louise is right there with him.

In this hopeful state of reverie and the optimism of rebirth, he stupidly enters the tournament under his real name.[3] On the application, he claims to be a professional from the Evergreen Golf Club. Since Evergreen is a daily-fee public course, he assumes that if anybody asks around for Vincent Gebardi, he will be unknown, the safest tack to take. Certainly his attorney, Ben Feldman, is far more realistic and has reminded his client that there is still a vagrancy warrant out for him. McGurn must expect to be arrested any minute, but the month before the tournament brings no cops to his door. As the first week of August approaches, McGurn is excited beyond measure.

Louise spends time choosing her outfits for the weekend of the Western Open. She makes up three elegant ensembles of golf wear for McGurn, certain that he will still be in the hunt on the final Sunday. He has beautiful, expensive golf clothing, preferring long pants and light shirts to the Bobby Jones–style knickers that are the popular fashion. Louise is counting on being photographed, while McGurn will do anything to avoid it, a most unlikely possibility since the Western Open is one of the grand events of golf and one of the most heavily covered sporting events of the year.

In 1933, Olympia Fields Country Club is the world's largest golf-course complex, with four eighteen-hole courses that are nestled together just east of the Illinois Central railroad tracks. The club is bordered on the western edge by Kedzie Avenue, on the south by Lincoln Highway (Route 30, which extends all the way south to Florida), and on the east by Western Avenue, the longest street in America. Butterfield Creek runs through the middle of the first course and then turns due north, eventually running parallel to the Illinois Central tracks. The first course is 6,395 yards, with a total par of seventy-four. The fourth course, on which half the contenders will play, is 6,490 yards long, also with a total par of seventy-four.[4] The lowest sixty scorers after the first two days of the tournament will compete on the fourth course in the deciding round on Sunday.

Vincent Gebardi, who believes he can put his alter ego of Jack McGurn in a drawer, is determined to be in the ranks of those sixty golfers.

The holes are large on either course, which presents more of a challenge for the long-ball hitters like MacDonald Smith and Tommy Armour. The first hole of the first course is a monstrous 465 yards, boomerang-shaped from the tee in front of the clubhouse to the green that is surrounded by giant oak and maple trees. There is a deep sand bunker two hundred yards out on the right side of the fairway, which catches a lot of drives, a natural magnet for golf balls. The pros know to take it out of play by fading their drive left and past it.

On Friday, August 26, McGurn must be thrilled to find himself teeing off for the qualifying round. Neither the governors of Olympia Fields nor the officials of the Western Open have any idea who he is, yet he has made a fatal miscalculation.

Established in 1900, the Western Open is the most important annual golf event in Chicago and one of the most exalted in the nation. It is played on a different course each year. The tournament has traditionally been open to the highest cut of professionals from the various golf associations as well as to any amateur who can qualify, such as McGurn. This year, the field starts out at 240 players. McGurn has been honing his game for over a year, and the practice pays off as he shoots a respectable eighty-three in the first qualifying round on Friday. He two-putts a few too many greens and duffs a couple of short shots, probably from the sheer pressure of competing in a professional tournament.

What he doesn't know is that on that evening, before the weekend of the tournament, chief of detectives William Shoemaker has spotted the name of Vincent Gebardi as an entrant of the Western Open, reading it on the *Tribune* sports page.[4] He immediately calls municipal judge Thomas Green, who issues a warrant for McGurn's arrest under Judge Lyle's new hoodlum-vagrancy law. Green knows that McGurn has no proof of any legitimate income and that this is another chance to grab him. To them, he is and always will remain Jack McGurn. Consequently, on Saturday morning, Shoemaker sends sergeants John Griffith and John Warren to pick up McGurn at the tournament in Olympia Fields.

The two cops are extremely nervous about approaching the now infamous McGurn; they call lieutenant Frank McGillen at the Homewood station of the county highway patrol for reinforcements. McGillen must also be timorous: he enlists five other officers to come with him. They all descend on the Olympia Fields clubhouse, check the starting order, and make their way out to course number one, searching for the man who is now referring to himself as Vincent Gebardi.

The flock of blue-uniformed officers catches up to the gangster on the seventh fairway. Their target is having a brilliant round. He is partnered with a solemn young man named Howard Holtman from Beecher, Illinois, who is completely unaware of McGurn's identity, believing him to be Vincent Gebardi. Louise follows along the fairway with the spectators, tanned and dressed in a tight white dress, white hat, and anklet stockings. A fair golfer as well, she has competed in the Women's Western Open the previous week. According to the *Tribune*, she flashes around a three-carat diamond ring on her hand.[5]

It is at this moment that a form of cosmic justice is meted out for Machine Gun Jack McGurn. Although he will eventually die by the gun, the police cause his spiritual death on the seventh green of Olympia Fields, course number one.

Resplendent in gray flannel, well practiced, and at the height of his gift, he sees his dream coming true. McGurn has wangled his way into the realm of champions, in the world that most thrills him—not the world of the trigger and the muscle but the tranquil emerald domain of the golf course. Jack McGurn the killer has temporarily disappeared; Vincent Gebardi is once again an honest pretender, the way he started out in the boxing ring as a teenager. This must seem like the most enormous second chance ever dangled before a Roman Catholic machine gun killer who might be seeking some form of absolution. He no longer intends to shoot other men; he is more interested in shooting with the pros, the fantasy of every dedicated golfer.

As the players approach the seventh green, Lieutenant McGillen steps forward, clears his throat nervously, and reads the warrant. Up to this moment, McGurn thinks he is anonymous. He is playing one stroke under par for the first six holes, tied with tournament leader MacDonald Smith for the day. It will be kinder if McGillen just shoots him.

Holtman and McGurn listen to the reading of the warrant. The impassive Holtman reportedly doesn't flinch when he hears the true identity of his partner. McGurn remains silent until the police officer is finished, then civilly asks permission to finish the tournament. There is a lot of pressure on the police at this point. A crowd gathered and has increased since the uniformed officers surrounded McGurn on the green. To his credit, McGillen displays his humanity by agreeing to let the gangster continue.

The temporary stay of execution is granted, but with the police lowering a pall on the course, McGurn's game falls apart. He three putts, getting a double bogie.

After McGurn and Holtman make their drives from the eighth tee, with the law enforcement entourage following them, Louise finally explodes. Seeing that the police have destroyed McGurn's game, she screams at the lieutenant who is shadowing her husband, "Whose brilliant idea was this?" That the lieutenant refuses to answer further angers her. She appears to be a victim of police brutality in her innocent white outfit. She has already sensed that the crowd might be sympathetic toward her and Jack.

On the eighth tee, McGurn becomes very flustered. A photographer appears and snaps several pictures of him as he tees off. All the way up the fairway, McGurn duffs one shot after another as police and reporters hang in his peripheral vision. He finishes the hole with an eleven, seven strokes over par, a decimating tournament killer. The boyish face with the innocence of a Caravaggio has turned dark and sullen. His features are flushed with a combination of humiliation and anger that is barely under control.

A heartbroken McGurn driving off the eighth tee at the Western Open, 1933.
CHICAGO TRIBUNE ARCHIVES

With the police feet away, McGurn runs over to the photographer who has taken his picture and grabs him by the shirt, shaking him. "You busted up my game," he yells into the man's face. "I'll break your head." And then he gestures around him, adding, "Is it a crime to play golf?"[6] The photographer suddenly reminds himself who he has just infuriated, turns, and runs as Louise tries to stop McGurn from chasing him down. Another photographer, the *Tribune*'s Henry Schaeffer, snaps a picture of this. It is like a wacky Mack Sennett silent comedy, with people chasing each other in truly ill humor. Somehow McGurn is able to regain his composure and play on. Inside, he is fighting the greatest battle of his life.

Closeup: the agony of defeat, 1933. *CHICAGO TRIBUNE* ARCHIVES

The circus continues up the course. One of the golfers in front of McGurn, overcome with frustration of his own, rips up his scorecard and leaves the tournament. The man's partner, a corporation lawyer named Arthur Tilley, is forced by tournament officials to join McGurn's twosome. Tilley is a member of Olympia Fields and has been the Chicago Bar Association champion. Even though policemen, reporters, photographers, and fascinated throngs of spectators breech the sanctity of a major sporting event, the rules of play dictate that any contestant found single must join the twosome directly behind him. Tilley must be less than thrilled to find himself playing golf with Machine Gun Jack McGurn and the carnival surrounding him.

Strangely, Tilley has a steadying effect on McGurn, who shoots fairly well from the ninth hole on in, but his features remain almost stricken, as if he's had several shots of Novocain. He ends with scores of 45 on the first nine and 41 on the second. He is just twelve over par, which, added to the 83 he shot on the previous day, makes 169 for thirty-six holes. This eliminates him from advancing in the playoffs the next day. His heart must be pounding with the effort to grasp this sudden tragic reality, this brutally abrupt death of his dream. He must be as close to tears as he can ever be. Here is the killer blown to ground with a sense of loss that is indescribable.

Visibly crushed, McGurn shakes hands with his opponents as Lieutenant McGillen comes up and officiously taps him on the shoulder. McGurn and Louise are in shock, seeming to wilt. There is no trouble as the police prepare to escort them to their automobile. But they have an old friend in the crowd; as they step off the green, Michael L. Igoe, whom McGurn "campaigned" for in 1924 against Dean O'Banion's man for state's attorney, is now the South Park commissioner. He is also an ex–state representative as well as a member in good standing of Olympia Fields. Igoe is infuriated at the mayhem created by the police. In a combination of perhaps old loyalty to McGurn and Capone and his own feeling of outrage as a dedicated golfer, he approaches McGillen: "What's the idea? You're trying to pull a publicity stunt on this club! Who ordered this? What's the idea of arresting this man at his play? If you wanted to take him, why didn't you do it outside?"

The lieutenant freezes up and does not speak, getting nervous at the surprisingly irritated citizenry, with the appearance of public opinion being on the other side. A reporter from the *Daily News* answers for him, announcing that orders for McGurn's arrest had been issued by Judge Green when he saw Vincent Gebardi's name in the tournament on the sports page. Igoe swears at the reporter with a comment that is "unreportable."

At this point, McGurn, who has been relatively cool since chasing the photographer up the seventh fairway, senses where the crowd's sympathies lie. He plaintively addresses those gathered, asking, "I broke the law? I was out playing golf, so they arrest me. Trying to suppress crime, hey? It's the punks out pulling stick-ups who shoot the policemen. Why bother me? I haven't done anything for a year."

McGurn is probably telling the truth for the most part: he's been playing a lot of golf to prepare for this day. His reference to punks pulling stick-ups and shooting policemen has to do with the killings of a dozen Chicago policemen by young hoodlums and robbers just since January.[7]

A few other voices echo displeasure with the police, and the surrounding crowd seems to be changing into an ad hoc town debate, complete with eager members of the press. To keep McGurn from getting any more excited, the nervous and wildly unpopular McGillen allows the couple to drive their own coupe to the Homewood police station. To the delight of the crowd, in a final tableau that leaves its own priceless image, McGillen and Griffith squeeze themselves into the rumble seat. Escorted by several police vehicles, McGurn and Louise drive away with the two cops in the tiny space behind them. When they arrive, Louise drives off to get their lawyer, leaving McGurn to fend for himself at the detective bureau.

It is at this moment that the true persona of Jack McGurn becomes apparent, as he allows a cynical, brokenhearted, self-parodying, and certainly emotional utterance to come out of his mouth. His intelligence shines through his words, worthy of the sharp rhetoric of the young defiants who will come along in the tumultuous 1960s. As he is taken to a holding cell, followed by many reporters, he calls out to them before the steel door slams shut: "Just put it down that I'm booked for carrying concealed ideas."[8]

32

Only You Were Singing
in the Silence

1933

Chief Shoemaker does indeed book McGurn for vagrancy. Everyone chuckles at the image of McGurn in his impeccable, expensive, Walter Hagen–style golf flannels being charged as a vagrant. When the reporters demand to know what is happening to the gangster, Shoemaker dramatically announces that after his arraignment before Judge Green, McGurn will be questioned by the Federal Bureau of Investigation, which, though relatively new, already has a fierce and somewhat exalted reputation.

Perhaps consciously, Shoemaker drives a wedge between Jack McGurn and the Outfit by creating a concern that the iron-handed methods of the FBI will get the cornered gangster to talk about something. Apparently, this stimulates all kinds of concern at Outfit headquarters. Because of his upcoming federal interview, McGurn is held without bond over the weekend.

On Monday morning, August 28, small newspapers all over America are keeping abreast of McGurn's arrest at the Western Open. J. E. Lawrence, humorist and editor of the *Lincoln Star* in Nebraska, and ardent golfer, represents much of the country's amusement:

The officers have no appreciation of the ancient and honorable game. There was McGurn, out matching shots with the best of them. For the first six holes, he reeled off five straight pars, and for good measure, poured in a birdie, to be one under par at the seventh [hole]. Perhaps the officers should be forgiven that they do not understand golf requires concentration. Thanks to their interruption, Mr. McGurn required six strokes at the par-four seventh and then needed eleven at the eighth. When he came to the ninth, he gave up golf, and resumed the occupation he was supposed to be more familiar with by taking after a photographer who had endeavored to take his picture.

Then Lawrence adds, "McGurn has been known to the police as one of Chicago's toughest. It has been said that golf takes a man's mind off his work."[1]

The vagrancy arrest seems to snowball into wild conjecture about extreme interrogations of McGurn for any crime in the last several months. The *Tribune* jumps in with the bold headline MCGURN FACES KIDNAP QUIZ.[2] The story centers on McGurn's scheduled appearance before federal agents regarding the kidnapping of Jake "The Barber" Factor and other victims of gang ransom demands. A gang war between Factor and Roger Touhy is being waged while McGurn has been faithfully practicing for the Western Open. He isn't singled out, though, for the respondents of twenty-five other vagrancy warrants are also being questioned. He calmly and repeatedly tells anybody who confronts him that he hasn't done anything for a year except practice for the golf tournament.

McGurn's vagrancy charge is part of yet another round of arrests under the newly passed "criminal reputation" law, the extension of Judge Lyle's original idea. Just as he was a pioneer for the sanity tests, McGurn is the first person arrested for being a vagrant with a criminal reputation. Chicago law enforcement hopes it will help convict gangsters by judging their guilt partially on their criminal histories. In other words, if a person is a known criminal and cannot prove the source of his livelihood, he can be arrested and judged on just that, without committing any new crime. It is judicially medieval. The word "vagrant" is from the Old French word *waucrant*, meaning a person who wanders idly from place to place without lawful or visible means of support. Judge Lyle has apparently decided that the only way to outsmart the gangsters who drive Lincoln sedans and wear hundred-dollar suits is to make them all into vagrants.

This obviously desperate maneuver will be short-lived, because civil libertarians will recognize it for the thinly clad Byzantine ploy that it is. It does indicate how stymied the honest part of the system is in their war with the gangsters. But that minority must face the fact that they are really combating their own associates. Since the federal government is now entering Chicago's war against the gangs and making its presence known, many of the people who were on Capone's payroll are turning over a new leaf, quickly distancing themselves from the Outfit and their own pasts.

Famed FBI agent Melvin H. Purvis—who will be given credit for the execution-style shootings of John Dillinger and "Pretty Boy" Floyd the following year—has been sent back to the Chicago office by J. Edgar Hoover, supposedly on the insistence of President Roosevelt. This does complicate things for the judges, state's attorneys, and law enforcement officers who have flown too close to Capone's flame. The feds are in town in full force to watch, so everybody is severing old ties and cleaning up his act. Of course, many will gravitate back to form even more lucrative deals with the new Chicago Outfit, but the abuses will never be quite as open in Cook County again.

In addition to the presence of the Department of Justice, a Senate committee on racketeering, led by New York Democratic senator Royal S. Copeland, is scheduled to begin public hearings on October 3.[3] The committee had held hearings a few months before, which brought Iowa Democratic senator Louis Murphy to Chicago to survey the rackets. Murphy meets with Chicago police officials, federal operatives, mayor Edward J. Kelly, and state's attorney's investigators. Afterward, Murphy concludes that thirty-five of the industries in Chicago that were victims of the rackets are engaged in interstate commerce. This information allows the federal government "an entering wedge for prosecution of gangsters," affecting McGurn. All those picked up under Chicago's new criminal-reputation gang law will also be subjected to federal inquisition to determine if they had any connection to kidnapping or racketeering.[4]

On Sunday, August 27, McGurn appears in a show up at the detective bureau on South State Street. He loudly complains to Chief Shoemaker that Judge Green's warrant included only the names of "minor" criminals; the leaders of the gangs are not being summoned. With Al Capone in prison, McGurn means Frank Nitti and his next-in-command, a pronouncement that must come as a shock to Nitti when he reads about it on Monday. The steadfast McGurn, a strict adherent to *omerta*, the Sicilian code of silence, seems to be quite alienated from his bosses. Shoemaker agrees with McGurn in front of several reporters, promising that more lists for warrants are being prepared with the names of "big shots." Such a prospect must make the hierarchy of the Capone Outfit very nervous; their biggest gun appears rattled and has told the newspapers that he wants everyone with him under the spotlight.

The seed of doubt so unknowingly planted by Chief Shoemaker begins to sprout, as it comes at a time when McGurn has made himself vulnerable, a man interested only in his sport but still very much considered a public enemy. The arrest and humiliation at his dream performance during the Western Open have clearly unnerved him. He has aspired to a different life through his athletic talents. The arrest at Olympia Fields is such a crushing defeat for McGurn that his entire outlook and attitude appear to have changed overnight. His words are resentful toward the people to whom he has been so loyal. With Capone in prison, he is apparently reassessing his entire affiliation with the Outfit and the ultraconservative Frank Nitti, who has never personally cared for McGurn, considering him much too gregarious.

On Wednesday, August 30, after a weekend behind bars, McGurn, still dressed elegantly but rumpled from his captivity, appears before Judge Green in felony court on the vagrancy charge. Having read about his well-publicized misfortune at the golf tournament, crowds of people try to catch a glimpse of the dapper killer. Benjamin Feldman announces, steps up, and immediately goes on the attack, belittling the vagrancy sham. He requests a delay: "This is a brand-new law. I must have time to determine the legality of such a legislative act which allows men like my client to be arrested while playing golf."[5]

Judge Green answers, "Your client was arrested because he has a reputation for being engaged in criminal practices against the good of society. You must bring in your witnesses to prove this is not so if you wish an acquittal. The law is not like it used to be."[6]

McGurn (far left) and attorney Benjamin Feldman (second from left) before Judge Green, 1933. COLLECTION OF JOHN BINDER

Green sets a new hearing date for September and refuses to reduce McGurn's bond, set at ten thousand dollars, which his attorneys immediately produce. McGurn returns on September 6, of course without any witnesses who can attest to the fact that he earns an honest living.

Nevertheless, Benjamin Feldman is waiting for Judge Green with one of the neatest little setups since Dean O'Banion sold Johnny Torrio the Sieben Brewery as it was due to be raided. Feldman has McGurn take the stand and pointedly, if not dramatically, asks him how a vagrant could possibly play golf with a judge.

Apparently Judge Green seems to have been afraid this would surface. His face reddening, he immediately interrupts: "I know what you are driving at. It is true that I once played with McGurn at the Evergreen public-fee course. I was with two men I knew, and McGurn joined us to make a foursome. I didn't know who he was. That might happen to anybody."[7]

McGurn's trials and hearings are big draws for reporters—they are hungry beasts who feed on hypocrisy. There is a burst of uncontainable laughter, which is ended by Judge Green's jackhammering gavel. The jury stays out nineteen minutes; they find Judge Green innocent of playing

An extremely unhappy McGurn giving "the look," 1933. COLLECTION OF JOHN BINDER

golf and McGurn guilty of the new vagrancy law, imposing the maximum penalty of six months in jail.[8] Before he can be led to the lockup, stalwart bondsman Louis Cowan appears and posts a cash appeal bond for the ten thousand dollars. Jack McGurn never serves another minute for vagrancy.

A humorous article in the *New York Mirror* a month later, which shows a picture of McGurn swinging a golf club, states, "The law grabs him frequently but doesn't seem to hold on."[9] Nevertheless, the law has done tremendous damage to the psyche and spirit of Jack McGurn, who was tantalizingly close to transforming himself into a professional athlete. He was within a hair of changing his life and his entire future along with it. Was this ever really possible? Could Machine Gun Jack McGurn and everything that he did simply disappear back into the persona of Vincent Gebardi, a pro golfer?

Perhaps the final, greatest insult to McGurn is that the trumped-up vagrancy charge, utilized with such pettiness, has interrupted such a grand dream. He has always been aware of the risks and penalties of his chosen profession, willing to accept the potential consequences of the life of the gangster. He isn't remotely naive; everybody who plays eventually pays. He is one of the denizens of the underworld who frequently proves that axiom. Still, justice apparently has its surprises in the same manner as injustice, a fact of Chicago life that he now must own for himself.

At this point, with luck seemingly abandoning him, events begin to suggest that nothing will ever be as good as when Al Capone was in control. The persona named Vincent Gebardi disappears, never to return. Moreover, life for Jack McGurn has just begun to go completely sour.

On October 27, petite bondsman Louis Cowan is shot dead by rival gangsters believed to be from the Touhy gang. This killing severs another link with the Capone legal machine of days of yore, and it tears another hole in the safety net that has protected McGurn from the law since 1925. It will end up a moot point, for Jack McGurn will never be arrested again.

On December 5, 1933, just in time for Christmas, the consumption and sale of hard liquor once again becomes legal. The Prohibition that conspired to create Jack McGurn and the beer wars is gone, like Al Capone. At first there isn't even enough alcohol to sell. Many of the watering holes, speakeasies, and blind pigs are boarded up. The Outfit is happy to sell off its remaining stocks at inflated prices, a farewell victimization of the Depression-stricken masses. As Edward Behr humorously notes in *Prohibition*, New Jersey governor Harry Moore solves the state's dearth of alcoholic products by announcing, "Liquor has been sold illegally for thirteen years and it will not hurt if this is done a few days more."

33

I Don't See Anyone, Anywhere

1934

On May 14, the Illinois Supreme Court rules that the state vagrancy law—or "the reputation law," as the press calls it—is unconstitutional. This immediately lets off the hook Louie "Two Gun" Alterie, James "King of the Bombers" Belcastro, and Jack McGurn. Many voices in the press are stunned that a law that has led to hundreds of arrests and has put many gunmen behind bars has been upset by the high court. The cries resound that just when Chicago seemed well on the road to eliminating its gangsters, the court has taken away one of its most important tools. But giving a man six months any time he can be picked up off the street cannot be tolerated in a democratic society. The Illinois Supreme Court holds that "before liberty or property may be taken from anyone, regardless of his reputation, there must be proof that he is in fact a habitual criminal."[1]

This is a shining moment for the US Constitution, which triumphs over "the worthy purpose" of the vagrancy act. The law had been in danger of going repressively overboard with legislative efforts to curb crime. The legislature, desperate to find a weapon in their war with the gangsters, tremendously endangered constitutional guarantees. As badly as Chicago wants Jack McGurn and the others of his sort, it is clear that there are sufficient laws for punishing criminal acts already on the books and that it is up to the police to work harder and produce greater vigilance in their tasks.

Of course, a little more honesty in law enforcement and the judiciary would also prove effective, but the traditional symbiotic relationship among ward politics, graft, and crime has always been the machinery underneath Chicago. It is a deeply entrenched, time-honored system that simply cannot evaporate overnight, for there are far too many people who have investments in the subterranean designs that make the city work.

As bad an idea as Prohibition was, striking down the vagrancy act shows a modicum of balance returning to America. Perhaps it is the Depression that is the catalyst for transforming the repressive atmosphere in government. People recognize that the "noble experiment" of dry laws and the attitudes that spawned them also created the bootleggers and gangsters, and Americans profoundly resent these attempts to legislate morality.

With booze legal and the possibilities of endless nightlife once again a reality, the Outfit turns more to gambling. Nitti and the powers that be throw McGurn a bone: they put him in charge of a new, swanky, and hopefully lucrative gambling den. Because McGurn is a celebrity in various Chicago crowds and especially the underworld, the thought is that he will attract the money and the gamblers. Working with him is his stepbrother Anthony.[2] They formally open the 225 Club on the Near North Side on Wednesday night, June 20. Invitations are sent to a lot of prospective customers, so undercover police officers attend, looking for any known Capone associates. There is a party with free drinks and a "preview" of the gambling facilities.

Sometime after midnight, a "carelessly discarded cigarette" starts a fire that ruins an estimated one thousand dollars' worth of new light fixtures and furniture. It's not clear if the fire is a warning of some kind or perhaps even the incendiary act of one of the detectives. The following morning, the press announces that Machine Gun Jack McGurn is reputed to own half interest in the club.[3] It's also not clear if this is correct or if McGurn is more of a manager and front man; whatever the truth, the club is damaged by smoke and doomed. Even if it is an accident, it is still an indication that McGurn's luck is beginning to go from bad to worse. He has also begun drinking more with the growing stresses of not having money.

Louise apparently has nurtured a golf fantasy of her own. After all, it is a form of show business; she was highly photographed at the Western Open, the outcome notwithstanding. Undaunted by that degrading experience, she attempts to accomplish what her gangster husband has not been able to do. She qualifies to play in the Women's State Public Parks Golf Championship in Lincoln Park in August 1934. Shooting a score of 106, she is only ten strokes off the leader, but she is still eliminated from the tournament, also signifying the end of her public golf career.[4]

The law is still afraid of the power of Al Capone. To make certain that the incarcerated Big Fella cannot communicate with his organization in Chicago, he is transferred from Atlanta to the rock of Alcatraz on August 22 as prisoner number eighty-five, living—if it can be considered that—in cell number eighty-one. He is no longer able to talk with anyone but his immediate family.

The axis completely turns as Frank Nitti, Louis Campagna, Curly Humphreys, and Paul Ricca now have unconditional control of the Outfit. At the same time, the FBI is growing into a police organization that has a presence in every large American city, especially Chicago. The Napoleonic J. Edgar Hoover is becoming as much a public hero as the gangsters are public enemies.

Hoover, who seems to be waging an almost personal war against any and all mobsters, has not forgotten Jack McGurn; however, he seems to have missed the fact that the US Supreme Court has put McGurn's Mann Act troubles to permanent rest. As it will be with all the high-profile criminals of the 1930s, Hoover is like a gila monster who won't let go of something until it's dead. Neither will the eager prosecutors who work for the Department of Justice. In a May 17 letter from Hoover to Alexander Holtzoff, special assistant to the attorney general, Director Hoover responds to Holtzoff's question whether Machine Gun Jack McGurn and Louise Rolfe should be further prosecuted for the Mann Act charges from their November 1, 1929, indictment: "The Bureau desires to be advised concerning the above pending indictment at your earliest convenience in order that, if additional investigation is desired, the same may be conducted without further delay."[5]

Of course eventually somebody who is more familiar with the "no means no" verdict of the high court straightens Hoover out. The director of the FBI realizes that he is not more important than the US Supreme Court and turns his attention to bank robbers and outlaws like Bonnie and Clyde and "Baby Face" Nelson, who are running around the country causing mayhem with their Thompsons and Browning automatic rifles. This particular widespread lawlessness is indicative of the desperate nightmare of the Great Depression.

As if things are not bad enough, McGurn and Louise lose their golf mentor, Willie Harrison, in January 1935. Harrison's charred body is discovered in a barn in Ontarioville, Illinois. The police theorize that he was killed by the infamous Alvin Karpis, whom Willie had joined in 1933 when he became a part of the kidnapping of St. Paul beer brewer Edward G. Brenner.[6] Harrison was in charge of laundering the ransom money and apparently shortchanged his pals.

34

February May Be Short, but It's the Worst Month

1935–1936

Like an Aristotelian character with a tragic flaw, Jack McGurn begins a descent in 1935 that will seal his fate. It is dramatic, pathetic, and Shakespearean in the blood that will be left on the stage when the final curtain falls. It will take an enormous toll on his family.

McGurn's robust, athletic body has been challenged in recent months as he begins suffering from an abscess over the wound in his lung, a left-over from the gunshots delivered by the Gusenbergs at the McCormick Hotel in March 1928. He is in constant, nagging pain. Certainly his poor state of psychological health and his tremendously increased alcohol consumption have begun to affect his immune system.

In the third week of February 1935, McGurn is admitted to Mount Sinai Hospital, where he is reported to be in serious condition. Dr. H. A. Gussin performs a surgical procedure on February 24 that finally offers relief.[1] McGurn begins to make a quick recovery, but his presence at Mount Sinai is accidentally discovered by a *Chicago Tribune* reporter when he "checks up" on the old Capone Outfit boys following chief bodyguard Frankie Rio's succumbing to heart disease the previous Saturday. The reporter notes that Louise Rolfe has been by her husband's bedside most of the time.

It seems that almost everything is falling apart for McGurn, who is at odds with Frank Nitti. Consequently, McGurn has become extremely paranoid. His house in Oak Park has been foreclosed. He and Louise have now moved into an apartment at 1224 North Kenilworth Avenue, with Louise's twelve-year-old daughter, Bonita, who lives with them off and on.[2] Perhaps Mabel Rolfe becomes unable to take care of a teenager again, or maybe Louise feels that Bonita's presence will help stabilize her husband and their shaky life. Unfortunately, with his income dwindling and his fortunes falling, McGurn has now begun drinking even more heavily and behaving more irrationally, which will be attested to by both the police and Louise. Confirming this, Oak Park police lieutenant Harry Wilson will later testify regarding McGurn's drinking and paranoia: "A dozen times McGurn has called us to say that his life was in danger. Last October we went to the house on a call and found him locked in a clothes closet. He wouldn't come out until he was sure we were policemen."[3]

This rather uncharacteristic behavior indicates that things have begun to go terribly wrong for Jack McGurn, especially in terms of his relationship with the Outfit. With the Depression at its peak and Nitti excluding him from his traditional duties, McGurn is involved in sports betting and small gambling venues. The Outfit is headquartered at the Morrison Hotel, where Nitti and the boys hold council. McGurn is conspicuously absent and constantly in need of money. In addition, the new Outfit hierarchy has learned that McGurn has asked for some kind of help from Albert J. Prignano, the state representative of the Seventeenth District and Twentieth Ward Democratic committeeman.[4] Prignano is linked closely to Chicago mayor Edward J. Kelly, who is appointed in 1933 after the murder of Anton Cermak.

Prignano, an old friend of Capone's, has an adversary for ward committeeman in Republican alderman William V. Pacelli, whom Frank Nitti is behind. With the Outfit's eye on national labor unions, their plan for expanding into the rest of the country includes first removing any obstacles in Chicago. There is growing tension between Nitti and Prignano; when the Enforcer learns that McGurn is seeking aid from Pacelli's opponent, Nitti is infuriated that the seemingly errant assassin has sidestepped him in order to get some kind of political support. Regardless of McGurn, the Outfit agenda is to get rid of Prignano, which happens on December 29, 1935, when the politician is gunned down in front of his family at his Bunker Street apartment by three men. This also sends a message to McGurn, who knows he has crossed the line; he certainly suspects that he is now on Nitti's short list.

McGurn has spent most of his afternoons at a handbook in Melrose Park, taking small bets. It is located in the defunct Citizens State Bank at Broadway and Main Street. Phone records will show that Louise frequently calls him there. Meanwhile, because of his erratic behavior, McGurn has become a perceived danger to his longtime employers. Nitti is probably convinced that Capone's favorite boy is now *squilibratu*—deranged. He is deemed a loose cannon and certainly a serious threat to them if he decides to talk about anything he shouldn't. Consequently, a plan is made to set things straight where Jack McGurn is concerned. It will have to be very good plan, because McGurn is still assumed to be an extremely dangerous man.

McGurn spends the Thursday evening before Valentine's Day at the wake of his close friend, Giuseppe Circella, Caponite Nick Circella's father.[5] Giuseppe is waked at his home on South Austin Boulevard. McGurn also attends the funeral for Circella on Valentine's morning at St. Francis Church, accompanying the family out to Hillside to Mount Carmel Cemetery where he sees several Outfit members and old friends. Somebody whom he still trusts from the old days suggests joining him for bowling later that evening. Lately McGurn has bowled regularly. He makes the date with two men, undoubtedly ones with whom he is close.

In an FBI wiretap recorded on January 28, 1960, Curly Humphreys will allege that Claude Maddox ("Johnny Moore") from the Circus Gang and another unknown man are the killers who accompany McGurn.[6] An excellent candidate for the second man is Capone shooter Willie Heeney, whom McGurn is still friendly with. They agree to meet at his favorite spot, the Avenue Recreation Rooms at 805 North Milwaukee Avenue, where the bowling alleys and pool room are on the second floor.

According to Louise's initial testimony, McGurn comes home and takes a nap after the funeral. He sleeps until almost 11:00 PM, when he awakens and has a Valentine dinner with her. After eating, he leaves to meet his two pals for a few drinks; there will be alcohol found in his stomach by the medical examiner, including signs that he'd been drinking steadily all day. The Avenue Recreation lanes are frequented by many gangsters, remaining open until the early hours of the morning. McGurn and the other two men enter the bowling alley at about 12:50 AM, not quite an hour past Valentine's Day.

There are only four bowling lanes, so McGurn and his two chums wait about ten minutes for one to become available. They are given lane number one, which is the closest to the stairway. They take off their coats and hats and begin to bowl. According to the witness accounts, three men quietly come up the stairway, arriving at about 1:05 AM.

Jack McGurn, the professional killer and recent paranoid, certainly has had that honed sixth sense since he was an adolescent. Unlike most people, he knows when somebody is standing on the other side of a door. His attention is drawn to supposedly empty spaces when they are not the voids they appear to be. When the Gusenbergs let loose on him and Nick Mastro in the McCormick Smoke Shop in 1928, he is inexplicably watching the doorway before they appear. Similar to his abilities in the boxing ring, he is able to feint to the left before the bullets can find his heart or his head. These are among the required talents of his chosen profession.

Outlaws like McGurn seem more connected with their reptilian brain and their primordial instincts. This ability is certainly out of fear as well as knowledge of the violent intentions of other men, a unique gift that is more indicative of combatants, something that most people have lost with evolution.

But at this particular moment, sporting with trusted friends, after many months of stress, misery, and too much alcohol, those instincts of survival are rusty, corroded over with a fuzzy patina like the terminals on an old automobile battery.

Several things happen simultaneously. One of the three men who have appeared at the top of the stairs shouts, "This is a stick-up! Nobody move!"[7] McGurn turns toward them as they follow the announcement with several shots fired into the ceiling, but this is purely a diversion—their real work is already finished. Everybody else in the small bowling alley dives for cover, a true Chicago instinct. At almost the same time, one

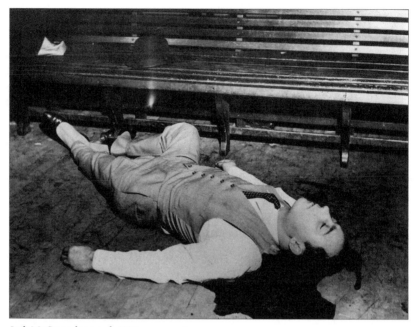

Jack McGurn deceased, 1936. UPI, AUTHOR'S COLLECTION

of his bowling partners walks up behind McGurn and fires two .45-caliber bullets into the back of his head. He never knows what hits him. He crumples onto his back; a fan of blood spreads from his decimated head onto the varnished planks of the bowling alley.

The three arrivals run back down the stairs. McGurn's two bowling partners grab their coats and the score sheet, which has their first names on it. They also disappear down the stairs and out onto Milwaukee Avenue. There are a total of twenty men in the bowling alley; seventeen of them run outside, following the shooters. The police will only find two souls alive when they arrive.

Vincent Gebardi and his alter ego, Machine Gun Jack McGurn, the professional killer who kills professional killers, will never see his thirty-fifth birthday.

In McGurn's pockets are a pack of cigarettes, $3.85, and two unused boxing tickets for the Bath-Burman fight that night at the Chicago Stadium. However, he is unarmed—not that a gun would have helped him.[8] Also found on McGurn's body is a 1936 Illinois automobile identifica-

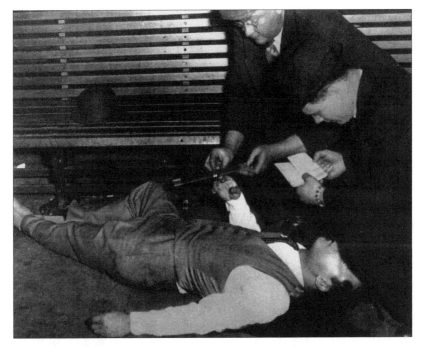

Coroner Schlagel taking McGurn's fingerprints, 1936. COLLECTION OF JOHN BINDER

tion card, except it is issued to William Belmonte of 5541 West Harrison Street. It lists a Ford coupe, which McGurn had driven to the bowling alley. It vanishes with the killers.

By the time the police are called at 1:07, everyone who had been in the room prior to the shooting has fled, except for proprietor William Aloisio and porter Tony Mascarella.[9] Police lieutenant Garrett Fleming responds, along with officers P. Ward, B. Walsh, H. Urban, and E. Mangan. Twenty minutes later, Deputy Coroner Schlagel arrives and takes McGurn's fingerprints from his dead hand.[10] Once his identity is confirmed, the word goes out. The people of Chicago are hardly surprised.

J. J. Kearns, one of the medical examiners under Frank J. Walsh, the Cook County coroner, performs the postmortem examination on McGurn. He notes that the first bullet entered the victim's neck at the first cervical vertebra, three centimeters to the right of the midline. It is a dev- astating wound; the bullet passed upward, extensively lacerating the right cerebral hemisphere, the corpus callosum, and the left temporal lobe of

Louise weeping for her Jack, 1936. COLLECTION OF JOHN BINDER

his brain. At that point looking more like a mushroom than a missile, the bullet exited to the right of the eye socket, its deadly path "through and through."

The second round was fired almost instantly, even before McGurn dropped to the floor. It entered the right side of his head, at the level of the tip of his nose and three centimeters to the back of where the jaw hinges to the skull, causing "extensive fracturing of the petrous portion of the temporal bone, perforating laceration of the temporal lobe of the right cerebral hemisphere." The .45-caliber copper-jacketed bullet is found in the parietal lobe of the right side of the brain. It was an immediate and painless death.[11]

Not even an hour after the shooting, police officers go to McGurn's apartment on Kenilworth Avenue in Oak Park. It is just after 2:00 AM, but surprisingly, Louise doesn't answer the door. Two more police officers go to Josephine DeMory's apartment on Morgan Street and tell the family that Jack has been shot and killed.

Two hours later, sergeant Francis Donohue of the coroner's office, accompanied by two police officers, returns to McGurn's apartment and tries again. This time Louise, half dressed and cinching a robe around her, opens the door, her mascara running down her cheeks in twin black streaks. Since their first visit, she has returned home, and a reporter from one of the Chicago papers has already told her that her husband has been shot. Donohue laconically asks her, "Heard about Jack?" Now she knows that her worst fear has materialized. She sobs, "My God, how bad is it?" Donohue, with the empathy of a stone, says, "He's gone."[12]

Louise gets dressed, putting on her beautiful ermine-collared coat. It is the coldest February in Chicago in thirteen years, with the temperature below zero, but she still has the presence of mind to look fashionable for the press. She weeps continuously.

Donohue takes her to the Racine Avenue police station, where she is interviewed in the detective division by captain Martin Mullen. Also present are lieutenant Richard Barry, sergeant Kyran Phelan, and police stenographer P. J. Broehl. Her answers to Mullen's questions will show that she is still the evasive, stonewalling moll:[13]

Mullen: What is your husband's name?

Louise: Vincent Gebardi alias Jack McGurn.

Mullen: How long have you been married?

Louise: Four years.

Mullen: What does your husband do for a living?

Louise: I don't know.

Mullen: When did you last see your husband?

Louise: Between 11:00 and 11:30 PM, February 14, 1936.

Mullen: Where did he say he was going?

Louise: He said he was going bowling.

Mullen: Do you know where he bowls?

Louise: No.

Mullen: Was anyone with him when he left the house?

Louise: No.

Mullen: Had he received any phone calls and did he make any phone calls before leaving the house?

Louise: No.

Mullen: Of your own knowledge, do you know if he had any trouble with anyone lately?

Louise: No.

Mullen: You know that he was shot and killed last evening?

Louise: Yes, a reporter came to my house and told me.

Mullen: Do you know of any reason why he should have been killed?

Louise: No.

Mullen: Do you know if he belonged to any secret or labor organization?

Louise: None.

By this time, Mullen and his men have rounded up at least three escapees from the bowling alley and taken their statements. They will not learn anything from any of them. They immediately follow the lead of the driver's license found on McGurn, visiting William Belmonte at his home on Harrison Street. Belmonte has just arrived with his friend Tony Lambert; they have been at the prizefights at the Chicago Stadium, the same fights for which McGurn had tickets but did not attend. They arrest both men and bring them to the Twenty-Ninth District station.

Belmonte turns out to be McGurn's tailor. When asked why the deceased gangster had a license issued in his name, Belmonte claims that in December 1935, when bringing McGurn some suits to try on, he was asked to be a "reference" for his client's prospective car purchase. Belmonte, the dupe, received the identification card by mail and then brought it to McGurn.[14]

None of the cops believe that Belmonte is that stupid or naive. Obviously, his extensive criminal history prevented McGurn from being able to acquire a legal driver's license. Because he was giving his tailor steady business, a deal was struck. Needless to say, Belmonte did not want to say no to the gangster and complied fully with his request. Belmonte explains that he always did business with his client in his home in Oak Park. When interrogated about the driver's license, Belmonte claims, "He [McGurn] asked me if he could use my name as a reference in buying an automobile and I told him he could." The detectives ask him if he signed any papers as a "reference" for McGurn, to which Belmonte answers, "Yes, but I don't know what it was that I signed."[15] When he is again questioned at the inquest, Belmonte confesses what the police obviously know, admitting, "I let him use my name because he was a good customer, and he said it wouldn't be easy for him to get them [the license plates and the identification card] under his own name."[16]

The thoroughness and thoughtful planning of McGurn's murder become more evident when his Ford coupe is discovered abandoned on Ada Street two days after his death. Police officers A. T. Linderman and I. H. Pearson find that the ignition leads have been hotwired and the car had been driven there shortly after the killing. They also find a key ring on the floor of the car with a key to a safety deposit box; it is numbered, but the bank identification, as usual, is unmarked.[17]

At 7:00 AM, Captain Mullen brings Louise to the Cook County Morgue, where she is shown Jack's body. It is a freezing cold morning, and she walks with her ermine-collared coat clutched around her. The only time she has been awake this early in the day is if she hasn't yet gone to bed, which is certainly the case on this dreadful morning. Her features are stricken and pale with exhaustion. After viewing her husband's corpse, she becomes hysterical and collapses, sobbing in a corner. She remains there with a white handkerchief over her mouth and nose until the coroner's inquest convenes four hours later at 11:00 AM.

As the inquest commences, assistant state's attorney Malachi Coghlan questions Anthony Gebardi and Louise while Josephine DeMory, short and stocky, weeps quietly throughout the proceedings. Mercifully, she is not forced to testify. When asked what his stepbrother did for a living, Anthony tells Coghlan that he was a golf pro at Maywood Country Club. Coghlan, apparently prepared for this from Anthony's statement to the police earlier that morning, calls up James Killgallon, the president of the club, who refutes Anthony. He claims that McGurn often played golf there but was never an employee.[18] Anthony's lie is ignored because there are more important issues at hand.

William Aloisio, the proprietor of the bowling alley, takes the stand. He tells the same story to the coroner's jury as he did to Mullen that morning.[19] Three men came in, announced a "stick-up," and began firing their guns. Aloisio ducked under a pool table until it was over. He can't identify any of the offenders, claiming he didn't know Jack McGurn even though the gangster frequented his establishment. He has nothing more to offer. Later in the day, Captain Mullen describes Aloisio's statement and testimony as "sheer poppycock," adding, "We can't blame Aloisio for lying and it won't do much good to question him again. He knew McGurn and he knew the men that were with him at the bowling alley. He is in danger of being murdered himself."[20]

Next in the witness chair is Aloisio's employee Tony Mascarella, who is the porter and maintenance man. Tony takes the unimpeachable tack of the "Chicago nap," claiming he was asleep, albeit twenty feet from where McGurn was standing when he was felled. He was awakened by the shots and saw a man backing out the door with a gun. Tony doesn't know McGurn or anybody who was with him. When asked who his employer is, he claims he doesn't even know Aloisio's name, only that he is called

Smokes. He is obviously terrified and nearly speechless. Earlier that morning, when Captain Mullen asked if his statement was true and correct, Mascarella answered, "The statement is true, but I refuse to sign it."[21]

Figuring discretion is the better part of valor, Tony the porter is smart enough to avoid perjury and is already coming down with a virulent case of Chicago amnesia. Following him is perhaps the worst witness, twenty-year-old Edward Bonarek, the pin setter of the bowling alley, who admits he had previously seen McGurn there two weeks before. The coroner and the police perk up at this candid illumination, eagerly expectant that similar truths are forthcoming. But young Bonarek claims he was focused on setting up the bowling pins at the far end of the alley. He keeps it short and simple: "I heard some shooting and I thought it was fire-crackers and I looked out again and seen a man sprawled out on the floor and I grabbed my coat and ran out and went home."[22]

Coroner Whalen asks Louise to take the witness chair. She sobs constantly, holding the handkerchief to her mouth, which Whalen politely asks her to remove so the stenographer can hear her answers. Coghlan asks her if it is true that she has a twelve-year-old daughter, to which Louise replies, "Oh, don't ask me. Can't you see how I feel?"

As her past has so amply shown, she knows how to play the victim, trying to convince the jury that she and McGurn were leading the familiar Depression-era life. "We were living quietly in the little flat when the police got me," she says, adding, "We were dirt poor." This statement gets a stifled chuckle from several people, as she sits in the witness chair in her expensive coat and costly waved hair.[23]

With a consistency like the progression of time, Louise gives the exact same replies to the state's attorney's questions as she did a few hours before to the police. So do all the witnesses who were at the bowling alley; they definitely know better than to say anything about anybody. Frustrated, Mullen and Coghlan's investigators ask for a continuance so they can gather more evidence, which is granted by Coroner Whalen, who announces that the inquest will reconvene on March 4.

Later that afternoon, back on Morgan Street, everyone in the Gebardi-DeMory family falls apart with grief. Anthony Gebardi pulls himself together and arranges for his stepbrother's body to be brought to Rago's

Funeral Parlor at 624 North Western Avenue. Capone's bodyguard and faithful lieutenant, Frankie Rio, who died of heart failure the previous February, was the last man to unite the old group at Rago's. Louise, distraught but still as fashion-conscious as ever, goes home and chooses a blue-checked three-piece suit, a light blue shirt, and a navy necktie for her husband's final journey. McGurn's body and his last elegant suit of clothes are reunited at Rago's.

The official statement from the undertaker is that there will be no wake and that the funeral home will be closed for the evening. But the press is almost as excited as they were on St. Valentine's Day. They know better about gangster obsequies. An undaunted *Herald Examiner* reporter makes a call to the funeral parlor and is surprised when Caponite and Circus Gang denizen "Tough Tony" Capezio answers the phone. The reporter asks Capezio if he is at the wake, to which the gangster replies, "Who did you say? McGurn? I don't know the party." "Isn't there a wake there?" asks the reporter. Capezio acquiesces, "Yeah, there are some people here." The reporter, pressing his luck, asks, "Is Louise there?" Tough Tony growls, "Aw, I said I didn't know any of these people."[24]

The wake, attended by several of the old Outfit boys, is held in a back room near the rear entrance of Rago's. Someone turns off the light over the door so that the watchful reporters cannot clearly identify the mourners as they go in and out through the alley. The boys send one of Rago's employees out a few times for seltzer water; they are apparently drinking heavily, toasting their fallen comrade.

The next morning at 11:00, the funeral is held at Rago's. Even though McGurn has allegedly died penniless—except for the $3.85 found in his pocket—the reported rumor is that the boys chip in and purchase a ten-thousand-dollar casket for their departed fellow. This comes to pass, as a magnificent bronze casket is provided from persons who remain anonymous. It will only cost one thousand dollars for the funeral, with everything but the casket included.

There are fifteen floral wreaths, with the largest marked FROM THE BOYS. Oddly, Louise, who claims she is still completely broke, purchases an extremely expensive four-foot-tall arrangement of red roses, which is shaped like a heart with a dagger through it. It stands at the head of

McGurn's hearse pulling away from Rago's Funeral Home, 1936. CHICAGO HISTORY MUSEUM

the coffin, inscribed TO MY HUSBAND. A large white heart—sent by his first wife, Helen, and their daughter, Josephine—is at McGurn's feet. Another arrangement, a six-foot column of white rosebuds and lilies, is inscribed FROM AL. It is provided by Capone's mother, Teresa, who is still close to Josephine DeMory.

Fifty people attend the abbreviated service. Josephine is ushered into the room with her daughter, Angeline, and her four remaining sons. Upon seeing the coffin, Josephine breaks everyone's heart, wailing, "My Jeemie, my Jeemie," as if mourning for a little boy. Angeline DeMory, also weeping uncontrollably, collapses, adding to the pathetic drama. Mafalda Capone, Al's sister, runs over and supports Angeline, with Frank Gebardi's help.

Six pallbearers carry the casket to a waiting hearse, which leads a cortege of twenty-seven automobiles to the familiar Mount Carmel Cemetery in suburban Hillside. McGurn has put many men there during his illustrious career. The temperature is hovering near zero when the mourners gather around the frozen rectangle of open earth near Angelo

DeMory's grave. It is a rather barren section of Mount Carmel. A small three-foot-high sapling is the tallest object near the grave.

Even though reporters and photographers are lined up in their vehicles on Roosevelt Road outside the cemetery gates, no pictures are ever taken. Beside the fact that it is almost too frigid to use their cameras, the hard-faced men who have come to bury their pal no doubt make it extremely clear that if anyone snaps a shutter, their equipment will end up a permanent part of their lower gastrointestinal tract.

Louise stands on one side of the grave, braced by detectives. She is across from the Gebardi-DeMory clan, who have never accepted her and never will. Standing with Josephine DeMory is Capone's mother, Teresa, and her daughter, Mafalda. The bronze casket is lowered into the waiting earth as tears literally freeze on the faces of those gathered. Nobody lingers for very long after Vincent Gebardi and Jack McGurn are laid to rest.

35

Why?

1936

The murder of Jack McGurn on the cusp of Valentine's night is morbidly poetic. Having successfully dodged culpability in the St. Valentine's Day Massacre in 1929, McGurn has no doubt been extremely careful on that anniversary each year. Now the holiday of lovers and romance is continually accompanied by reminders of the massacre in the newspapers, on the radio, and in scores of books. McGurn's name is mentioned in the Chicago press every year on the anniversary. By this time, in 1936, a Chicagoan might be in London, Paris, or Berlin, and inevitably, upon learning his or her city of origin, one of the natives will mimic a Thompson submachine gun using both hands with index fingers pointed. "Eh-eh-eh-eh-eh-eh! Chee-ca-go!" This is the unfortunate legacy that the Outfit and Jack McGurn have created for the great city.

It would have made a lot of sense had McGurn's shooting been carried out by someone he had wronged. The immediate scenario that comes to mind is that a friend or family member of one of his victims, especially one of the Moran gang, has patiently waited seven years for the opportunity to seek revenge. To further support this theory, a sardonic valentine card is found somewhere near McGurn in the bowling alley on the night of his murder, which he has apparently had a chance to read. According to William Aloisio, the alley manager, it had been left earlier that day by an unknown person. It is a cartoon of a typical Depression-stricken, scantily clothed couple standing behind a sign that reads SALE OF HOUSEHOLD GOODS in front of their foreclosed house. The accompanying poem is a sardonic reminder of blessings left to be counted:

You've lost your job; you've lost your dough;
Your jewels and cars and handsome houses!
Things still could be worse, you know . . .
At least you haven't lost your trousas!

The envelope of the valentine has been addressed to Jack McGurn. Both the *Tribune* and *Daily News* stories immediately link it to the shooting, as if it has been given to McGurn by the killers. The first reporters on the scene are shown the card, which has already been handled by several people—hence there are never any photographs by press or police photographers of its true proximity to McGurn's body.

After studying the crime scene and the various police affidavits, detectives determine that the valentine actually has no connection with the killing. A fact that seems to almost have been ignored is that five more valentines, the same as McGurn's, are discovered on the cigar counter of the bowling alley. They are all addressed in the same handwriting as that of McGurn's to Willie DeGrazia, Nick de John, Doc Pecaro, Jim Dyme, and Skippy. They had been left for William Aloisio to distribute. It seems fair to conclude that, given McGurn's already paranoid state, it is highly unlikely that the planners of the execution would have first left any kind of announcement that might tip off the already nervous intended victim.

The cause of McGurn's assassination must be directly related to his attempts to muscle his way back into the Outfit's lucrative businesses of 1936. The meager living that he is making out of running the handbook in Melrose Park isn't nearly enough for him, especially since he has known such an abundance of financial rewards in the past. He has allegedly sold off his and Louise's expensive jewelry one piece at a time. He knows that the real riches are still in labor racketeering, but he is antiquated, out of favor, and out of control. As he begins drinking and falling apart, even the humble drivers and buttons like Tony Accardo have moved past him in the Outfit.

The labor master Curly Humphreys has been sent to jail for labor racketeering; however, Humphreys's return in January after a two-year prison term has no doubt helped create a sense of challenge and perhaps even a flashpoint. Humphreys is a brilliant communicator and strategist, exiting Leavenworth like a hero and entering into Frank Nitti's embrace. Humphreys's reemergence and McGurn's murder the following month may be directly connected. Humphreys has always agreed with Nitti's example of keeping a low profile; he returns to find Jack McGurn drinking heavily and acting paranoid, a dinosaur left over from the flashy Capone era or, as the papers will describe him, "a useless mercenary."

McGurn has been doing too many things that endangered the mob's security, not the least of which is connecting with political adversaries. His unstable state of mind has Nitti concerned that he might talk to the wrong people. The question is, What would McGurn have done to anger Humphreys? The most logical conclusion is that McGurn has tried to muscle in on the unions, Humphreys's personal domain, his contribution to the future of the mob. This supposition would be problematic if it weren't for the huge crisis of the old culprit, the expanded and renamed Cleaners, Dyers, and Pressers Union, which seems to surround McGurn's death like the backdrop for a play. In the seven decades since McGurn was shot, there has been little mention of peripheral events that certainly seem far too coincidental to ignore.

On February 6, 1936, a little more than a week before McGurn's death, three armed men break into the Cleaners, Dyers, and Pressers Union headquarters for Local Number 17742, which is located at 1583 North Ogden Avenue. They hold Ivor Fitzgerald, the secretary-treasurer of the union, at gunpoint, force him to open the office safe, and take all the union records, including the entire membership roster. Fitzgerald has already complained to the state's attorney about threats and problems in his organization.[1] These may possibly have come from McGurn, who is far from satisfied with his sparse income from the sports booking that he is involved in with his stepbrother Anthony.

Since the failure of the 225 Club in 1934, McGurn knows that the unions are still where the big money is. With Outfit labor master Humphreys serving his time "away at college," McGurn has a propitious moment to grab some of the riches from labor away from Frank Nitti. He may be planning an independent invasion of the still-fat resources within the unions, which, despite the Depression, still maintain formidable coffers. Just as McGurn makes his move, Humphreys gets out of prison.

Curly Humphreys cannot let his old friend get involved in business the Outfit is counting on—these types of dealings require abilities that are certainly beyond McGurn's. At this point, according to Captain John Egan of the Maxwell Street police station, McGurn has almost completely renounced Nitti's Outfit. Police captain John Stege also agrees with Egan.[2]

The Outfit, headed by Nitti, Campagna, Ricca, and the newly liberated Humphreys, is poised to usher in a new era of expanded labor racketeering that will soon go national. This has been the master plan since 1929. There is no room for interlopers or competition. When they discover that McGurn is trying to beat them to the punch by muscling his way back into one of the largest and richest unions, his death warrant is issued. When Nitti orders the assassination, he gets lucky; the events of the past naturally lead the press to conclude that McGurn's death is linked to revenge.

But some are aware of the alternative possibilities. The day after McGurn is shot, United Press staff correspondent Robert T. Loughran boasts that he knows why the gangster has been killed. In an article full of assumptions and incorrect facts, Loughran will launch many of the myths and much of the misinformation regarding McGurn. Still, the reporter arrives at some interesting truths, disagreeing with the initial police theories that McGurn's murder is retribution: "I knew Jack McGurn when he was a palooka prizefighter. I watched him grow up in the Chicago rackets. I knew he had no part in the St. Valentine's Day Massacre seven years ago. Gangland knew it too." As unlikely as this is, Loughran significantly adds, "The killing last night was for something more recent."[3]

Loughran also acknowledges that Black Hand killers murdered McGurn's father when he was still a boy and that he swore by the Mafia oath to track down his father's assassins. This statement is the beginning of the revenge myths that actually end up erroneously transporting the story back to Brooklyn. McGurn will spawn lots of fanciful stories, for he has captured people's imaginations.

Many Americans have affection for the baby-faced killer, even to the extent where a few will fabricate relationships that didn't exist. On February 17, one of McGurn's biggest "fans" in Mansfield, Ohio—Mrs. C. J. Appleby—reports to the newspaper that "little Jack McGurn" used to be her newspaper delivery boy when she lived in Kilgubbin, the Chicago West Side neighborhood nicknamed "Little Hell" for the night glow from its blast furnaces, in the "early part of the century." In Mrs. Appleby's fantasy, Jack was "a little Irish kid," a freckled youngster who was always followed by his bulldog. She claims to have known him all his life, as well as "his father who owned McGurn's bowling alley and introduced hand ball to America."[4]

Of course, McGurn lived in Brooklyn until 1919, never had a freckle, and wasn't remotely Irish. In an ironic twist, Mrs. Appleby claims that the same McGurn from whom Vincent Gebardi actually took his nom de guerre was his father. Mrs. Appleby and many others contribute to the misnomers that will be McGurn's legacy.

There is a strange poignancy in the fact that average Americans have grown fond of the colorful gangster from Chicago. Bonding with outlaws has almost become fashionable in the 1930s, giving the traditional boost to the antiheroes like John Dillinger and Pretty Boy Floyd, who so excite the Mrs. Applebys. The newspaper will refute Mrs. Appleby a few days later when the editor realizes that McGurn was actually a Sicilian named Vincent Gebardi. But Mansfield is a small town, and the paper's editor lets her down gently.

Mrs. Appleby will be far from the last person to occlude the truth about Jack McGurn. The myths will grow, change, and be continually repeated by otherwise proficient researchers and writers who tend to propagate each other's mistakes. There will be constant errors regarding his name and his family's name, much of which is owed to his own elusiveness. The bizarre mythology of how police find nickels placed in the dead hands of McGurn's victims is one of the favorites, a romantic gangster tale suffusing a sense of Capone justice into the epic. This story is a complete fabrication; there isn't one piece of evidence in police reports, newspaper stories, or crime-scene photographs that even hints at this being true. In addition, none of the medical examiner's accounts mention anything remotely like it. It is a myth with a decidedly western style, a gunfighter who leaves a nickel as his personal metaphor, not unlike the way the Lone Ranger left his silver bullets.

The Brooklyn story of how young Vincent Gebardi's father was gunned down on the Lower East Side—a seminal event that supposedly led him to enter a life of murder—is also total fiction. Vincent's father, Tommaso, died of natural causes, and Josephine Gebardi married Angelo DeMory seven years before the family moved to Chicago. By the time Angelo was murdered by Genna gunmen in 1923, Vincent had already transformed into Jack McGurn and worked for the Torrio-Capone organization out of Cicero. There are no law enforcement records in Brooklyn or King's County indicating Vincent was anything but lawful and anonymous to authorities. This is also true about his birth father, Tommaso, who was never involved in anything except hard, honest labor.

There is also another myth that McGurn played the ukulele and sang. Sadly, there is no evidence that this is accurate, although it might still have been possible. It is a rather charming invention with no history, at least none that has come to light. It is conceivable that Louise played the uke and sang along, although she was never known for her vocal talents.

The boxing myth that McGurn had a glass jaw and lacked the fighting heart is certainly not correct—this is obvious from his pugilistic career statistics. He enjoyed modest success as a welterweight, although he did have trouble sustaining his dynamic energies into the matches that had more rounds. His overall record proves that he still fared well as a professional during a time when it was nearly impossible to fight for a living in Chicago. The prohibition of boxing made it unlikely for a fighter to make a decent, steady income, contributing greatly to the reason McGurn sought alternative employment.

McGurn's penchant for using the Thompson submachine gun has also been quite exaggerated. For the few times he utilized this weapon, there were many more killings when he chose handguns and especially revolvers, where his accuracy was almost always due to short-range proficiency. Although he was effective with the Thompson when he used it—such as on Hymie Weiss, Joey Aiello, and possibly on St. Valentine's Day—any American soldier who carried one in World War II will testify that, at a firing rate of six hundred to eight hundred rounds a minute, it did not require a special ability to puncture someone who wasn't moving.

Jack McGurn definitely earned his reputation as a killer with a prolificacy that still hasn't been completely accounted. There may have been many more victims who fell to his guns, including several who could have been credited to other gangsters. Even without the mythologies, he was deserving of the highest accolades for mayhem and murder; he was Al Capone's superstar in that arena.

36

Whoever Desires Too Much
Ends Up with Nothing

1936

L ouise Rolfe Gebardi is now standing alone in the spotlight. If she has ever been considered fascinating, aberrant, or eccentric, she is now totally enigmatic. With McGurn having taken his turn in the Cook County Morgue, Louise assumes center stage.

From the very moment when she receives the knock on the door by the police at three in the morning and hears her Jack has been shot, the indefatigable, searching eyes of law enforcement and the press are focused on her. Because she is still the Blonde Alibi to the public, she will get very little sympathy. She is interrogated, probed, pushed, and examined by no-nonsense men who demand answers to difficult questions. Moreover, with her string to Jack McGurn eternally severed, the Gebardi-DeMory family offers her no support or solace. The one exception is Anthony, with whom she is apparently close. She must feel extremely alone and eminently vulnerable.

On February 17, after McGurn's funeral, Sergeant Donohue brings Louise back to the detective bureau at the Racine Avenue station. Investigators have been very curious as to where Louise was when they attempted to notify her shortly after McGurn's murder. She isn't a direct suspect, but her absence from her home so late in the night tells them there's more to her story. To further inspire them, reporters seem to have caught a buzz of something rich, which doesn't take long to develop.

Detectives William Burns and Edward Le Fevre have found evidence that Louise's testimony about being home and waking up her husband on the night of his murder is completely false. Acting on a tip, they question a nineteen-year-old woman named Margaret Swift, who admits that she and Louise had been together for most of Valentine's Day, drinking that night until early Saturday morning.[1]

It turns out that "Margie" Swift is the granddaughter of the late George B. Swift, a former mayor of Chicago. She lives in a suite at the tony Streeterville Apartment Hotel at 195 East Chestnut Street with her eighteen-year-old lover, Mary Dickinson, a stenographer. To everyone's astonishment, Louise has recently been on the fringe of a clique of lesbians who meet at the Chestnut Street apartment for women-only parties. It is Dickinson who contacts the detectives, jealous of her roommate's relationship with Louise.

This new, extremely odd turn of events is a true challenge to the reporters, most of whom are loath even to touch the subject. The homosexuality of the new players in the drama is never honestly discussed, only implied. Dickinson and Swift are described by the press as "girl friends" and "mannish," both appearing in masculine clothing.[2]

Perhaps the papers are also wary of the power behind the Swift family and don't want to incur new liabilities. This strange revelation is lost on most people, although pictures appear in several Chicago papers of Swift and Dickinson; they are indeed masculine in their look and dress. Both women are aware that Louise is Jack McGurn's wife; Swift even appears to be in

The "mannishly attired" Margie Swift and Mary Dickinson, 1936. *CHICAGO TRIBUNE* ARCHIVES

Mabel Rolfe, Louise, and Margie Swift in court, 1936. COLLECTION OF JOHN BINDER

some kind of competition with McGurn. On the Saturday morning after his murder, Swift calls her friend Helen Berg on the telephone, commenting somewhat triumphantly, "Well, I see they got McGurn."[3]

Captain Mullen finally gets the truth out of Swift, who has been lying about her whereabouts with Louise because she doesn't want her girlfriend to know they were together.[4] When searching Swift and Dickinson's apartment, police discover two leather whips and a pair of child's handcuffs, which Swift claims "have no significance." Louise, Dickinson, and Swift are brought together and forced to confess their individual truths, which eventually match up. There are some uncomfortable and fairly ugly moments after Swift admits to police that "she liked Louise right from the start."[5]

After officers discover McGurn's Ford and the key to the safe-deposit box inside, they trace the box to the Oak Park Trust & Savings Bank on Lake Street, where it is registered to Louise, thus allowing her husband to remain anonymous. After checking the recent history of the box, they discover that at 11:30 AM on the Friday before the murder, Louise has made a visit and removed cash, claiming it was eight hundred dollars.[6] This finding raises lots of questions. Police also report that Louise has been "well cared for," which indicates that perhaps McGurn wasn't quite as desperate for money as they have assumed. They certainly wonder if eight hundred dollars is all she removed.

The detectives are now worried that Louise may be a target because of what she might know. They seclude her and twelve-year-old Bonita in an unknown location, providing her with twenty-four-hour armed guards.[7] On February 19, state's attorney's investigators and detectives accompany Louise to the Oak Park bank and open the deposit box. With them is E. C. Yellowley, who is the head of the federal alcohol tax unit in Chicago. He is there to view the suspected stacks of illegal bootleg and gambling cash.

The anticipation is enormous as the group of combined federal and local law enforcement officers gather around and expectantly peer inside the metal box. The lid is lifted like a treasure chest is being examined. It is frustratingly anticlimactic—they discover $950 in cash and a $7,000 furniture insurance policy.[8] They certainly suspect that Louise cleaned out the box, perhaps in anticipation of coming into sole possession of its contents. They will never determine if her timely visit before McGurn's murder is purely coincidental or if she might have suspected his approaching demise.

On March 21, the Hearst paper in New York, the *New York American*, gives Louise the printed buckwheats. The lead story claims that police are expecting her death because she knows gangland secrets that will certainly get her killed. In a show of truly outrageous tabloid journalism, they imply that she also knows who killed McGurn and list her greatest virtues as a gangster moll: "She had proven beyond all doubt that she could stand up under the most persistent official grilling without flinching."[9] If Louise does know anything, this article must make her even more paranoid than McGurn. Ironically, it will also get the message out that she is stalwart, keeping to the code of silence.

This jaundiced account actually may diffuse any worries that Frank Nitti might have about Louise singing songs that could incriminate the Outfit. She has already been forewarned by the excitable and irresponsible press as well as by the police. Therefore it will certainly be in her best interests to keep her mouth shut, just as she always has, concerning the exploits of her husband and his group.

Whatever people will say about the flamboyant Lulu Lou, she will forever prove to have acumen and a Mafia-like integrity in this regard.

37

I Feared He'd Come Back and Kill Me

1936

Even with McGurn interred in Mount Carmel, the bloodshed isn't finished. Perhaps his worst mistake in the last years of his life is to drag his young stepbrother Anthony into his activities. Anthony idolizes Jack, desiring only to follow in his footsteps. If McGurn had been a simple tailor, Anthony would have become proficient with a needle and thread. Although he is a DeMory, he even takes McGurn's real name of Gebardi. From the perspective of the Gebardi-DeMorys, McGurn's murder expands into a double tragedy when twenty-four-year-old Anthony is shot to death in a scenario that is very similar to the shooting of McGurn. It occurs two weeks after his stepbrother is killed.

Anthony is apparently quite vocal after burying McGurn, muttering about revenge and payback for the killers.[1] He utters these words of bravado in the wrong places, where the walls have ears. The threat to Frank Nitti reaches the Morrison Hotel. Nitti understands the Sicilian code; in the old country, when a man is murdered, the same fate is shared by the remaining male members of his family. Otherwise, it is incumbent on the surviving father or brothers to seek revenge. Anthony's youth and Sicilian machismo will be his undoing, for Nitti and the Outfit will eliminate him before he gets the chance to come back at them or relay to others any of the proprietary information McGurn might have entrusted to him.

On the evening of March 2, 1936, Anthony is playing cards in a pool hall at 1003 West Polk Street, near his mother's apartment on Morgan Street. There are approximately twenty people in the place. Anthony is playing rummy with Santo Cudia, the proprietor of the hall; his friend John Lardino; and Sam "Bobo" Nuzzio, another of his card buddies who is also a Twentieth Ward Democratic precinct captain and an employee of the county assessor's office. Lardino and Cudia are facing the door; Anthony is sitting with his back to the entrance, always a poor idea for a wannabe gangster.[2]

At 8:08 PM, three men burst in, the brims of their hats down low, holding guns and handkerchiefs to their faces. One man guards the door while the other two walk up to the card table. In almost exactly the same manner as the killing of Jack McGurn, one of the men announces, "This is a stick-up!" Everybody dives for the floor, but Anthony stands up, puts his hands in the air, turns and faces his killers in a gesture that conveys either a chilling sense of resolve or machismo symptomatic of his undoing. It is as if he knows they are really there for him.

One of the gunmen opens up with a .38-caliber revolver; the first shot severs Anthony's watchstrap from his wrist and continues into his neck. The watch stops as it falls, dutifully recording the time of death. Another shot is fired, and Anthony drops to the floor. The other killer then empties a .45 automatic into his prostrate body. There are a total of nine bullets in his head, neck, torso, and arms.[3] The three killers run back out the door and into a waiting automobile, which speeds west down Polk Street.[4] In seconds, all twenty of the patrons vanish in the familiar postmurder exodus.

Eighteen-year-old Joseph DeMory, who is near the front of the room playing pool, picks up his unconscious brother Anthony with the aid of two friends. They carry him a block and a half to Mother Cabrini Hospital, leaving the proprietor, Cudia, alone in his blood-spattered poolroom. Joseph then dashes home to his family's apartment, where police officers later find him with his mother, Josephine, and his twenty-three-year-old sister, Angeline, who are sobbing hysterically. Anthony never regains con-

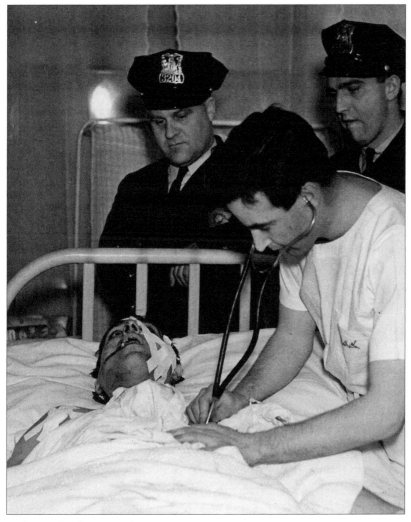

Anthony Gebardi-DeMory dying, 1936. COLLECTION OF JOHN BINDER

sciousness and dies on the operating table an hour later, after press and photographers appear, snapping a picture of the expiring youth.

Police take young Joseph to the station for questioning. Inconsolable, Josephine and Angeline throw their arms around Joseph as if to keep him with them. They say to the police officers, "They want to get him too. Take care of him!"[5]

Just after midnight, Louise Rolfe McGurn arrives at the morgue with her brother-in-law, Frank Gebardi. They identify Anthony's body—the second time in two weeks that they have watched a coroner's assistant remove the sheet from their loved one's face. This is nearly as devastating for Louise as McGurn's death. She leaves sobbing; a Twenty-Second District policeman snidely comments to the *Daily News* reporter, "She may be next."[6]

An hour after the shooting, Emma Lozano, a housewife who lives at 655 South Aberdeen Street, discovers the .38 revolver used to kill Anthony. It is lying near the sidewalk at the corner of Sholto Street and Vernon Park Place. She immediately takes it to the Twenty-Second District police station. An hour after that, fifteen-year-old Tony Lattanza and his friend Danny Grecco find the discarded .45 automatic near a vacant lot on Sholto Street and also bring it to the police station.

The serial numbers have been filed off the revolver. Sergeant Frank Ballou, who has examined dozens of murder weapons, finds the "secret" serial number inside the frame of the gun. This number and the still-extant serial number of the Colt .45 automatic are wired to the Colt Firearms Company in Hartford, Connecticut, to trace the original ownership. Both guns are immediately handed over to Calvin Goddard for ballistics testing. Since shortly after the St. Valentine's Day Massacre, Goddard has moved his entire forensics laboratory to Northwestern University in downtown Chicago to be near the center of the gangland storm.

After examination of the weapons and bullets at the Northwestern lab, Major Goddard determines that Anthony Gebardi and representative Albert Prignano, who was killed back on December 29, 1935, were murdered with the same Colt revolver. The police trace the gun to the Palace Loan Bank, the Depression-era name for a pawnshop, in nearby Gary, Indiana, where it was purchased in 1930 under a fictitious name.[7]

The best evidence that McGurn was killed by the remnants of the Capone Outfit is contained in this forensic epiphany. Captain John Egan of the Maxwell Street station, who is supervising the investigation, also concurs. He declares that there is strong evidence that the murders of Prignano, McGurn, and Anthony Gebardi have a "common origin."[8] He is probably in the know, for FBI director J. Edgar Hoover will note in a memorandum in 1937 that Egan himself was on the Capone payroll and received five thousand dollars a week.[9]

The coroner's inquest into the murder of Anthony Gebardi is convened on March 4 at 10:30 AM and conducted by assistant coroner James J. Whalen. A coroner's jury of six is sworn in. Representing Anthony's interests is assistant state's attorney John J. Phillips.

The first witness is Frank Gebardi, who last saw his stepbrother on the Thursday before he was killed. The most important part of his testimony is that he is a full brother to Jack McGurn and a stepbrother to Anthony Gebardi, thus confirming that Josephine Gebardi had indeed linked up with Angelo DeMory at least nine months before Anthony's birth in 1915. However, Frank has distanced himself from both of his brothers' criminal activities and knows nothing about Anthony's murder.

Next to be called is Officer T. J. Nolan of the Twenty-Second District station. He testifies that he and his partner answered a radio call and responded to the poolroom, where they found owner Santo Cudia standing over a huge pool of blood. Anthony had already been taken to the hospital, and the other patrons were long gone. Nolan offers absolutely nothing that is helpful.

By this time, the news of the weapons having been brought in changes the order of the hearing. Captain Egan announces that the police need to examine this new evidence. Consequently, the inquest is postponed until March 25 to give them more time.

In the final inquest session, Anthony's friend of seven years, John Lardino, is called to testify. He relates that his mob moniker is John Alcock. It is suspected that he was a bodyguard to Jack McGurn during McGurn's last year of life. Even though Lardino witnesses Anthony's murder, he is purposefully evasive, only answering the most basic questions put to him by the deputy coroner and the state's attorney. He is eventually excused, having contributed no useful facts.

The next to be called is Santo Cudia, the Sicilian owner of the pool hall. In his broken English, he explains that Anthony began coming into the hall about six months before, just after Cudia opened his business. Even though he too witnessed the shooting, he is unable to identify the killers. When he is asked what he was doing while the gunmen were firing, he answers, "Well, I sat in my chair, that is all. I no talk to them. Nobody talk to them."[10] Unable to shed any light on the murder, Cudia is also excused.

Lozano testifies about how she found one of the murder weapons, although it doesn't help in suggesting who the shooters might be. After she is excused, Officer Nolan is recalled. He claims that the testing of the gun and the ballistics is continuing, and that he isn't certain if the investigation has been completed. Deputy Coroner Whalen—frustrated and knowing full well that he is once again facing a Sicilian standoff—allows the medical examiner, J. J. Kearns, to summarize. The inquest is then formally brought to an end. The verdict, of course, is that Anthony DeMory, also known as Gebardi, was shot to death by persons unknown.

At this time there are four remaining Gebardi-DeMory sons. Josephine is completely terrified that the Outfit and those responsible for her boys' deaths will take Anthony's oath of revenge as a traditional Sicilian *vinnitta*. She immediately goes to Teresa Capone for help. Al's mother still has quite a bit of clout with Frank Nitti; she asks for an audience for Josephine, which is granted. An anonymous source who is quite close to the DeMory family suggests that during their meeting, Josephine pleads for her remaining sons' lives. She makes a promise that none of the boys will ever become involved in any illegitimate enterprise, nor will any of her family members even consider seeking revenge for the murders of Jack and Anthony. In a merciful gesture, Nitti, without confessing to any complicity, lets Josephine DeMory know that he will do whatever he can to ensure the safety of her surviving sons. In so many words, both uttered and unspoken, the deal is made; Nitti will keep his word.

Joseph DeMory will die in the Pacific on June 12, 1942, in the service of his country.[11] Frank, the last true Gebardi brother, will live into his eighties, dying of natural causes in 1989. The other family members will live out their lives in obscurity, leading a normal existence and bringing honor to their parents and grandparents. Josephine Verderame Gebardi DeMory will pass away in 1939, a beloved matriarch, at eternal rest with her family in Mount Carmel.

The section where they are buried is still tenderly supplied with red geraniums on their gravestones. The tree that was a tiny sapling in 1936 is now a mature, protective arbor that gives shade to the Sicilian American family resting near it. It is not a "gangster attraction" but a sacred place, as are all cemeteries, and should remain exempt from the inelegant visitations of the curious. It should also be reiterated that Vincent and Anthony Gebardi were but two members of a sizable brood who contributed myriad good things to their city and their country. They had children, grandchildren, and now great-grandchildren, who are all *bonu comu pani*, as good as bread.

38

Lulu Lou: What I Want, You Don't Have

1936–1995

For Louise, life after Jack McGurn's death doesn't turn out to be any less daunting. Wisdom eludes her in almost every way. Perhaps she is lonely, but she is rarely alone. Oddly, she stays in Chicago, where she is infamous; apparently the party isn't over yet for the indomitable doll Lulu Lou.

At first, after McGurn's death, she does go into seclusion for several months, dying her hair dark to avoid being recognized. She has certainly had too much of courtrooms and jails, and during the summer of 1936, she disappears from public scrutiny. She is also concerned with the press's spurious prognostication of her impending execution.

Her attempt at anonymity ends on October 7, when she kills her second man.

Driving with a license listing her as Louise De Vito, she is with three of her pals—Louise Cunningham, Marie Jarmer, and Patricia Lonquist. Jarmer and Lonquist live together on South Kedvale Avenue. Quite possibly Longquist has previously associated with Arthur "Doc" Barker, Ma Barker's son, in late 1934 and early 1935. FBI reports mention her as a friend of Doc's girlfriend, Mildred Kuhlman. The two Louises are together and have been partying all Saturday night. Early on Sunday morning, while the three others are with her, Louise Rolfe smashes her speeding automobile into another car at Pulaski Road and Fifty-Fifth Street. There are seven people in the large touring car, including the driver, Charles Fremarek; his father-in-law, fifty-three-year-old Vincent Zamiara; and Cecilia Zamiara, Vincent's forty-eight-year-old wife. The victim in Louise's second vehicular homicide turns out to be Vincent—he dies a couple of hours after the accident in Holy Cross Hospital. Cecilia survives after being in critical condition, while Charles and the others sustain minor injuries.[1]

Inebriated and terrified of any type of publicity, Louise and her pals manage to slip away from the scene. They disappear after the Oak Park police officer, to whom Louise has handed her driver's license, becomes distracted by the lifesaving efforts for the victims in the other car. The license, however, lists Jack McGurn's old address of 1234 Kenilworth Avenue, Oak Park, so warrants are immediately issued for Louise.[2]

She is found to have been living in the Cunningham woman's apartment, along with her daughter, Bonita, and another unknown woman. When the police come knocking at her door, she has already dyed her hair blonde again in an apparent attempt to confuse any witnesses.[3] She has already contacted one of McGurn's old friends, lawyer Robert Romano. After apprising him of the events, Louise spends the remainder of that morning in the Oak Park police lockup, characteristically chipping away at her red polished fingernails with her teeth and chain-smoking Pall Mall cigarettes.

Meanwhile, Romano contacts Charles Fremarek, the driver of the other car. Fremarek testifies at the inquest the next day, as Romano has made overtures to "settle" damages. Shortly after that, the ever-creative Louise perjures herself, testifying that another woman was actually the driver of her car. It is an act of stupidity that immediately turns against her. A few minutes later, Louise is identified by three people in the death car as the woman behind the wheel.

Felony court judge Edward Scheffler doesn't take this well; instead of throwing her in jail for perjury, he raises her bond from one thousand to ten thousand dollars, continuing the case to November 6. Louise spends the night in the lockup. The next day her stalwart attorney appears before acting chief justice John Prystalski, offering real estate in lieu of the bond, which the judge reduces to five thousand dollars.[4] Louise is released. Bernard Rolfe has bailed his daughter out for the last time.

On October 8, the coroner's inquest into the death of Vincent Zamiara begins, although assistant state's attorneys Patrick Daniher and Sam Papaneck ask for a continuance, pending the outcome of Cecilia Zamiara, who is still in critical condition and may die. Louise openly weeps in court, claiming, "I was not the driver."[5]

Louise is terrified that she will end up in prison. In an almost uncanny act of further stupidity, whether it is her idea or her lawyer's, she is somehow able to find a patsy. No doubt Romano has apprised her that a person with a clean record will draw much less time for accidental vehicular manslaughter. Louise's notoriety and the fact that she already killed someone with an automobile will ensure a much greater punishment. Before the November trial, someone, either Romano or Louise herself, is able to convince twenty-year-old Mildred McGarry to testify that she, not Louise, was the driver of the car. This indicates that Louise has some cash, for it will certainly take a goodly amount to get young Miss McGarry to perjure herself and then serve Louise's time.

To her great discredit, Louise stoops as low as she will probably ever go. She acts like a truly typical gun moll. Finding a patsy is a traditional gangster trick and certainly one of the lowest maneuvers, one without honor. Here, at the very height of the Depression, Louise is scrabbling in the dirt, clinging to the hanging threads of polite society. She is morally bankrupt to the extent where she will allow a destitute woman to ruin her own life and take the fall.

However, Miss McGarry never has to throw herself into the void. On November 25, the verdict of accidental death is ruled by the coroner's jury investigating the accident.[6] Somebody's money has certainly changed hands, not a surprise for such desperate times. Bernard Frank Rolfe, who is getting older, must doubt his daughter's sanity. It doesn't appear as if he will remain a contributor after this point. Louise has gone once too often to the well, yet she has again eluded a vehicular-manslaughter conviction.[7]

Her life after that seems to slide rapidly downhill. The Depression continues, and there doesn't seem to be much, if any, support from Frank

Attorney Robert Romano, Louise, and Bernard Frank Rolfe in court, 1936. A tearful
Mildred McGarry is in the background. COLLECTION OF JOHN BINDER

Rolfe, who may have fallen on hard times himself, along with most of the
advertising business. With Daddy gone and her last reserve depleted, she
moves back in with her mother so Bonita will have a home.

It seems that during this period, Louise is pure gold digger. Her only
focus in life is to locate a man whom she can seduce into taking care of
her. She is painfully aware that her beauty and charms are quickly eroding as she turns thirty. Her finances are dangerously depleted. She drinks
more heavily and begins to sink into a morass of low-life events, selecting
one bad male after another. Where she once was a Jazz Age nymph, her
slowly increasing weight and preference for heavy makeup have made her
feel like a constantly inebriated parody of herself. She is quickly running
out of any options she might have, but she still isn't totally out of luck.
Perhaps God does watch over fools and drunks, for she is able to snag an
unsuspecting man.

Louise marries Arthur F. Weibrecht on May 28, 1938. Arthur seems to
be an honest working man with no involvement in crime. Their marriage
lasts an astoundingly long two years, but her alcohol consumption is still
quite a serious problem and interferes with her ability to have any kind of
decent relationship. Weibrecht is hardly a stiff, but his wife is in another
league. Once again, Louise optimistically seeks greener pastures, leaving

Wiebrecht on July 5, 1940, after he "sought to dissuade her from habitual drinking."[8]

Sadly, Louise has been an alcoholic for many years. It is easy to see how she is transforming into a blousy, boozy barfly. She must absolutely shudder at the thought of her Jack seeing this hideous decline.

Ironically, on Valentine's Day in 1940, Louise is brought up for arraignment in Judge Joseph Drucker's felony court for disorderly conduct. She has been living on Sheridan Road in East Rogers Park, on the far North Side, with a small-time crook named Edwin Rozelle. Once again, she is flying near the flame, perhaps in an attempt to relive old times but more probably because the only men left in her environment are bottom feeders. The genius Rozelle leaves a revolver he used in a robbery in Louise's apartment on Sheridan Road. The cops track Rozelle to her door through witnesses in various bars, but the man isn't there—only his gun is.

Louise is inebriated and acts out when the police begin to question her, so they haul her in. To her dismay, she is immediately recognized. In the old days, she would pose for the cameras like Jean Harlow, wisecracking to the reporters who stand by to jot down anything she uttered. But this kind of attention has become much less desirable. Louise shuns the cameras, trying everything she can to hide her face. The *Tribune* loves the fact that it is the yearly anniversary of the massacre and gleefully announces a "Valentine Jinx on McGurn Widow."[9]

In court, Louise pathetically bats her eyelashes and convinces the judge that she knows nothing about her boyfriend's profession. By this time in her life, she has practiced her "presentation" in front of many a jurist. Still moderately attractive, she does her very best to project a modicum of innocence. She has also learned a few other lessons from her past performances; without the bravado of McGurn and Al Capone's money behind her, she is loath to talk back or display any attitude. She represents herself as Louise Wiebrecht, trying her best to appear reputable. This is not easy. The veteran reporters and photographers know better, snickering at her weak camouflage. Still, she is able to put on an effective show. Her attorney, James M. Burke, argues that it is no crime to have a gun in a home if the possessor doesn't know it was used for illegal purposes. Judge Drucker apparently buys it, and the charges are dismissed.[10]

On November 22, 1940, Louise loses her father, her last and best source of support. Bernard Frank Rolfe dies a few days before Thanksgiving.[11]

After the Japanese attack on Pearl Harbor—the beginning of US involvement in World War II—Louise's estranged husband, Arthur Wiebrecht, enlists and is sent overseas. Louise moves her meager belongings from one cheap hotel room to another. By this time, her daughter, Bonita, is eighteen and marries a twenty-four-year-old named Leo Rusetos in February 1943.[12] Apparently Bonita has carried on the tradition that she has learned from her mother and marries to escape her home. She avoids her mother at all costs; they will remain estranged until February 1973 when Bonita's grandson, John, is born.[13]

Louise successfully conducts her life and self-destructive romances without public notice until 1943, when she is once again arrested. This time, her foraging has brought up a young man who makes Jack McGurn seem like one of King Arthur's knights. She almost seems to be in competition with herself to link up with the most profoundly damaged, degenerate males imaginable. The Albany Park police appear at her hotel room at 827 West Lawrence Avenue; she has been witnessed passing rubber checks in the company of a suspected army deserter.

The cops have an easy time of it. The couple is tracked back to Louise's apartment, where they find the young man lounging naked in bed. He loudly rebukes the officers for the intrusion and, in a grandiose style, claims to be James O'Donnell, a sergeant major from Fort Knox, Kentucky. Under questioning, he quickly admits he is actually Harry Bernard, a private from Brooklyn, New York. He was on leave when he met Louise at a North Side nightclub.[14] They have lived together for four months, and now his money has run out. Consequently, several complainants have reported a brassy blonde and a soldier passing worthless checks.

Perhaps in the midst of World War II, with all that is occurring, Louise simply seems hapless and not even worthy of any retribution. Incredibly, she is released by judge J. M. Braude a few days later. He doesn't prosecute her on the disorderly conduct charge; somehow he is capable of sympathizing with Louise and finding empathy for her grievous state. Still, he refuses to buy her song and dance about being duped and unaware of her boyfriend's identity.[15] Braude's final admonition to her is "Stay out of trouble."[16]

The press is tough on Louise, recounting her sordid but once glamorous history and pointing out that "there was none of her glitter of gangland days . . . no strings of pearls, no squirrel coat, no fancy leather slippers." She is described as being plump and having bedraggled hair. While Americans are at war, Louise appears to be just as direly at battle with her pathetic limitations, clueless as to how to attempt to fight them.

Arthur Wiebrecht survives the war, returning to Chicago in 1945 to discover that his estranged wife has been living with a bartender named George Jawny for the last year. At this point, she seems to be forming her relationships with men based on their proximity to their source of alcohol. Arthur is tired of her abusing his name; now that he has helped defeat the Germans and the Japanese, he is finally up to dealing with Louise. He charges her with desertion, divorcing her on October 23, 1945.[17]

By early 1947, Louise is employed at the King of Clubs, a gambling dive at 2839 Broadway. She is a dice-game attendant, a "26 Girl." When her coworker Catherine Jacobs is found strangled in Benton Harbor, Michigan, two days after her wedding, detectives arrest Louise for questioning. Like Jack McGurn, she has begun to have usual-suspect status, which is inspired by her seedy past. She is immediately released, knowing nothing about the murder, but the press still remembers her and gives her enough of a mention to ensure some humiliation.[18] She continues to live with Jawny, finally marrying him in 1948. The union then begins to break down; she ends up leaving him in 1949.

That April, she moves in with a man named Richard King at 823 Lakeside Place.[19] On November 25, 1951, she shows up at the Town Hall police station with two black eyes and a split lip and files charges against King for assault and battery. The *Tribune* refers to her as "a bruised and slightly larger edition of the once beautiful Louise Rolfe."[20]

King, in what is essentially his idea of a moronic joke, snidely testifies that Louise "received her bruises when she fell off a bar stool." The next day, Roger Bramly, the bartender of Louise's favorite bar, testifies that it was King who was lying. Judge Emmett Harrington immediately issues a warrant for the perjurer King. Upon his return to court, he admits that he came home from work and found Louise drinking away the sixty dollars he had given her for rent, groceries, and the electric bill, so he "flattened her." Judge Harrington, who does not suffer fools or woman beaters, rules for Louise. He gives King sixty days in the Cook County House of Corrections.[21]

Because she attaches herself to often-violent men, Louise seems to be still searching for a man like her Jack. But she has no sense when it comes to tough guys, who inevitably turn out to be nothing like McGurn. They prove their hardness by being bullies and cheapsters. Louise must begin to realize that she needs someone a bit more civilized at this point in her life. Sadly, she also realizes once and for all that she will never be able to replace her Jack.

Louise in court after being beaten by Richard King, 1951. COLLECTION OF JOHN BINDER

In 1951 Bonita Boex, who is now twenty-eight, marries her second husband, a man named Sam Minerva.[22] She has little or no contact with her mother as Louise finally drops out of the news, marrying a Chicago man named J. Bernard Nash, presumably in 1965. Nash, who lives in San Francisco, moves to Sonoma in 1964.[23] He is yet another bartender, and though he has an alias—Bob Walsh—he appears to be a decent-enough fellow. Perhaps Louise cannot be happy with a man with just one name or identity. She calls him Bob. He is a good, enabling drinking partner for his wife, but eventually their marriage breaks up and they go their separate ways. In the new age of peace and love, Lulu Lou enjoys little peace and sporadic love.

At this point in her life, Louise is inspired to seek gainful employment. In 1973, she files for a Social Security number for the first time in Chicago.[24] Not long after this, she permanently moves back to her favorite place, Boyes Hot Springs in the Sonoma Valley in California, which she discovered in her Black Bottom dancing-tour days.

Bonita Boex and her grandson, John
Rusetos, 1973. COLLECTION OF JOHN RUSETOS

Bonita Louise Boex Rusetos
Minerva, perhaps the most unfortunate victim of all, passes away
around 1977. At a tender age,
poor Bonita witnessed the downfall of Jack McGurn as well as the
wild machinations of her mother.
Hopefully her life improved when
she found family through marriage. She does live to see her
grandson, John Rusetos, who is
born in 1973. At that time, she and
Louise, now a great-grandmother,
reconcile in time to share the few years Bonita has left.[25]

Mellowed by alcohol, cigarettes, and advancing age, Louise appears
briefly in an infamous television special in 1986 concerning the opening of
a vault underneath the old Lexington Hotel, Capone's headquarters. Host
Geraldo Rivera tries his charm on Louise, asking her if McGurn was really
with her the morning of the St. Valentine's Day Massacre. Louise, cagey
as ever, plays with Rivera from her living room somewhere in Boyes. She
coyly tells him nothing in a voice tempered by decades of tobacco and
booze. The show turns out to be quite a dud, although its ratings are

Geraldo Rivera and Louise, 1986.
AUTHOR'S COLLECTION

huge, testifying to the ever-fresh
appeal of the Capone era. One of
those millions of viewers is Louise's last ex, J. Bernard Nash.

Nash, who has recently retired
after forty years as a bartender at
the Oakmont Country Club in
Sonoma, is struck by the thunder-
bolt once again. For him, the magical Louise still has her ineffable
charms. He calls the producers of
the show and begs them to help
him contact his ex-wife. They agree

to convey a message with his phone number to her; she immediately calls him. They have lived only a few miles from each other for decades. They hook up and get married for the second time. Capone-era researcher Mario Gomes, in his interviews with Nancy Miller, Louise's last close friend, determines that it is Nash's tenth marriage and the eighth for the prolific Louise. The two of them are finally made for each other, because they've eliminated everyone else.[26]

Nancy Miller and her husband, Warde, are longtime friends of Nash's, whom Louise still calls Bob. They are witnesses at the secular wedding ceremony, and the two couples spend a lot of time together, eating, drinking, and trying to remember the past, or at least some of it. According to Nancy, Louise prefers to drink daiquiris. She loves to eat lobster, and her cigarettes of choice are still Pall Malls. In the 1980s and early 1990s, she gains more heft, still coloring her snow-white hair an indeterminate assortment of yellows. Bob, once robust, is a small, bald, elderly man in extremely ill health.

By 1993 Louise also suffers from a serious list of ills, and, as witnessed by Nancy Miller, Bob and Louise fall into an "extreme senior state." They both refuse to take their prescribed medications, essentially becoming like two sick, goofy children. Brave J. Bernard Nash, the man who married Louise Rolfe twice, passes away on June 4, 1994, leaving Lulu Lou alone once more.

The Blonde Alibi dies in Sonoma, California, on February 21, 1995. Her remains are cremated.[27] She had a good time for a very long time. When she was young, she invented and embodied the 1920s idea of "flaming youth." Unlike Clara Bow, the it girl who played unconventional, rebellious females on the silent screen, Louise Rolfe lived that life. She was beautiful, narcissistic, spoiled, carefree, and corrupt and drove automobiles with thoughtless, homicidal abandon. She was a perversely dedicated hedonist, and her one great love, Jack McGurn, was Al Capone's best killer.

Chicago gangster expert Michael Yore Graham is the last person to interview Louise in the late 1980s. In tandem with the century, she is in her eighties. As is her custom, she stays true to her famous alibi when Graham asks her about Jack McGurn and St. Valentine's Day.[28] She is either the paragon of loyalty and *omerta*, outshining even the most tight-lipped gangsters, or, more likely, she is simply telling the truth. Either way, her integrity concerning the massacre remains intact to the very end. The likeliest possibility seems to be that she slept through the morning of Valentine's Day in 1929, missing everything Jack McGurn did or didn't do.

Louise lived a very long life compared to her Jack; he died young and handsome at thirty-four. Her memories of him were certainly sweetened by those of her own youth. Even with her longevity, she remained a little-known legend, a reservoir of delicious secrets. She lived to see all of her hedonism and selfishness plowed under by the dubious gift of time. There is such history in this one woman, and yet she seemed to have learned to privately relish her personal past, not even tempted to talk about her incredible flaming youth to anyone but her closest pals. She had a long time to glean wisdom from her adventures, if indeed she cared about such things.

Louise was tough—a survivor of a time so fascinating that it will never be forgotten. Nobody gets out of this world alive, but Louise May Rolfe got away with almost everything else. If she learned anything in her eighty-nine years, certainly it was that the memories that last are of love.

Acknowledgments

I owe a tremendous debt to my friend John Binder for his generous support over the years. Mark Levell, my "brother in McGurn," is another expert whom I can never thank enough. It is Mark who so perfectly described Jack McGurn as "the professional killer who killed professional killers."

I also want to express my deep gratitude to two individuals who wished to remain anonymous; they knew Jack McGurn, Louise Rolfe, and their families very well. They spoke to me off the record, helping me tremendously to uncover many personal details. It is common for authors in this genre to find sources who desire to share their knowledge for posterity but who must also have their anonymity, even after their deaths. It is up to each author how to deal with that promise; I always keep mine.

A very special thanks to Jerome Pohlen, senior editor at the wonderful Chicago Review Press, and Cynthia Sherry, publisher, as well as to Kelly Wilson, Mary Kravenas, Gerilee Hundt, Rachel McClain, and Jonathan Hahn. Thanks also to Kathryn Tumen and her team at IPG.

There are many great books on the Capone era, some of the best surprisingly written by non-Chicagoans. Besides their information, which I have cited, I owe all of those authors an acknowledgment of fraternity. I am proud to have been able to build upon what they have already given us; I know it was not easy for any of them. I especially wish to thank writers Bill Helmer and Daniel Waugh for their friendship and the late, great gangster expert Rick "Mad Dog" Mattix for his invaluable help. I also thank my attorney, Beverly Berneman, and pathologist Mark Hayes in the United Kingdom, for finding a few facts that, until now, we all seemed to miss.

Thanks with love to Sande Noble, my graduate mentor; the late Dr. Rosemary Cowler, who first edited this book; and to my professors Drs. Carol Gayle, Dan LeMahieu, and the late Arthur Zilverschmit at Lake Forest College. My undergraduate mentor, Dr. W. S. E. "Doc" Coleman at Drake University, taught me that life is the best theater.

My wife, Ann, and my son, Sam, have always been my reason for continuing to breathe for the last thirty-four years. My brothers, Mark Staller and Donald Lipski, have always made me something other than an only child, and they both aided me on this journey. Thank you to David and Thyra Gusfield, for the excellent education and your unconditional love, and to my cousin MacKinlay Kantor, one of America's greatest writers, who instructed me very early in my life. I also owe an immense debt to my beloved teachers A. Doraine Anderson and Ralph Ciancetti.

My deepest gratitude also goes to my dedicated and helpful readers Jerrold Carl and Bob Swedlow; ace defense attorneys Bob Gevirtz, Barry Sheppard, and Donnie Brenner; Peter Wenrich of the Palatine Police Department; and Professor Steve Weinberg at the University of Missouri. I also wish to thank Mario Gomes, whose website is an inspiration. Thanks to Captain Bruce Jacobs and Jeffrey Erickson for their contributions, and to John Rusetos, Louise Rolfe's great-grandson, for supplying family information regarding his grandmother Bonita Boex Rusetos. My great appreciation goes to Thomas DiGanci, who so generously shared his information on Captain William Drury, Chicago's most honest cop. Thank you, Christine Heineise, for your blessing on behalf of the Gebardi family.

For a very long time, whatever the truth is, I have tried to find it. We learn as we go.

Notes

Preface

1. Anthony Berardi died on July 13, 2005, at the age of ninety-nine. Al Capone liked the tough young photographer because he was Italian and had boxed as a teenager. According to his obituary in the *Chicago Tribune*, he was the first person to take a picture of Capone for which the boss actually posed. In "Prohibition," first televised on the History Channel on January 9, 1999, Berardi recalled how, in a display of affection, Capone had one of his bodyguards (probably Jack McGurn or Frankie Rio) stuff a race ticket into the young photographer's pocket at the Maywood horsetrack. The horse came in at extraordinary odds, paying the five-dollar ticket out at three hundred fifty. Nevertheless, Berardi said of Capone, "He was no hero to me. He hurt the Italian people."

Prologue: Call Everybody! Valentine's Day, 1929

1. Loftus's wife, Wilma, and nine-year-old daughter, Margaret, are listed in the fifteenth census of the United States, which occurred in 1930. Their address was 2737 Carmen Avenue, Chicago.
2. There were two REO Speedwagon vans, a White, a Mack, a Ford Diamond-T, a Ford delivery van, and a Dodge. The only one of the vehicles that was legally registered was the Ford van—it was owned by victim

Adam Heyer, whose alias was Frank Schneider. Some historians believe that "SMC" stood for "Schneider Moving and Cartage."

3. Loftus stated from the very beginning that there were a hundred shell casings, perhaps suggesting the use of two fifty-round drums. Both drums were recovered from Fred "Killer" Burke and are in the Berrien County (Michigan) Sheriff's Department archives with the weapons.

4. The first doctor on the scene was Frederick M. Doyle, whose office was at 2314 North Clark Street.

1. I Came to America to Give a Better Future to My Children, 1906

1. According to the Ellis Island archives, the *Gregory Morch* was built by Fairfield Shipbuilding & Engineering Company, Glasgow, Scotland, in 1889. The ship weighed 4,801 gross tons and was 390 feet long and 46 feet wide. It was powered by a triple-expansion steam engine with a single propeller. The cruising (service) speed was thirteen knots. It held 1,758 passengers. There were thirty-eight cabins in first class, twenty in second (cabin class), and seventeen hundred double-stacked bunks in steerage class. It was built for the North German Lloyd Company under the German flag in 1889 and named *Munchen*. It served various lines including the Bremerhaven–New York service. Sold to Russian owners in 1902 and renamed the *Gregory Morch*, it began sailing the Mediterranean–New York service. It was scrapped in 1910.

2. Atti Di Nascita (birth notation) for Vincenzo Gibaldi, *Tribunale Di Agrigento*, Provincia Di Agrigento, Citta Di Licata, July 2, 1902.

3. Manifest of alien passengers for the US immigration officer at port of arrival, list 1, November 24, 1906.

4. Her grave in Mount Carmel Cemetery in Hillside, Illinois, reads JOSEPHINE GEBARDI DE MORY, BELOVED MOTHER, 1887–1939.

5. Manifest of alien passengers for the commissioner of immigration, list 19, April 19, 1903.

2. Sicily in Brooklyn, 1907

1. "Secret Wake Conducted by Capone Gang," *Chicago Herald and Examiner*, February 16, 1936, 2. That Vincent allowed only his mother to call him "Jimmy" yet again confused the press at McGurn's funeral.

2. My source close to the Gebardi family knew that Josephine also passed on her recollections of Licata and her outlaw tales to the younger children who were born in America.

3. Richard Gambino, *Blood of My Blood: The Dilemma of the Italian-Americans* (Guernica Editions, Toronto, 1996), 286.

4. 14th census of the United States: 1920, Addison Street Apartments, Chicago.

3. He's Capable of Learning Many Things, 1911–1917

1. Social Security Administration death record for Frank Gebardi, May 24, 1989.

2. Cook County coroner's certificate of death for Anthony DeMory, March 2, 1936. Frank Gebardi attested to Anthony's date of birth.

3. In the coroner's inquest after Vincent's murder in 1936, Anthony Gebardi attested that his brother went through only two years of high school.

4. The same source confirmed that Vincent's grades were slightly above average in high school and that his handwriting and English were excellent.

4. She Who Is Born Beautiful Is Born Married, 1918

1. My source close to the family suggested that this was originally a wish of Tommaso Gibaldi's because anyone who wasn't Italian or Sicilian heard "Gebardi" whenever he or Josephine said "Gibaldi." The family members actually did change it after Tommaso's death, but not legally in court.

2. J. J. Johnston and Sean Curtin, *Chicago Boxing* (Chicago: Arcadia Publishing, 2005).

3. Ten years later, before dying of tuberculosis, Gans confessed that he had taken a dive. Until then, McGovern had never been aware of this, believing he had knocked his opponent down.

4. 14th census of the United States: 1920, 571 Sangamon Street, Chicago.

5. Edward Behr, *Prohibition: Thirteen Years That Changed America* (New York: Arcade, 1996), 3.

6. Joseph R. Gusfield, *Symbolic Crusade: Status Politics and the American Temperance Movement* (Urbana, IL: University of Illinois Press, 1963), 7. Joe is my beloved cousin.

7. "Old Maxwell Station Just Won't Die," *Chicago Tribune*, January 23, 1975, W4.

8. Both John Binder and Mark Levell have always concurred that Vincent would have gravitated to the 42 Gang in his own neighborhood. There have always been vague suggestions that he may have worked closer to the North Side with the Circus Gang on North Avenue because he was always friendly with Claude Maddox, who owned the Circus Café—but I believe that Vincent didn't meet Maddox until he went to work for Torrio and Capone.

9. F. Scott Fitzgerald, "The Offshore Pirate," from *Flappers and Philosophers* (New York: Charles Scribner & Sons, 1920).

10. My source close to the Rolfe family recalls how Louise began rebelling against her mother long before her parents divorced, claiming Louise had "a smart mouth."

5. Boxing, 1921

1. "To the Colors," *Chicago Tribune*, April 17, 1917, 8.

2. Johnston and Curtin, *Chicago Boxing*, 39.

3. "Tribune Decisions," *Chicago Tribune*, October 1, 1921, 14.

4. Happy Gilmore was legendary in Chicago boxing for his twenty-eight-round battle in 1887. After that memorable epic, he retired from the ring and taught others to fight. Some of his protégés were Tommy White, Eddie Santry, Harry Forbes, and Jimmy "The Little Tiger" Barry. In 1897, the Tiger, who weighed one hundred pounds, became the first bantamweight champion in Chicago. To his misfortune, he went on to kill Walter Croot in the twentieth round of a match in London, England, for the championship of the world. These men were certainly heroes to McGurn.

5. My anonymous source close to the Gebardi family told of how Vincent was also prompted to adopt an Irish-sounding name by his trainers at Feretti's gym. None of his family members ever called him Jack. His mother continued to refer to him as Jimmy, and his siblings only called him Vincent.

6. "Dundee Drills Here for Bout with Lawler," *Chicago Tribune*, January 17, 1924.

7. "Moore Beats Puryear in Mill on Commodore," *Chicago Tribune*, November 5, 1921, 10.

8. Helen Canazzaro testified in court after the St. Valentine's Day Massacre, revealing that she and Vincent were married under the name Gebardi in 1921.

6. If You Don't Do What I Want, I Won't Be Happy, 1921

1. "One Machine Is Upset; Two Men May Die," *Chicago Tribune*, March 28, 1921, 1.
2. "Attorney Hurt in Triple Auto Collision Dies," *Chicago Tribune*, March 30, 1921, 2.
3. "Brundage Sues 3 for $15,000 for Injuries in Automobile Crash," *Chicago Tribune*, July 15, 1921, 1.

7. Everyone Wants to Earn More Money, 1922

1. "Burman-Schaeffer Forfeits Up for Go," *Chicago Tribune*, January 28, 1922, 8.
2. "Badger 'Comish' O.K.'s Burman and Schaeffer," *Chicago Tribune*, February 2, 1922, 14.
3. "Add 1,000 Seats to Aurora Bout Bowl," *Chicago Tribune*, May 18, 1922, 16.
4. Sam Hall, "Taylor Holds Moore Even in 10-Round Bout," *Hammond (IN) Times*, June 24, 1922, 8.
5. 14th Wisconsin state census, 1905.
6. Marriage certificate, September 23, 1922, for Harold Anthony Boex and Louise May Rolfe, Waukegan, Illinois.

8. Terrible Misfortune, 1923

1. Behr, *Prohibition*, 187.
2. "Salesman Shot to Death in Mystery," *Chicago Daily News*, January 8, 1923, 1.
3. John H. Lyle, "The Story Behind the St. Valentine's Day Massacre," *Chicago Tribune*, February 21, 1954, 17.
4. Coroner's inquest of the murder of Angelo DeMory.
5. Ibid.
6. Ibid.
7. *Chicago Tribune*, January 9, 1923, 2.
8. My source close to the Gebardi family suggested that it was common knowledge who the men were who shot down Angelo DeMory; this was later confirmed by Al Capone when the same four were marked for death in order to eliminate the Genna brothers' worst killers.
9. Burial record of Angelo DeMory, Mount Carmel Catholic Cemetery.

9. We Remain Tormented in This Land, 1923

1. Cook County coroner's statistical history of the deceased, Angelo DeMora [*sic*], signed by his stepson James DeMora (Vincent Gebardi).
2. Cook County coroner's inquest #110101, case #14, January 8 and February 1, 1923.
3. William Balsamo, in a phone interview with the author, January 12, 2007.
4. After 1926, as the public begins to consistently see the impeccably dressed McGurn accompanying Al Capone to sporting events and chic restaurants, the police and members of the justice system no longer buy into the ignorant-immigrant-boy performance.

10. I've Been Living in This City for Three Years, 1923

1. "Boxers Tangle in St. Malachy Benefit Tonight," *Chicago Tribune*, May 21, 1923, 18.
2. "Mexican Heran Whips Gory in Brophy Post Go," *Chicago Tribune*, May 22, 1923, 25.
3. Bonita Boex, Harold's sister, is listed in the Wisconsin state census of 1905.
4. Birth certificate for Bonita Louise Boex, July 6, 1923 (Clerk of Cook County, file #6027962).
5. William Howland Kenney, *Chicago Jazz: A Cultural History 1904–1930* (New York: Oxford University Press, 1993).

11. This Man Knows Precisely What He Wants to Do, 1924

1. According to my source close to the Gebardi family, Teresa and Mafalda would ask Josephine DeMory to mass at St. Columbanus Church.
2. John Kobler, *Capone: The Life and World of Al Capone* (New York: Putnam, 1971), 103.
3. Rose Keefe, *Guns and Roses: The Untold Story of Dean O'Banion, Chicago's Big Shot Before Al Capone* (Nashville, TN: Cumberland House Publishing, 2003), 62.

12. Dean Is More Clever than Intelligent, 1924

1. My mother, Thyra Kantor Gusfield, and my aunt Janis Kantor Burke were North Side contemporaries of Louise Rolfe at Senn High School. They knew her as one of the "unfortunate tramps."

13. You Don't Have to Say Anything, 1925

1. "Genna Brother Murdered," *Chicago Tribune*, May 26, 1925, 1.
2. Bundesen, Chicago police suspect list, 1929, 1.
3. Edward M. Burke and Thomas J. O'Gorman, *End of Watch* (Chicago: Chicago's Books Press, 2007), 280.
4. "Anthony Genna Murdered," *Chicago Tribune*, July 9, 1925, 1.
5. Bundesen, Chicago police suspect list, 1929, 1.
6. Chicago police department, case #612490, October 30, 1925.
7. Bundesen, Chicago police suspect list, 1929, 2.
8. Chicago police department record of Probation Officer Devine for McGurn, Jack, case #612490. This is the only probation record I've ever found for McGurn. The probation officers in his future vanish, as does their paperwork.

14. I'd Like to Buy a Hat, 1926

1. My source close to the Gebardi family claimed that McGurn knew the identities of the four men who shot down his stepfather soon after the killing and that Angelo DeMory suspected Tropea and his men had sent him the Black Hand letters.
2. "Booze War Blamed for Man's Death," (AP) *Iowa City Press-Citizen*, February 16, 1926, 1.
3. "Quiz Grand Opera People in Chicago Gangland Murder," *Helena (MT) Independent*, January 12, 1926, 1.
4. "Police Puzzled over Latest Mafia Slaying," (AP) *Appleton (WI) Post-Crescent*, February 22, 1926, 1.
5. Bundesen, Chicago police suspect gun list, 1929.
6. "Gangland Has an Exodus of the Gunmen," *Davenport (IA) Democrat and Leader*, February 25, 1926, 17.
7. "Chicago Police to Resume Raids on Gangsters," (AP) *Zanesville (OH) Times Recorder*, February 25, 1926, 2.
8. "Bullet Rips Through Hat of Ex-Pugilist," *Chicago Tribune*, March 30, 1926, 1.
9. Bundesen, Chicago police suspect gun list, 1929.
10. Ibid.
11. "Acquit Genna Gang Police Killers," *Chicago Tribune*, March 19, 1926, 1.
12. Bundesen, Chicago police suspect gun list, 1929, 4.

13. Robert J. Schoenberg, *Mr. Capone* (New York: William Morrow, 1992), 150.

14. *Chicago Daily News*, May 21, 1928, 1.

15. The More One Works, the More One Earns, 1926

1. "Slain Portuguese Identified in $80,000 Holdup," *Chicago Tribune*, July 15, 1926, 5.

2. "Chicago Gangland Again Opens Fire," *Canandaigua (NY) Daily Messenger*, July 14, 1926, 1.

3. "Kill No. 42 in Rum Feuds," *Chicago Tribune*, August 11, 1926, 1.

4. "Clerk Wounded in Gang Shooting," *Chicago Tribune*, August 11, 1926, 1.

5. Frederick C. Othman, "The Lighter Side," *Syracuse (NY) Herald-Journal*, March 2, 1948, 1.

6. Schoenberg, *Mr. Capone*, 177.

7. Traditional thinking was that Weiss's men fired blank rounds to lure Capone outside; however, .45-caliber blanks without projectiles did not have the power to recycle in the Thompson gun. They were all definitely "live" bullets.

8. *Chicago Tribune*, September 21, 1926, 1.

16. I'm Not Afraid of His Words, I'm Afraid of What He Can Do, 1926

1. Bundesen, Chicago police suspect list, 1929, 4.

2. In thirty years of researching McGurn, I have never discovered where the nickel myth came from. As ritualistically interesting as it would be to leave a nickel in a dead victim's hand, Jack McGurn never lingered near his targets long enough to do even that. As much as I like the myth myself, there is not one piece of evidence to support it, other than the creativity of a post-1930s writer.

3. *Chicago Tribune*, November 12, 1926, 3.

4. "Two Killed, Four Others Wounded in Gangland War," (AP) *Waterloo (IA) Evening Courier*, October 12, 1926, 1.

5. Schoenberg, *Mr. Capone*, 162.

6. *Chicago Tribune*, November 12, 1926, 3.

7. Bundesen, Chicago police suspect gun list, 1929, 3.

8. McGurn used the 1927 version of the Thompson, which fired eight hundred rounds per minute. A few years later, the US Navy commissioned

General Thompson's company Auto Ordinance to reduce the rate of fire to six hundred rounds to improve accuracy. In addition, a Cutts compensator was attached to the end of the barrels to keep the muzzle from climbing so severely.

9. "Gang War for Liquor Control," (AP) *Davenport (IA) Democrat and Leader*, October 12, 1926, 1.

10. "Shoot to Kill Orders Issued for Gangland," (UP) *Sheboygan (WI) Press*, October 13, 1926, 12.

11. "'Scarface Capone,' King of Underworld, Exposes Booze Ring," (AP) *Iowa City Press-Citizen*, October 13, 1926, 1.

12. "Cicero Restaurateur Missing," *Chicago Tribune*, December 5, 1926, 1.

13. Fred D. Pasley, *Al Capone: The Biography of a Self-Made Man* (New York: Ives Washburn, 1930), 68.

14. "River Dragged for Rum Gangster's Body," (AP) *Oakland (CA) Tribune*, December 5, 1926, 1.

15. Charles Thompson, *Bing* (London: Wyndham Publications, 1976), 30.

17. Aren't You Ashamed of What You Did? 1927

1. "Chicago Man's Body Found," (AP) *Salt Lake (UT) Tribune*, January 6, 1927, 1.

2. Kobler, *Capone*, 199.

3. "Retired Dentist Played Piano for Al Capone," *Suburban Life Citizen* (Chicago, IL), September 13, 1989.

4. William Roemer, *Accardo—The Genuine Godfather* (New York: Donald I. Fine, 1995), 19.

5. Bill Nunes, *Illinois in the Roaring 1920s* (St. Louis, 2006), 35.

6. "Unidentified Man Found Shot to Death in Street," *Chicago Tribune*, May 26, 1927, 3.

7. Bundesen, Herman N., coroner of Cook County, murder, suspect, and suspect weapon chart, annotated, 1929.

8. Roemer, *Accardo*.

9. "Body of Man Found Sewn in Burlap Bag," (AP) *Charleston (WV) Daily Mail*, July 18, 1927, 2.

10. "Arraign Suspect in Cinderella Death," (AP) *Wisconsin Rapids Daily Tribune*, August 2, 1927, 1.

11. "Man Arrested in Cinderella Death Released Today," (AP) *Sheboygan (WI) Press*, August 10, 1927, 12.

12. "Friends Are Saddened over Willie's Death," *Hammond (IN) Times*, October 17, 1935.

13. Milton Mezzrow and Bernard Wolfe, *Really the Blues* (New York: Random House, 1946).

14. My anonymous source who was extremely close to the Rolfes remembered how Louise always attended any shows or theatricals headlining famous performers, and that at this time she had essentially become a "gold digger," always searching for "sugar daddies" who could support her.

15. Mario Gomes, www.myalcaponemuseum.com.

18. Sometimes Cat and Mouse Dance Together, 1927

1. John H. Lyle, *The Dry and Lawless Years* (New York: Prentice-Hall, 1960).

2. James Doherty, "Texas Guinan, Queen of Whoopee!," *Chicago Tribune*, May 4, 1931, B4.

3. James Doherty, "I Remember Prohibition," *Chicago Tribune*, March 11, 1951, C6.

4. Recounted by Captain Bruce Jacobs, who grew up hearing the story of his grandfather's confrontation with Jack McGurn.

5. Danny Cohen denies McGurn had any interest in the Green Mill.

6. Art Cohn, *The Joker Is Wild: The Story of Joe E. Lewis* (New York: Random House, 1958), 4.

7. Ibid., 7.

8. Schoenberg, *Mr. Capone*, 294.

9. Cohn, *The Joker Is Wild*, 52.

19. We'll Come Back Later, 1928

1. "Beer Runner Slain; Body Found in Snow," *Chicago Tribune*, January 2, 1928, 1.

2. Ibid.

3. Bundesen, weapon/suspect list, weapon number 14, held in the Goddard laboratory.

4. "Goldberg Shot; Police Look for New Gang War," *Chicago Tribune*, February 15, 1928, 16.

5. Bundesen, Chicago police suspect list, 1929, 4–5.

6. "Arrested with Gun as He Seeks to Avenge Beating," *Chicago Tribune*, October 3, 1926, 12.

7. "Feud Opens Up in Hotel Shop; McGurn Victim," *Chicago Tribune*, March 8, 1928, 1.

8. "View McGurn Attack as Part of Gaming War," *Chicago Tribune*, March 9, 1928, 7.

9. "Gangland Breaks Lose Again; McGurn Is Shot," (UP) *Sheboygan (WI) Press*, March 8, 1928, 13.

10. Ibid.

11. "Gangster Shot in Chicago Row," (AP) *Reno (NV) Evening Gazette*, March 8, 1928.

12. "Lost Shipment of Machine Guns Now Sought by Chicago Police," (AP) *Reno (NV) Evening Gazette*, March 9, 1928, 9.

20. Do You Know Who I Am? 1928

1. David E. Ruth, *Inventing the Public Enemy: The Gangster in American Culture, 1918–1934* (University of Chicago Press, 1996), 134.

2. "Machine Gun Spray Laid to Capone's North Side Invasion," *Chicago Daily News*, March 8, 1928, 1.

3. "View McGurn Attack as Part of Gaming War," *Chicago Tribune*, March 9, 1928, 7.

4. Ruth, *Inventing the Public Enemy*, 133.

5. Photograph of the bullet holes in McGurn's 1928 Lincoln L sedan, *Chicago American*, May 18, 1928, 1.

6. "McGurn Again Gun's Target; Escapes Unhit," *Chicago Tribune*, April 18, 1928, 1.

7. "Chicago Gangster Becomes Realtor," (AP) *Bismarck (ND) Tribune*, May 15, 1928,

21. When Love Knocks, Be Sure to Answer, 1928

1. "Texas Guinan," *Chicago Tribune*, March 4, 1951, B4.

2. This was recounted by Roy Erikson on July 12, 1997. During the day, Erikson worked at Patton's Garage, repairing some of the more exotic automobiles, many of which belonged to the Capone Outfit. They appreci-

ated his talents and his mature attitude; he was offered a job driving a beer truck. When Erikson politely turned it down, they offered to make him a "chauffeur." Smart enough to know where this would lead him, he said, "No, thank you."

3. "Captured Gangster's Girl Friend Revealed a Divorcee and Mother of 5-Year-Old Child," *Chicago Tribune*, March 1, 1929, 2. Louise tells reporters that she has known McGurn for three years.

4. According to my anonymous family source, McGurn found it difficult to sit still for the entire length of a movie and could be found smoking and pacing out in the foyer once every half hour.

5. Bundesen, Chicago police suspect list, 1929, 3.

6. "Police Sergeant's Son Mysteriously Shot: Won't Talk," *Chicago Evening Post*, November 14, 1928, 1.

7. "Former Fireman Shot, Pulls Fire Box to Call Aid," *Chicago Tribune*, November 14, 1928, 1.

8. "Hunt McGurn in Davern Slaying," *Chicago American*, February 16, 1929, 1.

9. William J. Davern Jr., *Chicago Tribune*, January 1, 1929, 63.

10. "Gang Massacre Inquiry Shifts to Dyers Feud," *Chicago Tribune*, February 20, 1929, 1.

11. William J. Helmer and Arthur J. Bilek, *The St. Valentine's Day Massacre* (Nashville: Cumberland House, 2004), 231–32.

12. Laurence Bergreen, *Capone: The Man and the Era* (New York: Simon & Schuster, 1994), 306.

13. Bundesen, Chicago police suspect list, 1929, 4.

22. Who Looks for a Quarrel Finds a Quarrel, 1929

1. Roemer, *Accardo*, 52.

2. Chicago police statement of Mrs. Minnie Arvidson, February 18, 1929, recorded by officers Connelley and Devane.

3. Helmer and Bilek, *The St. Valentine's Day Massacre*, 103–104.

4. George Brichet testifies to what he saw in the coroner's inquest, but the transcript mysteriously "disappears," including a copy that ends up at the Chicago Crime Commission.

5. Ted Newberry is the most likely suspect to have been the inside informer to Capone; he joined the Outfit soon after Valentine's Day.

6. Chicago police department document C.O. #42, March 28, 1930, 2.

7. FBI agent William Roemer heard Accardo claim to have been with McGurn on the wiretap device known as "Little Al" two decades later.

8. "Seize M'Gurn for Massacre," *Chicago Tribune*, February 28, 1929, 1.

9. My second cousin, Julius Schaefer, head of the Chicago ASPCA in the 1950s and 1960s, claimed in a 1968 interview that the euthanasia of Highball was carried out in the early spring of 1929.

10. Walter Trohan, *Political Animals: Memoirs of a Sentimental Cynic* (Garden City, NY: Doubleday, 1975), 25.

11. Bergreen, *Capone*, 312.

12. Thomas Donnelly, *The Plain Truth*, Chicago Employer's Association pamphlet, Chicago Historical Society (Chicago History Museum).

13. John H. Lyle, *The Dry and Lawless Years* (Englewood Cliffs, NJ: Prentice-Hall, 1960), 187.

14. "2 Capone Men Seized as Gang Massacre Aides," *Chicago American*, February 28, 1929, 1.

23. The Wicked Man, 1929

1. Robert V. Allegrini, *Chicago's Grand Hotels* (Chicago: Arcadia Publishing, 2007).

2. "McGurn Seized in Hotel Hideout," *Chicago Tribune*, February 28, 1929, 1.

3. "Dentist Charges Capone Aid Held Him with Machine Gun," *Chicago Tribune*, February 23, 1929, 1.

4. "Kidnapped Man Names Suspect in Massacre," *New York American*, February 23, 1929, 1.

5. Ibid., 2.

6. "Net Drawn Around Gunman Tightens," (UP) *Lincoln (NE) Evening Journal*, March 1, 1929, 5.

7. "2 Capone Men Seized as Gang Massacre Aides," *Chicago American*, February 28, 1929, 1.

8. "Louise Denies Her Jack Was in Massacre," *Chicago Tribune*, February 28, 1929, 2.

9. "Captured Gangster's Girlfriend Revealed a Divorcee and Mother of 5-Year-Old Child," *Chicago Tribune*, March 2, 1929, 5.

10. "The Golfing Gangster Can't Make It Now Under 180 [Days]," *New York Mirror*, October 8, 1933, back page.

11. "The Ace of Chicago Gangster Killers Is Identified," (AP) *Oshkosh (WI) Daily Northwestern*, February 28, 1929, 1.

12. "'Ace' of Gang Gunmen Held in Massacre," (AP) *Oakland (CA) Tribune*, February 28, 1929, 3.

13. "Jack Greets Louise in Fleeting Embrace," *Chicago Tribune*, March 2, 1929, 2.

14. "Blond Beauty Hope of Massacre Suspect," *Davenport (IA) Democrat and Leader*, March 1, 1929, 1.

15. "Louise Denies Her Jack Was in Massacre," *Chicago Daily News*, February 27, 1929.

16. "McGurn's Blond Alibi Doesn't Spill Secrets," (AP) *Sheboygan (WI) Press*, March 1, 1929, 17.

24. This Doesn't Suffice to Remove All Suspicions, 1929

1. "Two Men Charged with Gang Killing," (UP) *Stevens Point (WI) Daily Journal*, March 2, 1929, 7.

2. "Three Named Wielders with Machine Gun," (AP) *Syracuse (NY) Herald*, March 5, 1929, 1.

3. "Hide-and-Seek Terrors of the Wistful Boy Gangster," *Helena (MT) Daily Independent*, March 10, 1929, back page.

4. "M'Gurn Accused in Gang Slaying," (AP) *Reno (NV) Evening Gazette*, March 11, 1929.

5. Helmer and Bilek, *The St. Valentine's Day Massacre*, 93.

6. Bundesen, Herman N., coroner of Cook County, letter to Major Calvin Goddard, April 1, 1929.

7. Ibid., 1.

8. "Machine Guns Found Sold to Rival Gangsters," (UP) *Coshocton (OH) Tribune*, April 20, 1929, 1.

9. "Officers Plow into Evidence from Massacre," (AP) *Sheboygan (WI) Press*, May 2, 1929, 28.

25. Mind Test, 1929

1. In his diary, police lieutenant William Drury mentions that the famous alienist Hickson had been consulted concerning the gangster violence.

2. "Girl Psychiatrist Upsets Chicago Gangster; Dapper Suspect Loses Poise in Sanity Test," *New York Times*, August 17, 1929, 10.

3. William John Drury, personal diary entry, August 16, 1929, provided by Thomas Edward DiGanci, January 29, 2003.

4. Schoenberg, *Mr. Capone*, 186.

5. Federal grand jury indictment #20592 against James Gebardi and Louise Rolfe for interstate commerce for immoral purposes.

6. "Jack M'Gurn, Blond Sweetie Face White Slavery Indictment," *Chicago Tribune*, October 30, 1929, 2.

7. Karen Abbott, *Sin in the Second City* (New York: Random House, 2007), 207.

26. See You Soon! 1930

1. "Charge Capone Aide Received Kidnap Ransom," (AP) *Wisconsin Rapids Daily Tribune*, January 18, 1939, 12.

2. "Seek Woman in Slaying of Loesch Sleuth," *Chicago Tribune*, February 2, 1930, 1.

3. "Rosenheim Is Shot to Death by Gangsters," (AP) *Lima (OH) Sunday News*, February 2, 1930, 22.

4. Roemer, *Accardo*, 55.

5. "M'Gurn Loses Battle to Keep Gun from Jury," *Chicago Daily News*, June 24, 1930, 1.

6. "M'Gurn and Pal Seized," *Chicago Tribune*, February 1, 1930, 1.

7. "Take Steps to Correct Crime," *Havre (MT) Daily News*, February 8, 1930, 1.

8. "Two Held After Gangsters Kill Chicago Sleuth," (AP) *Decatur (IL) Evening Herald*, February 1, 1930, 1.

9. "Unpaid Police Stand Between Gang Killings and Chicago Millions," (UP) *Sheboygan (WI) Press*, February 6, 1930, 2.

10. F. Richard Ciccone, *Chicago and the American Century* (Chicago: Contemporary Books, 1999), 174.

11. "Jack McGurn Arrested on Miami Golf Course," (AP) *Bismarck (ND) Tribune*, April 1, 1930, 1.

12. "Chicago Authorities Credit McGurn with Being Deadliest, Most Ruthless of Gangsters," *Miami Daily News*, April 1, 1930, 1.

13. "Miami Bags Big Shots for Chicago," *Chicago Tribune*, April 1, 1930, 2.

27. I'd Send You to Jail, 1930

1. "Charge Capone Aide Received Kidnap Ransom," (AP) *Wisconsin Rapids Daily Tribune*, January 18, 1939, 12.
2. "Chicago Gangs Put on Thriller, 1 Dead, 3 Hurt," (AP) *Jefferson City (MO) Post-Tribune*, May 31, 1930, 2.
3. "Chicago Killer Slain, Wounds Two Companions," (AP) *Kokomo (IN) Tribune*, May 31, 1930, 2.
4. Ray Walsh, *Fox Lake Police Association and Village of Fox Lake History, 1907–1962* (Fox Lake, IL: Fox Lake Publishing, 1982).
5. "Round Up 200 Men in Drive on Gangsters in Chicago—Two of Capone's Men Captured After Chase," (AP) *Elyria (OH) Chronicle-Telegram*, June 3, 1930.
6. "Jack McGurn No Sooner Out than He Is Tossed In Again," *Chicago Tribune*, June 2, 1930, 1.
7. "Seize Jack M'Gurn," *Chicago American*, June 2, 1930, 1.
8. "Crack Gunner of Al Capone Must Serve One Year," (UP) *Oshkosh (WI) Daily Northwestern*, June 26, 1930, 9.
9. "M'Gurn Guilty; Second Gunman Headed to Jail," *Chicago Tribune*, June 25, 1930, 1.
10. "Putting Them Away," *Oakland (CA) Tribune*, July 2, 1930, editorial page.
11. "Al Capone 'Absorbs' Rivals to Form Co-operative Bootleg Organization," *Port Arthur (TX) News*, September 11, 1930, 10.
12. Even though forensics from Goddard connects one of the guns that killed Zuta to Danny Stanton, he walked away from the charge.
13. Raphael W. Marrow and Harriet I. Carter, *In Pursuit of Crime: The Police of Chicago, 1833–1933* (Sunbury, OH: Rats Publishing, 1995), 630.
14. "Ex-Unione Siciliane Leader Gunned Down," *Chicago Tribune*, October 24, 1930, 1.

28. Nothing Lasts Forever, 1931

1. "Pubic Enemy McGurn Seized on Lyle Charge," *Chicago Tribune*, February 2, 1931, 1.
2. "McGurn Faces Court—Given a Jury Trial," *Chicago Daily News*, February 4, 1931, 2.
3. "Status of Public Enemies," (UP) *Sheboygan (WI) Press*, March 19, 1931, 8.

4. "Yes, Jack M'Gurn Buys Oak Park Home 'On Time'!" *Chicago Tribune*, October 21, 1932, 2.

5. "Capone Sought as Suspect in Torch Slaying," (AP) *Lima (OH) News*, May 2, 1931, 1.

6. "Wed 3 Days After Wife Gets Decree," *Chicago Tribune*, May 6, 1931, 1.

7. Lake County marriage license of Vincent Gebardi and Louise Boex, issued May 3, 1931.

8. "Dapper Gangster Gets 2 Years—Wife 4 Months," *Chicago Tribune*, July 22, 1931, 2.

9. Ibid.

10. "McGurn Given 2-Year Term; Wife to Jail," *Chicago Herald-Examiner*, July 22, 1931, 1.

11. "Cleaning Up Chicago," (UP) *Oshkosh (WI) Daily Northwestern*, July 23, 1931, 12.

12. "Capone Gets 'Bronx Cheer' as He Sees Football Game," (AP) *Reno Nevada State Journal*, October 4, 1931, 1.

13. Schoenberg, *Mr. Capone*, 315.

29. The Bad Intention, 1932

1. "McGurn Mann Act Conviction Upheld by Court," *Chicago Tribune*, April 3, 1932, 2.

2. "Machine Gun Jack's Conviction," *New York American*, April 3, 1932.

3. Walter Winchell (syndicated), "You've Got the Wrong Slant, Capone Told Man Who Jailed Him," *Mansfield (OH) News-Journal*, May 13, 1950, 5.

4. Ibid.

5. "Court Refuses McGurn Hearing," *Circleville (OH) Herald*, May 4, 1932, 1.

6. Thompson, *Bing*, 58.

7. Ibid., 59.

8. This also explains why Louise gave her name as De Vito when she was involved in the fatal accident in 1934.

9. "Court Dismisses 6 of 7 Charges Against Jack McGurn, Kin," *Chicago Sun-Times*, August 30, 1932, 3.

10. "Machine Gun M'Gurn Freed; Brother Fined," *Chicago Tribune*, August 31, 1932, 2.

11. "McGurn Explains Police Radio Calls, Freed," *Chicago American*, August 30, 1932, 1.

30. A Great Victory, 1932

1. "Arrest Wife of Jack M'Gurn in Auto Chase," *Chicago Tribune*, November 1, 1932, 2.

2. *Brief for the United States: Jack Gebardi, alias Jack McGurn, alias Jim Vincent D'Oro, and Louise Rolfe, vs. United States of America, Thomas D. Thacher, Nugent Dodds, & James Wharton*, filed July 5, 1932, case no. 97 (Supreme Court Archives).

3. Letter from US attorney Dwight H. Green to assistant attorney general of the United States Seth W. Richardson, September 27, 1932, 2 (National Archives).

4. Letter from US attorney Dwight H. Green to the attorney general of the United States, October 1, 1932 (National Archives).

5. Letter from US attorney George E. Q. Johnson to assistant attorney general Nugent Dodds, October 2, 1932 (National Archives).

6. "Pair Convicted Under Mann Act Win Reversal," *New York Tribune*, November 8, 1932, 2.

7. "Chicago Gangs Decimated and Funds Depleted," (UP) *Oshkosh (WI) Daily Northwestern*, November 23, 1932, 7.

8. Mars Eghigian Jr., *After Capone: The Life and World of Chicago Mob Boss Frank "The Enforcer" Nitti* (Nashville, TN: Cumberland House, 2006), 222.

9. Behr, *Prohibition*, 235.

10. "Compile New List of 'Undesirables,'" *Ironwood (MI) Daily Globe*, January 10, 1933, 1.

11. "Halt Hoodlums' Trip and Seize Six Doughnuts," *Chicago Tribune*, February 15, 1933, 3.

12. Gus Russo, *The Outfit* (New York: Bloomsbury Press, 2001), 94.

31. I Am Innocent! 1933

1. "Capone Gunman Reported Shot on Golf Links," *Chicago Daily News*, July 17, 1933, 1.

2. "Gangster M'Gurn Refutes Reports That He Is Dead," (AP) *Lincoln (NE) Star*, July 18, 1933, 2.

3. "Western Open Starts Today with 18 Holes," *Chicago Tribune*, August 25, 1933, sports page.

4. Olympia Fields Country Club, correct diagram of the completed four courses, 1933.

5. "McGurn Found Playing in Golf Title Match," *Chicago Tribune*, August 27, 1933, 1.

6. "Golfing Gangster's Game Disrupted," (UP) *Reno Nevada State Journal*, August 27, 1933, 1.

7. Edward M. Burke and Thomas J. O'Gorman, *End of Watch: Chicago Police Killed in the Line of Duty 1853–2006* (Chicago: Chicago's Books Press, 2007), 367–76. McGurn's comment here refers to the shocking fact that eleven Chicago police officers had been shot down since January. They were patrolmen Maurice Marcusson and Roscoe C. Johnston on January 20; Arthur D. Mutter on April 18; Stanley J. Lutke on April 30; Oscar E. Brosseau on June 1; Harry J. Redlich, who left a wife and four daughters, on July 8; Elmer R. Ostling and John Skopek on July 22; John G. Sevick on July 24; Patrick J. Ryan on August 8; Joseph P. Hastings on August 14; and Miles Cunningham on September 22.

8. "Arrest M'Gurn as He Golfs in Western Open," *Chicago Tribune*, August 27, 1933, 1.

32. Only You Were Singing in the Silence, 1933

1. "From Par to Boxcars," *Lincoln (NE) Star*, August 28, 1933, 4.

2. "McGurn Faces Kidnap Quiz," *Chicago Tribune*, August 28, 1933, 1.

3. "Federal Power Is Put Behind War on Gangs," *Chicago Tribune*, August 28, 1933, 1.

4. Ibid.

5. "Lawyer Attacks Law Invoked by Police," *Chicago Tribune*, August 30, 1933, 1.

6. Ibid.

7. "Gangster Sentenced by Judge He Played Golf with in Chicago," *New York Sun*, September 7, 1933, 3.

8. "Machine Gun Jack Jailed as Vagrant," *Chicago Tribune*, September 6, 1933, 2.

9. "The Golfing Gangster Can't Make It Now Under 180 [Days]," *New York Mirror*, October 8, 1933.

33. I Don't See Anyone, Anywhere, 1934

1. "Caution Needed," (AP) *Newark (NJ) Advocate and American Tribune*, May 15, 1934, 1.

2. "Jack McGurn's Brother Shot to Death," *Chicago Tribune*, March 3, 1936, 1.

3. "Chicago Club Gets a Fire at 'Preview,'" (AP) *Oakland (CA) Tribune*, June 21, 1934, 3.

4. "McGurn's Wife Seeks Crown," *Chicago Tribune*, August 14, 1934, 3.

5. J. Edgar Hoover, letter to Mr. Holtzhoff, special assistant to the attorney general, May 17, 1935 (FBI files).

6. "Friends Are Saddened over Willie's Death," (AP) *Hammond (IN) Times*, October 17, 1935, 1.

34. February May Be Short, but It's the Worst Month, 1935–1936

1. "Rio Death Bares Capone Offer in Lindbergh Case," *Chicago Tribune*, February 25, 1935, 8.

2. "Machine Gun M'Gurn Slain," *Chicago Tribune*, February 15, 1936, 1.

3. "Capone Chief Shot Down in Bowling Alley," *Chicago Tribune*, February 16, 1936, 1.

4. Eghigian, *After Capone*, 301.

5. Death notice for Giuseppe Circella, *Chicago Tribune*, February 12, 1936, 28.

6. Federal Bureau of Investigation wiretap transcript #CG 92-795, recorded January 28, 1960, HH (Chicago Crime Commission).

7. Cook County coroner's inquest, #167302, case #15, February 15, 1936, 18.

8. "Valentine Guns Kill Capone Thug," (AP) *Newark (NJ) Advocate and American Tribune*, February 15, 1936, 2.

9. City of Chicago police department offense report #89991, February 15, 1936, filed by commanding officer Martin E. Mullen.

10. Chicago police department homicide section, circular order #42—murder of Vincent Gebardi, alias Jack McGurn, February 29, 1936, 2.

11. Autopsy statement for Vincent Gebardi, D.O.A., February 15, 1936.

12. "Gang Slaying of Jack McGurn Is Seen as Climax of Alky War," *Chicago Daily News*, February 15, 1936, 1.

13. Statement of Louise Gebardi relative to the murder of Jack McGurn, taken in the captain's office of the Twenty-Ninth District police station, 6:00 AM, February 15, 1936.

14. Chicago police department homicide section, circular order #42—murder of Vincent Gebardi, alias Jack McGurn, February 29, 1936, 5.

15. Statement taken from William Belmonte relative to the murder of Vincent Gebardi, taken in the captain's office of the Twenty-Ninth District police station, 4:45 AM, February 15, 1936.

16. "Gang Menace Hides M'Gurn Killers," *Chicago Herald-Examiner*, February 16, 1936, 1.

17. Chicago police department bureau of identification report #244, February 17, 1936.

18. "'Machine Gun McGurn Slain by Three Gunmen," *Chicago Daily News*, February 15, 1936, 3.

19. Statement taken from William Aloisio relative to the murder of Vincent Gebardi, taken in the captain's office of the Twenty-Ninth District police station, 4:15 AM, February 15, 1936.

20. "McGurn Slain by Two Companions, Theory," *Chicago Daily News*, February 18, 1936, 1.

21. Statement taken from Tony Mascarella relative to the murder of Vincent Gebardi, taken in the captain's office of the Twenty-Ninth District police station, 3:10 AM, February 15, 1936.

22. Statement taken from Edward Bonarek relative to the murder of Vincent Gebardi, taken in the captain's secretary's office of the Twenty-Ninth District police station, 12:45 PM, February 15, 1936.

23. "Slain Capone Gunman's Aim Too High," *Chicago American*, February 15, 1936, 18.

24. "Secret Wake Conducted by Capone Gang," *Chicago Herald-Examiner*, February 16, 1936, 2.

35. Why? 1936

1. "Three Gunmen Raid Union Headquarters; Steal Records," *Chicago Tribune*, February 6, 1936, 4.

2. "Trace Gebardi and Prignano Death Weapons," *Chicago Tribune*, March 5, 1936, 1.

3. "Veteran Gangland Writer Tells Theory in Death of 'Machine Gun' Jack M'Gurn," (UP) *Coshocton (OH) Tribune*, February 16, 1936, 10.

4. "Mansfield Woman Tells of Slain Gangster as Newsboy in 'Little Hell,'" *Mansfield (OH) News-Journal*, February 17, 1936, 1. This is both an amusing

and a pathetic fantasy by a woman who obviously felt a kinship to McGurn, produced more from nostalgic feelings for her Chicago childhood than from any reality.

36. Whoever Desires Too Much Ends Up with Nothing, 1936

1. "M'Gurn's Widow Held by Police; Confesses Lies," *Chicago Daily News*, February 17, 1936, 1.
2. "Quizzed in McGurn Slaying," *Chicago Daily News*, February 17, 1936, 1.
3. "Girl Pals of Mrs. McGurn in Death Quiz," *Chicago Tribune*, February 17, 1936, 1.
4. "Mrs. McGurn Faces New Quiz as Friend Tells of Spree," *Chicago Daily News*, February 17, 1936, 1.
5. "McGurn Widow Faces Girls in Slaying Inquiry," *Chicago Tribune*, February 18, 1936, 1.
6. "Reveal M'Gurn Widow's Visit to Bank Vault," *Chicago Tribune*, February 19, 1936, 1.
7. "Blond Alibi in Hiding," *New York Times*, February 17, 1936, 1.
8. "Bullets Chief Clues to M'Gurn Slaying," *Oshkosh (WI) Northwestern*, February 20, 1936, 11.
9. "Killers Try to Silence Pretty Wife of Gangster," *New York American*, March 21, 1936, 1.

37. I Feared He'd Come Back and Kill Me, 1936

1. "Blame Boasting for Slaying of M'Gurn Brother," *Chicago Daily News*, March 3, 1936, 2.
2. Inquest on the body of Anthony De Mory by the coroner of Cook County, final session, March 25, 1936, conducted by James J. Whalen, deputy coroner, 4.
3. Coroner's certificate of death #9216, James J. Whalen, deputy coroner of Cook County, March 26, 1936.
4. "Jack McGurn's Brother Shot to Death," *Chicago Tribune*, March 3, 1936, 1.
5. "Crimes Linked to Battle over Unione Siciliano," *Chicago Herald and Examiner*, March 3, 1936, 2.
6. "Round Up 'Punks' in M'Gurn Death," *Chicago Daily News*, March 3, 1936, 4.

7. "Gebardi Gun Is Traced to Gary Store," (INS) *Hammond (IN) Times*, March 5, 1936, 2.

8. "Trace Gebardi and Prignano Death Weapons," *Chicago Tribune*, March 5, 1936, 1.

9. Hoover, J. Edgar, "Memorandum for Mr. Joseph Keeman, Acting Attorney General," 1934.

10. Inquest on the body of Anthony DeMory by the coroner of Cook County, final session, March 25, 1936, conducted by James J. Whalen, deputy coroner, 11.

11. Death certificate for Joseph DeMory, June 12, 1942 (Clerk of Cook County, file #16960).

38. Lulu Lou: What I Want, You Don't Have, 1936–1995

1. "Hunt Mystery Woman in Fatal Auto Collision," *Chicago Tribune*, October 8, 1936, 2.

2. "'Blond Alibi' Is Sought as Death Driver," *Chicago Daily News*, October 8, 1936, 1.

3. "Blond Alibi Provides Own: Wasn't Driving," *New York Daily Times*, October 9, 1936, 1.

4. "Louise McGurn Weeps as She Denies Driving Death Car," *Chicago Daily News*, October 10, 1936, 1.

5. Ibid.

6. "McGurn's Widow Cleared as Driver," *Chicago Herald and Examiner*, November 26, 1936, 2.

7. "Blond Alibi Manslaughter Charges Dropped," *New York Daily Times*, November 26, 1936, 2.

8. "Mate Divorces M'Gurn Widow for Desertion," *Chicago Tribune*, October 24, 1945, 3.

9. "Valentine Jinx on McGurn Widow," *Chicago Tribune*, February 14, 1940, 3.

10. "Blond Alibi Freed in Court," *New York Daily Times*, February 16, 1940, 2.

11. Death record for Bernard F. Rolfe, November 22, 1940 (Clerk of Cook County, file #32375).

12. Marriage license for Bonita L. Boex and Leo Rusetos, February 11, 1943 (Clerk of Cook County, file #1763475).

13. John Rusetos, Bonita Boex Rusetos's grandson, writes that Louise and Bonita reunited after his birth in 1973.

14. "McGurn's Widow Jailed," *Chicago Daily News*, March 3, 1943, 2.

15. "Blond Alibi Released in Army Deserter Case," *Chicago Sun-Times*, March 5, 1943.

16. "Glamour Gone, Blond Alibi Is Just a Working Girl Now," *Chicago Daily News*, March 4, 1943, 2.

17. "Mate Divorces M'Gurn Widow for Desertion," *Chicago Tribune*, October 24, 1945, 3.

18. "Police Seek Her Husband and Ex-Mate," *Chicago Sun-Times*, September 22, 1947, 2.

19. *Chicago Sun-Times*, November 26, 1951, 6.

20. "'Blond Alibi' Turns Up Again—to Complain," *Chicago Tribune*, November 26, 1951, A6.

21. "Blond Alibi Wins Again in Court Case," *Chicago Sun-Times*, November 29, 1951, 3.

22. Marriage certificate for Bonita L. Rusetos and Sam Minerva, 1951 (Clerk of Cook County, file #2197670).

23. Obituary for J. B. Nash, *Sonoma (CA) Index-Tribune*, June 7, 1994, A-4.

24. US Social Security Administration death records.

25. John Rusetos, grandson of Bonita Boex and great-grandson of Louise Rolfe, has photographs taken of Louise and Bonita together at the time of his birth.

26. Mario Gomes, interview with Nancy Miller, 2007, www.myalcaponemuseum.com.

27. Social Security death record, February 21, 1995.

28. Michael Yore Graham, in a phone interview with the author, June 12, 1996.

Bibliography

Abbott, Karen. *Sin in the Second City.* New York: Random House, 2007.

Allegrini, Robert V. *Chicago's Grand Hotels.* Chicago: Arcadia Publishing, 2007.

Allen, Frederick Lewis. *Only Yesterday: An Informal History of the 1920s.* New York: Harper & Row, 1931.

Anonymous. *X Marks the Spot.* Chicago: The Spot Publishing, 1930.

Asbury, Herbert. *Gem of the Prairie: An Informal History of the Chicago Underworld.* Dekalb, IL: Northern Illinois University Press, 1986.

Barkow, Al. *The Golden Era of Golf: How America Rose to Dominate the Old Scots Game.* New York: St. Martin's Press, 2000.

Behr, Edward. *Prohibition: Thirteen Years That Changed America.* New York: Arcade Publishing, 1996.

Benton, Barbara. *Ellis Island: A Pictorial History.* New York: Facts on File, 1985.

Bilek, Arthur J. *The First Vice Lord.* Nashville, TN: Cumberland House, 2008.

Binder, John J. *The Chicago Outfit.* Chicago: Arcadia Publishing, 2003.

Bonner, J. K. *Introduction to Sicilian Grammar.* Brooklyn, NY: Legas, 2001.

Bukowski, Douglas. *Big Bill Thompson, Chicago, and the Politics of Image.* Urbana, IL: University of Illinois Press, 1998.

Bunce, Steve. *Boxing Greats: Legendary Boxers, Fights and Moments.* Surrey, England: Quadrillion Publishing, 1990.

Burke, Edward M., and Thomas J. O'Gorman. *End of Watch: Chicago Police Killed in the Line of Duty 1853–2006.* Chicago: Chicago's Books Press, 2007.

Candeloro, Dominic. *Italians in Chicago*. Charleston, SC: Arcadia Publishing, 1999.

Ciccone, F. Richard. *Chicago and the American Century*. New York: McGraw-Hill, 1999.

Cohn, Art. *The Joker Is Wild: The Story of Joe E. Lewis*. New York: Random House, 1955.

Demlinger, Sandor, and John Steiner. *Destination Chicago Jazz*. Chicago: Arcadia Publishing, 2003.

Eghigian, Mars Jr. *After Capone: The Life and World of Chicago Mob Boss Frank "The Enforcer" Nitti*. Nashville, TN: Cumberland House, 2003.

Fitzgerald, F. Scott. "The Offshore Pirate," from *Flappers and Philosophers*. New York: Charles Scribner & Sons, 1920.

Gambino, Richard. *Blood of My Blood: The Dilemma of the Italian-Americans*. Toronto, Canada: Guernica Editions, 1996.

Green, Paul M., and Melvin G. Holli, eds. *The Mayors: The Chicago Political Tradition*. Carbondale, IL: Southern Illinois University Press, 1995.

Gusfield, Joseph R. *Symbolic Crusade: Status Politics and the American Temperance Movement*. Urbana, IL: University of Illinois Press, 1963.

Helmer, William J. *Al Capone and His American Boys: Memoirs of a Mobster's Wife*. Bloomington, IN: Indiana University Press, 2011.

———. *The Gun That Made the Twenties Roar*. Toronto, Canada: Collier-Macmillan Canada, 1970.

Helmer, William J., and Arthur J. Bilek. *The St. Valentine's Day Massacre: The Untold Story of the Gangland Bloodbath That Brought Down Al Capone*. Nashville, TN: Cumberland House Publishing, 2004.

Helmer, William J., and Rick Mattix. *The Complete Public Enemy Almanac*. Nashville, TN: Cumberland House Publishing, 2007.

Hoffman, Dennis E. *Scarface Al and the Crime Crusaders: Chicago's Private War Against Capone*. Carbondale, IL: Southern Illinois University Press, 1993.

Hostetter, Gordon L., and Thomas Q. Beesley. *It's a Racket!* Chicago: Les Quinn Books, 1929.

Johnson, Curt, and R. Craig Sautter. *Wicked City—Chicago: From Kenna to Capone*. Highland Park, IL: December Press, 1994.

Johnston, J. J., and Sean Curtin. *Chicago Boxing*. Chicago: Arcadia Publishing, 2005.

Keefe, Rose. *Guns and Roses: The Untold Story of Dean O'Banion, Chicago's Big Shot Before Al Capone.* Nashville, TN: Cumberland House Publishing, 2003.

———. *The Man Who Got Away: The Bugs Moran Story.* Nashville, TN: Cumberland House Publishing, 2005.

Kenney, William Howland. *Chicago Jazz: A Cultural History 1904–1930.* New York: Oxford University Press, 1994.

Kobler, John. *Capone: The Life and World of Al Capone.* New York: Putnam, 1971.

Lindberg, Richard C. *Return to the Scene of the Crime: A Guide to Infamous Places in Chicago.* Nashville, TN: Cumberland House, 1999.

———. *To Serve and Collect: Chicago Politics and Police Corruption from the Lager Beer Riot to the Summerdale Scandal.* New York: Praeger, 1991.

Lyle, John H. *The Dry and Lawless Years.* New York: Prentice-Hall, 1960.

Marrow, Raphael W. *In Pursuit of Crime: The Police of Chicago, 1833–1933.* Sunbury, OH: Rats Publishing, 1995.

Mezzrow, Milton, and Bernard Wolfe. *Really the Blues.* New York: Random House, 1946.

Morreale, Ben, and Robert Carola. *Italian Americans: The Immigrant Experience.* New York: Hugh Lauter Levin Associates, 2000.

Murray, George. *The Legacy of Al Capone: Portraits and Annals of Chicago's Public Enemies.* New York: Putnam, 1975.

Nunes, Bill. *Illinois in the Roaring 1920s.* Glen Carbon, IL: Nunes, 2006.

Pasley, Fred D. *Al Capone: The Biography of a Self-Made Man.* New York: Ives Washburn, 1930.

Peterson, Virgil W. *Barbarians in Our Midst: A History of Chicago Crime and Politics.* Boston: Atlantic Monthly Press/Little, Brown, 1952.

Privitera, Joseph F. *Sicilian Dictionary & Phrasebook.* New York: Hippocrene Books, 2006.

Roemer, William F. *Accardo—The Genuine Godfather.* New York: Donald I. Fine, 1995.

———. *Man Against the Mob: The Inside Story of How the FBI Cracked the Chicago Mob by the Agent Who Led the Attack.* New York: Ivy Books, 1989.

Russo, Gus. *The Outfit.* New York: Bloomsbury Press, 2001.

Ruth, David E. *Inventing the Public Enemy: The Gangster in American Culture, 1918–1934.* Chicago: University of Chicago Press, 1996.

Schoenberg, Robert J. *Mr. Capone: The Real and Complete Story of Al Capone.* New York: William Morrow, 1992.

Shadwick, Keith. *The Illustrated Story of Jazz*. New York: Crescent Books, 1991.

Theoharis, Athan G., ed. *The FBI: A Comprehensive Reference Guide*. New York: Oryx Press, 2000.

Thompson, Charles. *Bing*. London, England: Wyndham Publications, 1976.

Thrasher, Frederick M. *The Gang: A Study of 1,313 Gangs in Chicago*. Chicago: University of Chicago Press, 1927.

Trohan, Walter. *Political Animals: Memoirs of a Sentimental Cynic*. Garden City, NY: Doubleday, 1975.

Walsh, Ray. *Fox Lake Police Association and Village of Fox Lake History, 1907–1962*. Fox Lake, IL: Fox Lake Publishing, 1982.

Ward, Geoffrey C., and Ken Burns. *Jazz: A History of America's Music*. New York: Alfred A. Knopf, 2000.

Waugh, Daniel. *Egan's Rats: The Untold Story of the Prohibition-Era Gang That Ruled St. Louis*. Nashville, TN: Cumberland House Publishing, 2007.

Wendt, Lloyd, and Herman Kogan. *Lords of the Levee: The Story of Bathhouse John and Hinky Dink*. Evanston, IL: Northwestern University Press, 2005.

Index